Beyond Foreign Economic Policy

Beyond Foreign Economic Policy

The United States, the Single European Market and the Changing World Economy

Brian Hocking and Michael Smith

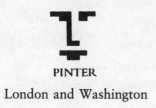

PINTER

London and Washington

PINTER
A Cassell Imprint
Wellington House, 125 Strand, London WC2R 0BB, England
PO Box 605, Herndon, VA 20172, USA

First published in 1997
© Brian Hocking and Michael Smith 1997

British Library Cataloguing in Publication Data
A catalogue record for this book is available from the British Library.
ISBN 1–85567–268–5 (Hardback)
    1–85567–269–3 (Paperback)

Library of Congress Cataloging-in-Publication Data
Hocking, Brian.
    Beyond foreign economic policy : the United States, the single
European market and the changing world economy / Brian Hocking and
Michael Smith.
        p. cm.
    "A Cassell imprint."
    Includes bibliographical references and index.
    ISBN 1–85567–268–5 (hc.) — ISBN 1–85567–269–3 (pbk.)
    1. United States—Foreign economic relations—European Economic
Community countries. 2. European Economic Community countries—
Foreign economic relations—United States. 3. United States—
Foreign economic relations—European Union countries. 4. European
Union countries—Foreign economic relations—United States.
5. Europe 1992. 6. United States—Foreign economic relations.
7. International economic relations. I. Smith, Michael, 1947– .
II. Title.
HF 1456.5.E825H63 1997
337.7304—dc21
                                                            96-52965
                                                            CIP

Typeset by BookEns Ltd., Royston, Herts
Printed and bound in Great Britain by Biddles Ltd, Guildford and King's Lynn

Contents

Introduction

In focusing on US responses to the Single European Market[1] initiative and the patterns of interaction which they generated, this book has the central aim of examining the changing nature of foreign economic policy. The discussion rests on the belief that significant developments at both international and domestic levels are fundamentally changing the management of this policy area. It is, for example, almost conventional – if not undisputed – wisdom that foreign economic policy is as much about domestic politics as it is about international policy. Hence the claims frequently made by trade diplomats – particularly in the USA – that their time is as much devoted to negotiating with domestic interests as it is with the representatives of other countries.

Our approach, as we explain in Chapter 1, seeks to build on a substantial literature dealing with the character of trade politics and to suggest that one way of conceptualizing the changes wrought by the patterns of 'boundary erosion' discussed there is to view the changing policy milieu in terms of a 'multilayered' policy environment. This is characterized by diversity and fluidity in terms of the actors involved in the policy processes, the strategies deployed to achieve specific goals and the arenas in which policy is conducted. Such an image, of course, challenges traditional assumptions regarding the automatic primacy of government in the conduct of international policy. But our analysis of US–European Community (EC) interactions in the context of the Single European Market (SEM) seeks to go beyond the debate over state-centric versus pluralistic approaches to policy-making.

The discussion might have been pursued in a variety of contexts and geographical settings. We have chosen to focus on transatlantic economic relations for two main reasons. On the one hand, they are highly significant within the context of the global economy. Second, the density and complexity of interactions within this policy arena lend themselves to the kind of analysis with which the book is concerned. Hence the second, more specific, objective: the examination of US–EC relations at a critical phase in their evolution.

As we attempt to demonstrate, the nature of the SEM raised central issues concerning internal structures and processes, as well as foreign economic policy in its traditional form. When the implications of the SEM began to be debated in the USA, the initial response in some quarters was one of alarm, partly generated by the European Commission's attempts during 1988 to counter claims that the project would benefit non-European business interests by arguing that it was to EC firms that the advantages of the Single Market would primarily accrue. In turn, this had the effect of sounding warning bells outside Europe. The phrase 'Fortress Europe' began to be heard as business and governments outside Europe took the Commission at its word.

The fear that the EC was bent on the creation of an inward-looking trade bloc was certainly voiced within the USA as the prospect of 'Europe 1992' gained wider currency. But this was only one response and was to be quickly modified, reflecting the complexity of issues and the range of interests, both public and private sector, which were involved. In fact, as Chapter 2 suggests, the SEM came to be viewed as a multidimensional set of challenges and opportunities which interlocked with US concerns over growing vulnerability in the face of the processes associated with globalization. This, it is argued, has to be seen in the context of a general shift in the agenda of world politics away from preoccupations with control over, as distinct from access to, international environments. Thus, for the USA, the SEM emerged at a time when the 'declinist' debate was in full flood and the concern with economic competitiveness high on the agenda. But it also coincided with the final phase of the Cold War, the upheavals in Eastern Europe and the prospect of a reunified Germany. In this sense, the future of a 'unified' Europe (whatever the final state implicit in the phrase might be) posed some alarming prospects for policy-makers which spanned the realm of the economic and military security agendas.

Consequently, the prospect of the SEM appeared to move US–EC relations into a new phase. Of course, the familiar irritations characteristic of transatlantic trade relations remained part of their fabric. Alongside specific disputes (such as hormone-treated beef and aerospace), the underlying issues of market access – reciprocity, rules of origin, technical standards, government procurement – were familiar items on the agenda. However, the prospect of a unified market in Europe raised their salience. Furthermore, the timing was critical in the context of the Uruguay Round General Agreement on Tariffs and Trade (GATT) negotiations. For Washington, the relationship of these two processes posed issues both of substantive policy and of strategy. To what extent did the emergence of the Single Market proposal represent a lessening of European commitment to a successful outcome in the GATT negotiations? Did it strengthen the Europeans' hand? And to what extent should the administration seek to deal with key issues within the GATT framework as opposed to direct bilateral negotiations? Different US interests offered varying answers to these questions.

It is in examining the inputs into the US responses to the SEM that the twin objectives of the book come together. As the following chapters illustrate, these responses were diverse and manifested themselves in differing conjunctions of interests depending on the issue involved. To this extent, the distinction between state-centred and societal-oriented explanations of foreign economic policy becomes less significant than the linkages between them. Rather than a uniform and hierarchical pattern of interactions presided over by national government, the picture that emerges is one of networks of interactions and relationships which cross the subnational/national/international and the public/private sector divides. Explaining policy thus becomes a more differentiated task, as Chapter 7, which considers public procurement and standards setting as two issues on the US–EC SEM agenda, demonstrates. Interactions generated by the procurement debate accorded more closely with government-oriented explanations of foreign economic policy, while the technical standards issue, by its very character and the arenas in which policy is formulated, provided a greater role for business.

Structure

Given the assumptions on which the discussion rests, we have sought to analyse the differing interests of the key US players as they responded to the challenges and opportunities that the SEM proposals presented. Following the outline of our approach to foreign economic policy in Chapter 1, Chapter 2 'sets the scene' for the subsequent discussion by sketching the background to the Single Market Programme, the issues which it posed for 'outsiders' such as the USA and the character of US–EC relations. Chapters 3 to 6 then consider the responses of the federal agencies, Congress, the states and regional interests, and business. As indicated above, Chapter 7 takes the form of a case study focusing on two key issues, technical standards and public procurement, and analyses the pattern of interactions which each generated.

The overall aim is to provide readers with a reasonably detailed overview of how US policy was shaped and implemented on a specific agenda and during a short time-span – from 1988 to 1993. It is not our objective to develop a model of policy-making applicable to all contexts. Rather, it is our assumption that each issue will generate its own pattern of roles and interactions within the multilayered policy environment and to that extent will be unique. Thus, for example, readers will become aware that the 'cast of players' here is somewhat different from that which developed around the ratification of the North American Free Trade Area

(NAFTA) agreement. The SEM did not excite the attention of environmental and labour-related pressure groups and thus become an issue high on the popular domestic political agenda. At the same time, we believe that the events and issues described in the following chapters cast valuable light on the changing environment in which foreign economic policy is conducted and, more specifically, the evolution of US–EC relations.

Sources and acknowledgements

As is evident from the footnotes and bibliography, information for the book came from two main sources: (a) secondary materials comprising books, articles and newspaper coverage during the period 1988 to 1993; (b) primary sources constituting official publications and interview data. Both authors had substantial information relevant to this study from earlier projects, but this was supplemented by some fifty interviews conducted in the USA and Europe. It would not have been possible to undertake the project without the help of a variety of people. However, a particular debt is owed to Edward Hodson, who worked as research assistant over several years. Not only did he undertake bibliographical research and interviews in Europe, he also produced the first drafts of the case studies in Chapter 7. We are also very grateful to Elizabeth Mily, who, while a research student at Georgetown University, undertook bibliographical work in the USA and provided us with useful contacts. Her supervisor, Professor John Kline, was kind enough to introduce us and to oversee the arrangements. In addition, we are, of course, indebted to those who agreed to be interviewed, not all of whom can be identified in the text. We gratefully acknowledge the financial support provided by Coventry University under its Research Initiative programme. Without this, the study could not have been undertaken. And finally, in this as in earlier projects, we owe an immense debt to our families for their support, patience and understanding while the book was being prepared and written. As is always the case, errors of fact and interpretation are the sole responsibility of the authors.

Notes

1   Throughout the book we have used 'Single Market Programme' and 'Single European Market' interchangeably. In addition, we have in places employed the terms 'Europe 1992' and 'EC-92', which were frequently used in the USA as shorthand references. Given the time period of the study, we have consistently referred to the European Community (EC) rather than the European Union (EU).

1

Beyond foreign economic policy

In terms of relationships between the member states of the then European Community (EC) and non-member states, the prospect of a Single European Market (SEM) was at once understated yet critical: understated in the sense that the White Paper published by the EC Commission in 1985, which heralded the Single Market Programme (SMP), made little mention of the outside world.[1] The White Paper was concerned with the removal of the remaining barriers to trade within the Community by such means as the elimination of border controls and the harmonization of standards. Through these and other measures, the 1988 Cecchini Report estimated, the EC member states would benefit to the tune of increased output and GDP of between 2.5 and 6.5 per cent.[2] True, references were made to other areas of the world, particularly the USA and Japan, in establishing the case for the SEM. And Cecchini noted that one consequence of the SEM would be enhanced competition within the enlarged market for European companies from competitors outside the EC.[3] But both the White Paper and the Cecchini Report were silent on issues of obvious concern to these and other countries, such as the levels of protection against non-EC goods and services after the advent of the Single Market in January 1993.

Nevertheless, the relationship of the Community and its member states to the outside world was critical in the sense that the whole rationale of the SEM enterprise was founded on the recognition that, in economic terms, Europe lagged behind other countries and regions, whose rates of growth outstripped those in Europe and whose industries were more competitive. These issues will be taken up in the next chapter, but it is important to note here that such concerns, epitomized in the belief that the rise of the newly industrializing countries (NICs) of the Asia-Pacific region would lead to the eclipse of Europe in the coming 'Pacific Century', underpinned the logic of the SMP. Whereas progress had been made in the years since the signing of the Treaty of Rome in terms of tariff reduction and the removal of quantitative restrictions on trade, significant obstacles in the shape of non-tariff barriers remained. Unless these were removed, so the argument ran, Europe was doomed to the condition of 'Eurosclerosis' which many had come to fear was its lot.

For 'outsiders', however, the prospect of the SEM, while it certainly offered opportunities, also presented the prospect of a dominant trading area to which access might be considerably more difficult, represented in the image of a 'Fortress Europe', inward looking and unheedful of the concerns of others. This view, and the perception of EC officials' responses to it, are epitomized in the words of one American observer: 'The official EC position is that fears of Fortress Europe are nothing more than silly paranoia on the part of foreigners (mainly Americans!) who do not understand how the EC works. The EC, Community officials believe, will become a global hegemonic leader, guiding the world toward freer trade.'[4] Such anxieties, of course, did not develop in a vacuum. Indeed, the significance of the SEM agenda, and the external responses to it, can only be understood in the context of the broader trade and political agenda of the 1980s.

In the case of EC–US relations, for example, the concerns engendered by what the Americans often referred to simply as 'EC-92' fitted into the broader issues examined in more detail in Chapter 2. Concerns with market access, the competitiveness of US industries and, particularly, conflict with Japan over a succession of trade issues had helped to stimulate a reawakening of domestic interest in foreign economic policy, symbolized by the growing protectionist sentiment on Capitol Hill.

At the multilateral trade level, the launch of the Uruguay Round of trade negotiations within the General Agreement on Tariffs and Trade (GATT) at Punta del Este in 1986 reflected concern at the erosion of the multilateral trade regime, together with the fact that increasingly important items on the trade agenda – such as trade in services and protection in intellectual property rights – were outside the remit of the GATT. But this was only part of the US trade strategy picture. Alongside a commitment to a new GATT round, Washington engaged in extensive bilateral trade negotiations, not least with Japan, negotiated the Canada–US Free Trade Agreement and launched negotiations which were to lead to the North American Free Trade Area, initially embracing the USA, Mexico and Canada. Furthermore, an increasingly aggressive Congress adopted the Super 301 trade provision in the 1988 trade bill intended to punish countries adopting 'unfair' practices against US exporters, in an attempt to pressure the White House over its conduct of trade talks with Tokyo.[5] US responses to the SMP were, therefore, conditioned by this broader agenda.

Against this background, it became very clear that it was not merely at the federal level but also at state and business levels that US responses were to be formed and articulated. Additionally, these interests were responding to events within an even more complex policy milieu, that of the EC. As we aim to demonstrate, the character of the resultant linkages challenges key traditional assumptions regarding both the nature and conduct of external policy. Before we turn to consider the background to the US–EC relationship in the next chapter, our aim here is to consider the changing character of what is usually designated as 'foreign' policy and 'foreign economic' policy.

Boundary erosion and the policy processes

Foreign policy and foreign economic policy

One way of doing this is to approach such changes in terms of shifting boundaries demarcating critical aspects of the 'real world' in which policy is conducted, and of the analytical perspectives brought to bear on the interpretation of that world. In the context of this discussion, a key boundary requiring examination is that between what have traditionally been regarded as these two domains of international policy. Seen in its purest expression, foreign policy possesses a clear agenda with distinctive policy processes characterized by a focus on military security. Here, the concern with territorial defence implies a collective 'national' interest, marking off one community from another and symbolically expressed in geographical borders. Foreign economic policy, on the other hand, has – at least in its post-mercantilist manifestations – often reflected a disunity of interests with its counterpart to the geographical border, the tariff, the subject of contention between free trade and protectionist interests. The growing concern with non-tariff barriers has underscored such differences as regional economic interests, expressed, for example, in regional development policies, have assumed a growing significance in international trade negotiations. Additionally, the politics of scarcity and the resultant rise of resources diplomacy generated by the ecopolitical agenda of the 1970s have served to sensitize domestic interests to the differences which can divide communities when they are reacting to their external environment.

Traditionally, this difference has been expressed in terms of a distinction between 'high' and 'low' policy, reflecting distinctiveness in character but also implying a hierarchy of importance. For several reasons, the two forms of external policy have become increasingly interlinked. Of course, foreign policy has always reflected economic objectives, but their relative significance and impact on other issues has dramatically increased. With the end of the Cold War, the relative importance of economic as distinct from military security issues has increased.[6] However, this development was one which also marked the Cold War era as it evolved through its various phases. Thus, in the 1980s, Rosenau, in an overview of the changing character of foreign policy, noted that the heightened significance of economics – attributable to nuclear stalemate and Third World demands for a greater share of the world economic cake – was one of two particularly noteworthy changes to the foreign policy environment.[7] Even before the events of the late 1980s and early 1990s, then, the high–low dichotomy was looking increasingly frayed, not simply in the sense that what had hitherto been designated as low was becoming more prominent, but because the very distinction appeared to be losing its utility as a means of describing the substance of the policy environment. Changing perceptions of the nature of security among publics as well as policy-makers were a key element of this development and was underpinned by the heightened salience of economic issues generated by the resource scares of the 1970s and 1980s.[8]

At the same time, the nature of foreign economic policy has become a far more complex issue area as new problems crowd upon it. The trade policy area, for example, is being affected by growing concerns with environmental issues as the goal of free trade increasingly confronts environmental objectives such as sustainable development.[9] Taken alongside the growing importance of politically sensitive non-tariff barriers to trade, as noted earlier, the whole character of this policy area is changing as it becomes more politicized, linked to human rights and environmental agendas and open to participation by an ever-expanding collectivity of non-governmental organizations (NGOs). Each of these interrelated developments has helped to bring what might be seen as the 'old' and the 'new' foreign policy agendas together.[10]

The domestic and international divide

Closely related to the developments outlined above is the erosion of a second boundary: that separating the domestic and international policy arenas. Recognized as one of the consequences of the processes accompanying interdependence and globalization, this has now become an accepted point of departure for any discussion of contemporary foreign policy processes. Nevertheless, it is worth reflecting on what its implications are, and these can be considered under three closely related headings. First, the domestic and international policy environments are more closely linked in terms of the *sources of policy inputs*. The globalization of markets ensures that the conduct of what have been regarded as national economic policies is subject to forces that are decreasingly within the control of individual governments. Goals relating to inflation, employment and interest rates are as much, if not more, determined by factors that lie outside a given nation state.[11]

To the forces represented by these forms of globalization have to be added those created by the emergence of international civil society operating between the individual and the state and across national boundaries. This is the product of the range of 'new' issues, such as those relating to the environment, which have already been referred to. Around them, an expanded cast of players, particularly NGOs, feed into the policy processes, operating across national boundaries, frequently forming transnational coalitions and, thereby, placing added demands on national governments.[12] These developments impact on socio-political as well as economic systems. Studies of the GATT negotiating environment, for example, clearly illustrate that enhanced interdependence subsumes interactions between the whole fabric of national and international legal and constitutional systems.[13]

The second perspective on the eroding domestic–international boundary is the reverse side of the first. Just as the internationalization of the domestic policy environment, and vice versa, create added pressures on governments over which they may have little control, they also represent *resources for action*. At one level, these are constituted from the web of international organizations in which governments are increasingly enmeshed. They are supplemented by the consultative networks which engage national agencies and bureaucratic departments in international interactions, without which much contemporary policy management would be impossible.[14] But the phenomenon extends beyond patterns of intergovernmental relations. Just as NGOs may be seen as a challenge to governments, so in other contexts they join in strategic alliances based on their possession of knowledge and expertise which state bureaucracies may not be able to emulate. Thus, in such areas as development aid, the transnational networks of which NGOs are a part become a significant element in the pursuit of national objectives.[15] In another sense, the internationalization of public policy provides national policy-makers with the opportunity to develop strategies for the attainment of objectives which are based on this very linkage. The deployment of what Putnam has referred to as 'two-level games', where policy-makers operate at the interface of the two environments, relies on their existence.[16] We shall return to this point later in the chapter.

A third dimension of the domestic–international relationship focuses on what might be termed *arenas of activity*. The point here, which follows logically from what has already been said, is that the political arenas in which policy objectives are pursued are increasingly porous in the sense that both governmental and non-governmental actors find themselves operating in subnational, national and international environments simultaneously. This, of course, requires the relaxation of one of the key assumptions of the 'traditional' image of foreign policy, namely that there is a hierarchy of arenas in which the international stands supreme, guarded by foreign ministries acting in the name of national governments. If this was ever an accurate depiction of reality, it certainly does not accord with the present-day situation. Groups and even individuals are now able to operate at all three levels, thanks in part to the revolution in communications technology.[17] Regional and local governments compete with one another internationally for scarce foreign investment; business finds itself involved with various layers of foreign governments in determining the character of taxation and investment regulations which affect its operations.[18]

Consequently, we are no longer able to think in terms of a single international environment in which states are located. Rather, a growing plurality of interests within these states have their own international environments, partly determined by external pressures and partly autonomously defined by their individual concerns. This is not to say that national governments are incapable of unified and purposive action, but that such action becomes increasingly demanding as policy-makers seek to balance external and internal pressures.

The effect of this growing international–domestic nexus can be variously interpreted. One of the most influential characterizations has been Manning's suggestion that a third type of policy – 'intermestic' – has joined the conventional designation of domestic and international.[19] While suggestive of the forces at work here, this does tend to obscure the fact that we are not necessarily presented with new categories of policy, but with a continuum of policy types which blend together differing elements of domestic and international influences, variously located in subnational, national and international arenas. Some areas of policy, especially those relating to military security, will tend towards the end of the continuum in which policy-making is the preserve of a restricted cast of players and the inputs from the domestic environment are more controlled. On the other hand, issues on the environmental agenda, for example, will be marked by a plurality of influences and a high degree of domestication, often projected across national boundaries through linkages between groups in different national settings.

States and non-state actors

A further boundary which the foregoing discussion requires us to bridge is that which separates the world of states from that of non-state actors. In the debate between competing perspectives on international relations, there is a notable tendency to stress the discontinuities between the domain of states and their concerns and that of the diverse groupings of non-state actors. This is based on the belief that one perspective more accurately reflects the realities of international relations and is bound to triumph over the other, with the state eventually incorporating the forces perceived as challenging it, or the latter eclipsing the sovereign state.[20]

There is another possibility: namely that neither outcome will eventuate and that states and non-state actors will be locked together in increasingly complex patterns of interactions. This is the logic of Seyom Brown's 'global polyarchy', comprising a variety of actors and interests focusing on a multitude of issues 'in which conflicts are prosecuted and resolved primarily on the basis of *ad hoc* power plays and bargaining among combinations of these groups – combinations that vary from issue to issue'.[21]

This reflects, of course, the domestic–international linkages which we have just described, but extrapolates from them the mutual dependencies that characterize the needs of governmental and non-governmental actors. Thus, in one context, Strange has described the emergence of a triangular diplomacy linking firms and governments as the latter pursue the quest for competitiveness and increased market shares, and the former, in pursuit of their own agendas, are constrained to interact both with government and with one another.[22] This serves to emphasize the fact that governmental and non-governmental actors possess resources that the others require but are unable to secure for themselves. Here, we are confronted with one of the central conundrums of contemporary international politics: the nature and significance of sovereignty.

As actors whose characteristics are largely defined in terms of this concept, it is clearly the case that governments enjoy major advantages in the pursuit of their international policies in an environment whose practices are conditioned by sovereignty-derived norms and rules. But sovereignty in many contexts is no longer enough to guarantee success and, indeed, may be a disadvantage where this requires other characteristics of 'actorness' associated with 'sovereignty-free' actors. Hence the advantages assigned to NGOs, whose qualities – such as legitimacy in the eyes of the public and transparency of motive and operation – enable them to defy many of these sovereignty-determined rules with considerable effect.[23] The central point to be made here, then, is that the demands of contemporary policy-making often require the maintenance of linkages and the striking of bargains between governments and non-governmental actors which transform the nature of diplomacy as an activity, and certainly as one wherein governments act alone and occupy an unquestioningly privileged position. This underpins the image of the international environment as corresponding to that of a mixed actor system, in which a variety of functions relating to regulation and governance are performed by both states and non-state actors, by public and private agencies, frequently in conjunction with one another.[24]

The erosion of these various forms of boundary has, therefore, had a major impact on the ways in which international policy is conceived, going far beyond the heightened relative importance of economic as contrasted to military security issues. Their significance is reflected in the debates regarding the appropriate perspectives to employ in analysing the conduct of international policy. The application of insights from international political economy and foreign economic policy has reinforced this debate, focusing, for example, on the nature of the state and the motivations – economically rather than security related – which explain the ways in which different states behave both domestically and internationally.[25] While the balance in explanations varies in terms of the significance assigned to the impact of factors derived from the nature of the international system, those related to the character of the state and those which flow from the character of societies, there is a general, if limited, consensus to the effect that explanations derived from any one level are unsatisfactory as descriptions of reality.[26]

Systemic theories, whether these are related to traditional foreign policy or foreign economic policy, can do little other than explain very broad policy characteristics. Statist approaches may not go much further in aiding our understanding, in the sense that they fail to penetrate the complexities that determine the way in which states formulate and express their policies. The value of societal approaches is to be found in the fact that they offer a richer tapestry and recognize that external policy usually reflects conflict between domestic constituencies rather than societal unity based on an indivisible national interest. Their danger, on the other hand, is that they may lead to the assumption that policy is simply the expression of such interests, with policy-makers acting as their voice, exercising little or no autonomous interest over the framing of policy. Hence the emphasis on 'integrative' approaches, which seek to give due weight to the importance of domestic influences and interests in international negoti- ations but, at the same time, argue the case for recognizing the role of the policy-maker operating at the interface between the domestic and international arenas and capable of influencing both.[27]

Multilayered policy

This study of US responses to the emergence of the SMP in the latter part of the 1980s is conditioned by the factors outlined above. It is not concerned to argue that in some sense state-related foreign, and foreign economic, policy has either withered away or been rendered irrelevant by the forces outlined above. Rather, we are suggesting that the relaxation of boundaries which these demand reflects the emergence of a more complex policy milieu which is neither contained by conventional boundaries demarcating political arenas nor responsive to assumptions regarding who are effective and legitimate actors within those arenas. The term 'multilayered' is deemed appropriate in the sense that it suggests a more densely textured policy process, in terms of the actors involved and the points at which they interact. While not denying the significance of the state, its agencies and representatives, it seeks to set them alongside a diversity of public and private actors who are increasingly able to mobilize at both domestic and international levels for the attainment of political goals, whether in support of or in opposition to governments. Furthermore, as noted earlier, it also stresses the absence of hierarchy in the sense of the presumed importance of issues on the policy agenda and the arenas in which they appear.

In several senses, this image is appropriate to a study of relationships between the USA and the EC, given the fact that each stands in a different position with regard to the forces which are transforming the policy environment. The USA, as a state actor, provides a specific example of the processes of foreign policy diffusion. Although it may not confront problems of state autonomy to the degree experienced by lesser states, nevertheless it finds the conduct of external policy a more taxing activity than even a quarter of a century ago. This reflects external challenges, as the management of international policy has to be conducted through a variety of bilateral, multilateral and plurilateral channels. At the same time, internal pressures affecting the administration's capacity to conduct a coherent set of policies towards the outside world have increased as the nexus between domestic and foreign policy is strengthened.[28]

On the other hand, the EC might be regarded as progressing towards the development of its capacity to project its voice within the international system, whatever the final state of the integrationist enterprise might be.[29] However, the very character of its decision-making processes ensures that this capacity is unlikely to bear any strong resemblance to the classical modes of foreign policy. Indeed, the fact that the EC political system is itself frequently presented in terms of a 'multilevel governance' model, reflecting the complexities of the political relationships which its structures have established, lends added substance to the concept of multilayered policy processes.[30] Put another way, each polity occupies points towards opposite poles on the continuum along which foreign policy is being redefined. The character of multilayered policy processes can be viewed along several related planes, those of *objectives, interactions* and *process*. We now consider each of these before turning to the specific case with which this study is concerned.

The objectives of multilayered policy: access and control in world politics

The background against which multilayered policy processes are emerging is one wherein the fundamental objectives of diplomacy are changing alongside the actors engaged in it. They are associated with a change in the balance between two fundamental concerns characteristic of international politics, and of particular relevance to the trade agenda: on the one hand, the desire to gain access to actors and theatres of activity perceived as crucial to the achievement of interests; on the other, the desire to control the ability of others to do likewise. Writing in the 1970s, Hanrieder was conscious of the shift towards access and away from control as a major feature of the changing character of international politics:

> Access rather than acquisition, presence rather than rule, penetration rather than possession have become the important issues. Often one gains the impression that negotiations over such technical questions as arms control, trade agreements, technology transfers and monetary reform are not only attempts at problem-solving but also re-examinations of the meaning and sources of power in the last third of this century.[31]

While it would be over-simplistic and misleading to suggest that growing concerns with access are replacing totally older preoccupations with control, they are certainly modifying the latter, especially where they focus on territorial separateness.

A major reason for this, particularly among the advanced industrialized states, is to be found in the complex patterns associated with transnationalism and transgovernmentalism. These reflect not only the impact of enhanced communications technologies within the framework of economic interdependence, but a more general recognition of a shift in the fundamental character of international politics which such developments presaged. Thus the imperative of control over rigidly defined territorial space has been modified by new needs. Underlying this, as noted above, lies a marked shift in the character of the dominant issues around which international politics cluster. The frequently proclaimed relative ascendancy of economic issues over the traditional military–security agenda, certainly within the advanced industrialized states, focused attention on a broader range of actors, more intricate patterns of interaction and more diverse modes of exercising influence.

Rather than exclusivity epitomized by the capacity to assert sovereign control over territory, an increasing number of problems – tackling ozone depletion and global warming, battling against terrorism and drugs cartels, searching for answers to the spread of AIDS – imply the need for access to a range of resources beyond the reach of any single actor. Thus each problem demands the increased sharing of scientific knowledge, technical expertise and money if any progress is to be made in managing it.

Even those state structures most associated with control and denial of access, the intelligence services, are responding to the challenges presented by a changing political environment. Hence the comment of a senior

Italian secret service official concerned with developing links with East European counterparts in the fight against the Mafia: 'The conquest of markets these days is more important than the defence of territory.'[32] The central lesson here is that even where control is a desired goal – as in the case of the fight against organized crime – its achievement demands access to resources residing outside national communities. Thus the links between the British domestic security service, MI5, and its equivalent in Germany, the BfV, are believed to have curbed Irish terrorist attacks against British army bases in Germany.

A key part of the growing significance of access lies in the development of the communication technologies which permit it to occur. As Kennedy notes, even the most authoritarian of governments now find it virtually impossible to seal off their countries from the flow of global communications. 'In a world with more than 600 million television sets, viewers are as much consumers of news and ideas as they are of commercial goods.'[33] At the minimum, almost instantaneous access to information, often in the form of televisual images, can pose real challenges to the ability of governments to control their societies, as the Chinese government discovered in the wake of Tiananmen Square. At the maximum, it can become an agent of political delegitimization capable of uprooting even the most repressive of regimes, as in the case of Eastern Europe during 1989–90.

The rapidly growing processes associated with economic globalization have added fresh impetus to the demands for access if governments are to share in their benefits, while, at the same time, denying them many of the traditional modes of control over their economies. Within what Ohmae terms the Inter-linked Economy of the Triad (the USA, Europe and Japan), international business is creating what he regards as a 'borderless world' in which many of the familiar policies designed to manage national economies – such as interest rates and the money supply – have been rendered ineffective.[34] The most dramatic example of growing globalization is to be found in the financial markets, where the revolution in communications technology permits virtually instantaneous movements of money across the foreign exchanges on a round-the-clock basis in the order of one trillion dollars a day.[35] As Bergsten argues, the 'pervasive growth in market interpenetration makes it increasingly difficult for any country to avoid substantial external impacts on its economy'.[36]

Moreover, in an environment marked by high mobility of capital, attempts by government to regulate the flow of goods and money become self-defeating, as they will lead to a decline in national living standards by discouraging investment and creating uncompetitive industries. Hence import controls on the US economy in the 1980s, which succeeded in enhancing the competitiveness of the foreign rivals of the protected US industry, in certain instances – such as the steel industry in the early 1970s

– damaged other industries by driving up the price of imported materials.[37]

Against this background, the role of government *vis-à-vis* international business has become one of agent of access as much as one of control:

> From a focus on political sovereignty and constrained economic interdependence in the 1960s and 1970s, there is now a need to be competitive in a global economy characterized by an easy movement of key ingredients of growth across national boundaries. In the 1990s, nations have begun to realise that to achieve many of their non-economic goals they have to offer at least as attractive facilities for production and market access to the main wealth creators as their main foreign competitors.[38]

This is not, however, to suggest that the state has ceased to be a significant actor but, rather, that it is confronted by competing role demands. Hirst and Thompson argue that whereas processes of economic internationalization have limited the effectiveness of national economic management, many regulatory mechanisms remain in place even if their 'nature, level and function have changed'.[39]

For some observers, notably Reich, 'globalization' has rendered it hard to identify 'national' companies as exemplified by the oft-cited case of US forklift truck manufacturer Hyster. In pressing for action to limit Japanese imports, the company was undermined by the revelation that its products contained more foreign components than its Japanese rivals. Similarly, Congressional attempts to punish Toshiba for illegal sales of US-designed milling machines to the USSR collapsed in the face of pressures from US firms such as Tektronix, Hewlett-Packard and Compaq, which were either dependent on Toshiba products (particularly semiconductors) or sold Toshiba goods under their own brand labels.[40]

Similarly, within the tariff-free EC, attempts by, say, the French government to limit imports of Japanese cars run up against the fact that Japanese vehicles assembled in the UK with more than 80 per cent local content cannot be excluded. Furthermore, where Japanese vehicle manufacturers export from plants located in the USA, French protectionism may well arouse the ire of the US government. Kennedy uses such instances as these to reinforce the argument that national control has been rendered virtually redundant, arguing that 'the real "logic" of the borderless world is that nobody is in control'.[41]

However, such a conclusion overlooks the complex relationships between government and business that the imperatives of access create. In dismissing the Reich concern with 'who is us' as a distinctively American preoccupation, Kapstein argues that the very firms often portrayed as anational frequently act in support of state needs and functions, relying on government in turn to provide them with crucial requirements for their successful operation:

Only the state can defend corporate interests in international negotiations over trade, investment and market access. Agreements over such things as airline routes, the opening of banking establishments, and the right to sell insurance are not decided by corporate actors who gather around a table; they are determined by diplomats and bureaucrats.[42]

Put another way, the logic of access in the global market place demands the maintenance of a local alongside a global perspective. Indeed, Kapstein argues that rather than 'establishing transnational structures with global ownership, global employment, and global products', large corporations are becoming increasingly sensitive to their home 'bases'.[43] The argument is sustained by Michael Porter's thesis that leading firms have stable ties with specific localities which provide them with 'home bases' from which the firms define their strategies.[44] In this context, the persistence of what Golden refers to as 'network nodes' or home bases from which firms operate provides an opportunity for public policy to influence the location of economic activity, notwithstanding the impact of globalization.[45]

The complexities of relationships between the forces of globalization and localization are being reinforced by the growing recognition of the significance of regions as points of access within the international political economy. Noting the relationship between developments in the global and in national economies, Ohmae has modified his 'borderless world' thesis to embrace the concept of what he terms 'region-states' whose essential characteristic is that their 'primary linkages ... tend to be with the global economy and not with their host nations'.[46] Thus region-states are seen as 'natural economic zones', which may be located within national economic borders (Catalonia or Northern Italy) or across national boundaries – such as Hong Kong and Southern China before 1997 or the 'growth triangle' comprising Singapore and adjacent Indonesian islands. As such, they perform a particular function which is of growing significance in the post-Cold War world of international regionalization, namely points of access to centres of economic activity.

In terms of gaining market access, Ohmae has pointed to the advantages experienced by Nestlé and Proctor and Gamble in penetrating the Japanese market through the Kansai region rather than Tokyo, where competition is far more intense. And, of course, the creation of economic groupings such as NAFTA, or their strengthening, as in the case of the SMP, is likely to enhance the significance of such access regions and cities. Kresl has noted the effects of the lowering of national borders in Europe on the role of cities and regions and the growth of competitiveness between them as they redefine their relationships in the European and global, as opposed to the national, economic space.[47] Hence cities such as Amsterdam and Lyons become important 'gateway' cities within the global economy and develop appropriate strategies in pursuit of such roles.

The changing environment of the post-Cold War world is, as noted above, reinforcing such trends as the structures and assumptions of that world are challenged. This in part reflects, as noted earlier, the relative strengthening of the economic over the military–security agenda. Second, the dynamics of access are beginning to apply to those areas of the international system previously insulated from them, as the countries of the former Eastern bloc seek integration into the world economy. Symbolic of these changes is the evolving role and structure of one of the key control-oriented mechanisms of the Cold War era, the Co-ordinating Committee on Multilateral Export Controls (CoCom).

Since its inception, the rationale of this organization has been the denial of access by the former USSR and its allies to military and dual-use technology. It was, of course, an increasing irritant in US–European relations, as Washington tended to adhere to more draconian listings of prohibited goods than was thought appropriate in Europe, but the end of the Cold War has demanded that its role be re-evaluated in the light of new realities and a more subtle range of threats to international stability. In adopting new ground rules for the organization in November 1993, the 17 member states of CoCom adopted a regime reflecting the need to adopt more flexible, access-oriented procedures based on the need to pool information and identify trends rather than the rigid control policies of the past. In the words of one CoCom official, predicting that licences will be needed on some 5 per cent of products on the current CoCom lists, 'We will be controlling hardly anything anymore.'[48]

We have dwelt at some length on the theme of access as an objective in world politics simply because it serves to explain one of the conditioning elements of the multilayered policy processes with which we are concerned. Moreover, in the specific context of market access, it is of particular relevance to an understanding of the relationships between the USA and the EC, providing the backdrop against which strategies and patterns of interaction surrounding the SMP developed.

Process and interactions

Part of the picture here is the changing nature of international negotiation which has accompanied the developments outlined in this chapter. Rather than the traditional image of negotiation as involving interactions between two or more actors, each with clear and defined interests, gradually moving towards a point of convergence between those interests, a good deal of contemporary negotiation is more akin to what Winham has likened to a management process. Here, actors are locked together in the management of complex problems which are marked by their technical nature, complexity and uncertainty in terms of content and outcome, and the bureaucratization of the processes through which negotiations proceed.[49] As we shall see in Chapter 2, this is certainly true of the interactions between the USA and the EC in the context of the SMP as it developed in the late 1980s.

The policy environment which these developments are helping to establish is one in which the key test of success for actors, both governmental and non-governmental, in achieving their objectives seems to be the capacity to develop strategic and tactical relationships to meet specific needs and to do so rapidly. Michael Lind has suggested that this is a key quality of what he terms the 'catalytic state', marked by the inability of governments to achieve their goals through reliance on their own resources and requiring the mobilization of coalitions comprising other states, international and transnational organizations and private sector interests. 'The challenges of twenty-first century diplomacy will inspire ingenious new methods of short-term collaboration, to accomplish more with fewer resources,' he writes.[50]

At the administrative level, this alters significantly the context in which the consequences of internationalization have to be dealt with. Over the past twenty years or so, this has been expressed in terms of an emphasis on the demands for coordination within national bureaucracies as the management of external relations has passed out of the sole control of foreign ministries.[51] Although linkages within bureaucratic systems remain important, the test of success in managing policy in many areas is related to the capacity to build linkages with a growing range of interests and organizations. To use Nye's term, the test of governmental success will increasingly become the capacity to develop 'co-optive power' through links with a diverse range of non-state organizations.[52] Thus, instead of thinking of international policy as an area dominated by governments – and a relatively small group of players within government – we are presented with policy networks comprising a diversity of actors, often dependent on the nature of a specific issue, and constructed to serve particular objectives. Moreover, these networks embrace a diversity of actors located in various political arenas and not determined by national boundaries.

Because of the changing environment of public policy, the conduct of many aspects of external relations is now more akin to the domestic policy processes than some ideal type of a 'foreign policy' process. Three points are worth noting in particular. First, the character of the policy process will vary depending on the issues involved; second, the role and influence of actors will vary between the stages in the policy-making cycle, from agenda-setting to implementation;[53] third, the traditional conception of the point at which the domestic arena fits into the overall conduct of external policy needs to be adapted to these changing realities. Rather than a sequential process, where domestic interests are consulted at the final stages of negotiation for purposes of formal ratification, there is an ongoing 'dialogue of ratification' between policy-makers and affected interests as negotiations unfold.[54]

This is not so much a restatement of the oft-heralded 'decline of the state' as a redefinition of the relationship between the state and society on one side and the nation-state and a galaxy of non-state actors on the other. It reflects mutual needs as each actor, whether in the governmental or non-governmental sphere, possesses resources that the others need to achieve their policy goals. As has been suggested earlier, this is bound up with a shift in the balance between the goals of access and control which embraces both domestic and international politics. Nor is it being suggested that all policy-making will reflect these characteristics in equal measure. Indeed, some areas of policy will continue to resemble the more traditional images of foreign policy.

But these trends, it can be argued, pose problems for bureaucratic organizations whose inherent characteristics are more oriented towards the tasks of control than to those of gaining access to a variety of political and social arenas. Not only does the changing global environment present challenges to national bureaucratic structures whose mode of operation may be more attuned to the problems of control over external linkages rather than developing them and thereby gaining access to policy networks, it also enhances the familiar problems which may flow from the desire of individual government departments to control their boundaries with other sections of national bureaucracies.

The growing concern with access, and the consequent need to develop linkages outside the confines of the bureaucratic system in the pursuit of the creation of policy networks, marks a lessening in the traditional distinctions between the public and private worlds of administration and diplomacy and the creation of linkages between government agencies and what might be termed 'agents of access' located in the non-governmental sphere. One manifestation of this trend is the emergence of 'epistemic communities' or 'networks of knowledge-based experts' operating across national and international networks.[55] These reflect the growing need for specialist knowledge which is no longer the preserve of government. This demand for knowledge in the conduct of policy is also reflected in the relationship between government and NGOs and 'think tanks', and is seen as growing in the uncertain environment following the end of the Cold War.[56]

Another manifestation of the agent of access is the political consultant or 'lobbyist'. To a considerable extent their true role and significance has been masked by the frequently tendentious treatment accorded to them in the media, particularly in the USA, where they are portrayed as agents of foreign influences.[57] In one sense, the emergence of the political consultant is the epitome of the politics of access, offering not the specialist advice characteristic of epistemic communities, but information as to how other policy arenas operate and the points within them where influence can be applied for maximum effectiveness.

In performing this role, they are developing lobbying networks comprising short-term working arrangements between interests located in different national settings linked by a common set of objectives, or the growing phenomenon of the international consultancy, with branches in several countries, or regions as in the case of the EC. From the point of view of this discussion, however, the significant point is that they frequently work alongside officials and private sector interests in the pursuit of common objectives, and are increasingly essential components in achieving those objectives. Indeed, in some senses, they become partners in a world where the distinctions between public and private diplomacy appear increasingly shadowy.

Conclusion

This chapter has sought to sketch the outlines of a policy milieu in which both the participants and the modes of interaction linking them are changing in important respects. Although the post-Cold War environment has (particularly in the context of US–EC relations) contributed to these developments, in many ways they predate it. Thus, for example, the growing permeability of the boundaries between foreign and domestic policy is a phenomenon whose consequences have been debated for many years. However, the development of the multilayered policy environment has moved the discussion beyond this familiar terrain. What appear to confront us in many policy contexts are not so much well defined developments marking the predominance of any one political arena, but a bewildering network of linkages between those arenas through which actors relate to one another in a variety of ways. In other words, policy-makers are required to operate in an environment spanning subnational, national and international arenas, where the achievement of goals at one level of political activity demands an ability to operate in the others.

Partly because of this, the traditional distinctions between domestic and foreign policy are becoming harder to sustain. Strategies for accomplishing external policy goals often require, therefore, that negotiators conduct diplomacy in several environments simultaneously, weaving together threads from each into a single tapestry. In this sense, what was regarded as a phenomenon of international politics – diplomacy – has assumed a notably domestic dimension. At the most extreme, it could be argued that the growth of redistributive issues in international politics has rendered both the content and the processes of 'foreign' policy indistinguishable from those characteristic of 'domestic' policy. It is important to note, however, that these developments do not apply to all interactions or affect all actors in equal measure. There are issues, particularly those on the military–security agenda, which accord far more to the traditional intergovernmental patterns of international relations than to the multilayered policy configurations. Similarly, it is clearly the case that areas of the international system marked by high levels of economic interdependence, notably those inhabited by the advanced industrialized states, will display the characteristics outlined in this chapter. Relationships between the USA and the EC obviously fit into this category.

The following chapters elaborate on these points and illustrate the ways in which this style of policy interaction operates by focusing on the trade agenda generally but, more specifically, by examining the complexities marking the relationship between the USA and the EC in the context of the proposal to establish a Single European Market. In essence, our argument is that the demands for creative responses to the kinds of challenge that the SMP has presented to the USA (and other 'outside' governments) are resulting in the development of a policy environment which brings together a variety of actors located in a multiplicity of arenas – some in the public, some in the private sectors. As roles and relationships are redefined in consequence, so are notions concerning the fundamental nature of foreign and domestic policy.

Notes and references

1   European Commission, *Completing the Internal Market: White Paper from the Commission to the Council*, Brussels, Commission of the European Communities, June 1985.
2   P. Cecchini, *The European Challenge 1992: The Benefits of a Single Market*, Aldershot, Wildwood House, 1988.
3   *Ibid.*, p. 89.
4   J. A. C. Conybeare, '1992, the Community, and the world: free trade or fortress Europe?', in D. L. Smith and J. L. Ray (eds), *The 1992 Project and the Future of Integration in Europe*, Armonk, NY, Sharpe, 1993, p. 144.
5   A brief introduction can be found in D. M. Snow and E. Brown, *Puzzle Palaces and Foggy Bottom: US Foreign and Defense Policy-making in the 1990s*, New York, St Martin's Press, 1994, pp. 125–40. For a more detailed discussion see: I. M. Destler, *American Trade Politics* (second edn), Washington, DC, Institute for International Economics with The Twentieth Century Fund, 1992, Chapter 4.

6   S. Brown, *New Forces, Old Forces, and the Future of World Politics* (post-Cold War edn), New York, HarperCollins, 1995.

7   J. N. Rosenau, 'Introduction: new directions and recurrent questions in the comparative study of foreign policy', in C. F. Hermann, C. W. Kegley and J. N. Rosenau (eds), *New Directions in the Study of Foreign Policy*, Boston, Allen and Unwin, 1987, p. 3.

8   The redefinition of security thus became a notable theme of international relations, as can be seen in R. Ullman, 'Redefining security', *International Security*, 8(1), 1983, pp. 129–53; and J. T. Mathews, 'Redefining security', *Foreign Affairs*, 68(2), 1989, pp. 162–77.

9   Among the growing literature on trade and the environment, see S. Harris, 'International trade, ecologically sustainable development and the GATT', *Australian Journal of International Affairs*, 45(2), 1991, pp. 196–211; and D. Brack, 'Balancing trade and the environment', *International Affairs*, 71(3), 1995, pp. 497–514.

10 The issue of 'new' and 'old' agendas in international politics is discussed in B. Hocking and M. Smith, *World Politics: An Introduction to International Relations* (2nd edn), London, Prentice Hall/Harvester Wheatsheaf, 1995, Chapters 7 and 8; and F. Halliday, 'International relations: is there a new agenda?', *Millennium*, 20(1), Spring 1991.

11 J. A. Scholte, *International Relations of Social Change*, Buckingham, Open University Press, 1993.

12 Discussions of the role of NGOs in the context of environmental policy can be found in T. Princen and M. Finger (eds), *Environmental NGOs in World Politics: Linking the Local and the Global*, London, Routledge, 1994; and P. Wapner, 'Politics beyond the state: environmental activism and world civic politics', *World Politics*, 47(3), 1995, pp. 311–40.

13 See, for example, J. H. Jackson, J. V. Louis and M. Matsushita, *Implementing the Tokyo Round: National Constitutions and International Economic Roles*, Ann Arbor, University of Michigan Press, 1984.

14 Ougaard refers to these developments as the 'international political superstructure'. M. Ougaard, 'The US state in the new global context', *Cooperation and Conflict*, 27(2), 1992, pp. 131–62. See also D. Held, 'Democracy, the nation-state and the global system', *Economy and Society*, 20(2), 1991, pp. 138–72. On the development of transgovernmental relations, see R. F. Hopkins, 'The international role of "domestic" bureaucracy', *International Organization*, 30, 1976, pp. 405–32.

15 Princen and Fingen, *op. cit.* Wapner (*op. cit.*, p. 312) suggests that there is a tendency to overstate the linkages between NGOs and the state as distinct from societal forces. The point here, however, is that

they are capable of developing a variety of roles and relationships in relation to both governmental and non-governmental actors. No one perspective is either intrinsically right or wrong.

16   R. D. Putnam, 'Diplomacy and domestic politics: the logic of two-level games', *International Organization*, 42(3), 1988, pp. 427–61.

17   C. F. Alger, 'Local, national and global politics in the world: a challenge to international studies', *International Studies Notes of the International Studies Association*, 5(1), 1978, pp. 1–3.

18   B. Hocking, *Localizing Foreign Policy: Non-central Governments and Multilayered Diplomacy*, London/New York, Macmillan/St Martin's Press, 1993.

19   B. Manning, 'The Congress, the executive and intermestic affairs', *Foreign Affairs*, 55(2), 1977, pp. 306–25.

20   Rosenau has described this tendency as the tension between two 'worlds', the state-centric and the multicentric. See J. N. Rosenau, *Turbulence in World Politics: A Theory of Change and Continuity*, Hemel Hempstead, Harvester Wheatsheaf, 1990.

21   Brown, *op. cit.*, p. 140.

22   S. Strange, 'States, firms and diplomacy', *International Affairs*, 68(1), 1992, pp. 1–15.

23   Princen regards these as two of the key advantages possessed by environmental NGOs. See Princen, *op. cit.*, pp. 41–2.

24   On the nature of the international system as a 'mixed actor system', see Hocking and Smith, *op. cit.*, Chapter 5.

25   B. E. Moon, 'Political economy approaches to the comparative study of foreign policy', in Rosenau, *op. cit.*, pp. 33–52. A similar discussion can be found in Simon Mercado, 'Towards a new understanding of international trade policies: ideas, institutions and the political economy of foreign economic policy', in J. Macmillan and A. Linklater (eds), *Boundaries in Question: New Directions in International Relations*, London, Pinter, 1995.

26   D. Skidmore and V. M. Hudson, 'Establishing the limits of state autonomy: contending approaches to the study of state–society relations and foreign policy-making', in D. Skidmore and V. M. Hudson (eds), *The Limits of State Autonomy: Societal Groups and Foreign Policy Formulation*, Boulder, CO, Westview, 1993. An excellent survey of differing approaches to the analysis of US foreign economic policy can be found in G. I. Ikenberry, D. A. Lake, and M. Mastanduno, 'Introduction: approaches to explaining American foreign economic policy', *International Organization*, 42(1), 1988, pp. 1–14. See also their conclusion to this special issue of the journal.

27   See, for example, P. B. Evans, H. K. Jacobson and R. D. Putnam (eds), *Double-Edged Diplomacy: International Bargaining and Domestic Politics*, Berkeley, University of California Press, 1993.

28 B. Hocking, 'Globalization and the foreign–domestic policy nexus', in A. McGrew (ed.), *The American Empire*, London, Hodder and Stoughton, 1994.

29 See, for example, M. Smith, 'The European Community: testing the boundaries of foreign economic policy', in R. Stubbs and G. R. D. Underhill (eds), *Political Economy and the Changing Global Order*, Basingstoke, Macmillan, 1994.

30 See G. Marks, 'Structural policy and multilevel governance in the EC', in A. F. Cafruny and G. G. Rosenthal (eds), *The State of the European Community Volume 2: The Maastricht Debates and Beyond*, Boulder, CO, Westview, 1993; and D. L. Smith and J. L. Ray, 'The 1992 project', and B. B. Hughes, 'Delivering the goods: the EC and the evolution of complex governance', both in D. L. Smith and J. L. Ray (eds), *The 1992 Project*, *op. cit.*

31 W. F. Hanrieder, 'Dissolving international politics: reflections on the nation-state', *American Political Science Review*, 72(4), 1978, pp. 1276–88.

32 'Secret services unite against crime', *The Financial Times*, 22 November 1993, p. 3.

33 P. Kennedy, *Preparing for the Twenty-first Century*, New York, Random House, 1993, p. 52.

34 K. Ohmae, *The Borderless World: Power and Strategy in the Interlinked Economy*, London, Fontana, 1992, pp. xi–xiii.

35 Kennedy, *op. cit.*, p. 51.

36 C. F. Bergsten, *America in the World Economy: A Strategy for the 1990s*, Washington, DC, Institute for International Economics, 1988, p. 60.

37 *Loc. cit.*

38 J. H. Dunning, 'A new multinational-government partnership?', *Atlantic Outlook*, 51, 30 July 1993, p. 7.

39 P. Hirst and G. Thompson, 'The problem of "globalization": international economic relations, national economic management and the formation of trading blocs', *Economy and Society*, 21(4), 1992, p. 370.

40 Hocking, *Localizing Foreign Policy*, *op. cit.*, p. 89.

41 Kennedy, *op. cit.*, p. 55.

42 E. B. Kapstein, 'We are US: the myth of the multinational', *The National Interest*, Winter 1991/2, p. 56.

43 *Ibid.*, p. 58.

44 J. R. Golden, 'Economics and national strategy: convergence, global networks, and cooperative competition', *The Washington Quarterly*, 16(3), 1993, p. 103.

45 *Op. cit.*, p. 104.

46 K. Ohmae, 'The rise of the region-state', *Foreign Affairs*, Spring

1993, p. 80; K. Ohmae, *The End of the Nation State: the Rise of Regional Economies*, London, HarperCollins, 1995.

47   P. K. Kresl, 'The response of European cities to EC 1992', *Journal of European Integration*, 15(2/3), 1992, pp. 151–72.

48   David Dodwell, 'Cocom: a brute turned super sleuth', *The Financial Times*, 16 November 1993.

49   G. R. Winham, 'Negotiation as a management process', *World Politics*, 30(1), 1977, pp. 87–113.

50   Michael Lind, 'The catalytic state', *The National Interest*, 27, 1992, p. 10.

51   For a discussion of these issues see: L. Karvonen and B. Sundelius, *Internationalization and Foreign Policy Management*, Aldershot, Gower, 1987.

52   Joseph S. Nye Jr, *Bound to Lead: The Changing Nature of American Power*, New York, Basic Books, 1990, pp. 31–3.

53   H. M. Ingram and S. L. Fiederlein, 'Traversing boundaries: a public policy approach to the analysis of foreign policy', *Western Political Quarterly*, 41(4), 1988, pp. 725–47.

54   Putnam, *op. cit.*

55   Peter M. Haas, 'Introduction: epistemic communities and international policy coordination', *International Organization*, 46(1), 1992, pp. 1–35.

56   The need for knowledge enabling 'new thinking' on US foreign policy, and the role of think tanks, are discussed in B. Roberts, S. H. Burnett and M. Weidenbaum, 'Think tanks in a new world', *The Washington Quarterly*, 16(1), 1993, pp. 169–82. A useful general survey of think tanks is to be found in W. Wallace, 'Between two worlds, think-tanks and foreign policy', in C. Hill and P. Beshoff (eds), *Two Worlds of International Relations: Academics, Practitioners and the Trade in Ideas*, London, LSE/Routledge, 1994, pp. 139–63.

57   For example, Pat Choate, *Agents of Influence: How Japan's Lobbyists in the United States Manipulate America's Political and Economic System*, New York, Knopf, 1990.

2

The USA and the Single Market Programme

In the previous chapter we have suggested that the traditional portrayal of foreign and foreign economic policy needs to be revised to accommodate patterns of relationships which no longer accord with the assumptions on which it is based. The emergence of more complex multilayered policy processes embracing a greater diversity of actors, both governmental and non-governmental, in political arenas linked by densely textured patterns of interaction, encapsulates these changes. But, of course, this image remains as much an abstraction as does that of the images against which it is set. All it can do is to provide the broadest of outlines of the way in which relationships are conducted and policy is formulated and implemented. In order to add flesh to the skeleton, we need to consider the nature of a particular set of issues, the actors involved and the context which conditions their relationships.

With this in mind, the aim of this chapter is to outline the background to US–EC relations as they developed in the context of the 1992 programme, and to expand the concept of the multilayered policy environment discussed in the previous chapter. It is not our aim to provide a detailed account of the development of the SMP but, rather, to outline some of its features which help to explain the ways in which US interests responded to it.[1] Nor is it our intention to engage in a detailed history or analysis of US–EC relations. Both can be found elsewhere.[2] But before we explore the responses generated within the USA by developments in the EC during the mid-to-late 1980s, it is necessary to say something about each of these.

The nature of the Single Market Programme

As one would expect, views on the character of the SMP and the influences shaping it vary. To take but one example, Moravcsik has argued that the negotiation of the Single European Act was the product of 'intergovernmental institutionalism'; that is to say, bargaining among the three largest

EC member states, France, Germany and the UK.[3] By contrast, Sandholtz and Zysman suggest that 1992 represented a dramatic break in the evolution of the EC, in which policy entrepreneurship on the part of the EC Commission generated elite bargains among the member states, the outcome of which was the SMP.[4] Although the distinction might seem of limited significance in terms of external responses to the SMP, in the case of the USA interpreting the forces producing this policy development helped to condition responses. Beyond these interpretations of the dynamics under-pinning the process, however, a considerable consensus can be found as to the motives for, and the implications of, the SMP. For purposes of analysis it is possible to distinguish between the narrower, EC, context of the 1992 proposals and their broader, global, dimensions.

In the context of the development of the EC, the motivations for the SMP, as we noted in Chapter 1, have to be interpreted in terms of the evolution of European integration since the 1950s and, in particular, a growing belief among many that further integration – both economic and political – was essential if the challenges to Europe in the global economic order were to be met. The dynamism that had marked the development of the Community in the early 1970s evaporated during the decade, with little progress on the various proposals for further integration such as those contained in the Tindemans Report of 1975. This reflected not simply divergent views as to the direction that the EC should move in but an inhospitable international environment following the energy crisis and subsequent recession which were the products of the OPEC oil price rises. To the strains created by differing responses to the energy crisis were added those related to enlargement of the EC, disputes over the Common Agricultural Policy (CAP) and the Community's budget. Thus during the late 1970s and early 1980s, a 'Europessimism' developed which derived from concerns with the internal development of the EC and its decision-making structures and processes as well as the place of Europe in the global economy.[5]

Here, Europeans were confronting a far more challenging environment than that which had alerted observers to the dangers of the 'American challenge' in the 1960s.[6] The emergence of the third industrial revolution based on microelectronics and information technology posed the dangers not simply of growing trade competitiveness but of access to the key technologies themselves. In this context, the growing pre-eminence of Japan was critical. By the mid-1980s, the Japanese had assumed a dominant role in key high-technology areas, eclipsing the USA and dominating production of memory chips, for example. Not only did this mean reliance on Japan for components in the manufacture of electronic goods, it also gave the Japanese a potential source of leverage over competitors in the battle for market share in those goods. Furthermore, the Japanese challenge encouraged US manufacturers to be more protective of their new products, thus making the USA a less certain source of high-technology products for the Europeans. When combined with growing protectionism in the USA and the difficulties of gaining access for its exports to the Japanese market, the situation confronting Europe appeared increasingly critical.[7]

But the debate was not simply economic in nature, for alongside it ran the accompanying theme of the character of the EC as a set of institutions and the future of the integrative processes. The linkages between economic dilemmas, political choices and institutional structures are continuing themes in the evolution of European integration. However, they acquired a new resonance from the mid-1980s onwards, not least as a result of the efforts of the President of the Commission, Jacques Delors, but also as a consequence of the stimulus provided by the introduction of direct elections to the European Parliament in 1979. Thus the SMP has to be seen as significant in terms of the status of the EC member states within the global economy but also as part of the debate about the future of the EC, one in which the respective Bruges speeches of the then British Prime Minister, Margaret Thatcher (1988), and Jacques Delors (1989) stood in sharp contrast.

This economic and political duality was reflected in the events leading up to, and in the character of, the Single European Act (SEA) enacted in July 1987, following several years of debate within the EC on economic, social and political issues. In economic terms, the major provision of the SEA was the proposal to create a barrier-free internal market based on the blueprint set out in the 1985 White Paper entitled 'Completing the Internal Market' presented to the 1985 Milan meeting of the European Council. The purpose here was to demolish those non-tariff barriers (NTBs) to trade which had survived the removal of tariffs and quantitative restrictions in the years since the signing of the Treaty of Rome in 1958. The argument was that NTBs – such as border controls, differential standards regulating products within the EC and controls over the award of government contracts to firms in other EC member states – constituted a major obstacle to EC economic development. Their removal would enhance intra-European trade and, in a single market of some 320 million people, allow firms providing goods and services to enhance their competitiveness on the world market. Approximately 300 deregulatory proposals were contained in the 1985 White Paper, to be put into place by 31 December 1992.

It was understood within the EC Commission and by many – but by no means all – within member state governments that the success of the economic agenda was dependent on progress on the political front. Indeed, Delors and others stressed that the first would not succeed without the second. Thus the SEA was concerned with more than the removal of internal trade barriers. It set out the objectives and processes for European political cooperation which stood outside the original Treaty of Rome, and reformed the decision-making processes, particularly the voting arrangements within the Council of Ministers, and the legislative relationship between the Council and the European Parliament.[8]

Taking the broader perspective, as we noted at the start of Chapter 1, despite the silence of the 1985 White Paper on the implications of 1992 for the international community, the entire enterprise was rooted in perceptions of the changing nature of the international system and Europe's place in it, as the concept of 'Eurosclerosis', so widely discussed in the 1970s and 1980s, underscores. The principal concern – and one which we shall examine in some detail in the context of US–EC relations – was the extent to which the SMP represented a decreasing commitment to the multilateralism of the GATT and the emergence of a creeping protectionism on the part of the EC. Japan, for example, was concerned by rumours that 1992 might lead to greater controls over Japanese car imports. Addressing the Royal Institute of International Affairs in October 1988, the Japanese Deputy Foreign Minister pointed to Tokyo's anxieties over the issue, which it regarded 'as a test case of the EC's sincere commitments to truly opening its market to the outside world, in conformity with the rules of GATT'.[9] The meeting of EC heads of state and government held in Rhodes at the end of that year appeared to recognize these concerns when it stressed that the Community was in no sense becoming inward-looking.

Nevertheless, there was a tension here which reflected the context in which the SMP and the SEA had emerged. At the same time that the SMP reflected the desire to reinvigorate the EC and its industries, it revealed the underlying insecurities of European governmental and industrial elites. From an early stage, there was a fear that forces of globalization would undermine the 'Europeanness' of the Single Market, and that American and Japanese corporations would come to dominate it. Within the European Commission, there was a perception among some that the Single Market should not be 'given away', and that concessions should be extracted from those outsiders who might benefit from a newly expanded economic space. Economic insecurity thus came to coexist with the bullishness of many European enterprises; the result was a strange mixture of confidence in the transforming effects of the SMP and defensiveness about the possibility that the market might be taken away from those who were most entitled to benefit. It was these considerations that led the EC Commissioner for External Trade Relations, Willy de Clercq, to observe that the SEM, while not overtly protectionist, would be looking for concessions from those seeking access to it: 'We want to open our border, but on the basis of a mutual balance of advantages in the spirit of GATT.'[10]

The symptoms of this unease were magnified by precisely the dynamic effects that had been expected of the SMP. During the late 1980s, investment by American and Japanese corporations in the EC spurted, although on the whole the Americans were perceived less as outsiders than the Japanese; after all, many of the corporations concerned had been operating in the EC since its early years. The move from boom to recession in the early 1990s, and the perceived failure of some European industries to respond to the changing environment, led to a combination of calls for a new industrial strategy (implicitly entailing intervention and subvention), while governments proved relatively unready to take significant stimulatory measures.

But the developments of the late 1980s held implications for the EC's political as well as economic role and relationships. As Lodge has noted, the development of the SMP, together with the politicization of international trade, helped to erode the increasingly tenuous distinction between the EC's external competences and the security and defence interests of member states.[11] Moreover, events in Eastern Europe as the decade drew to a close, to be followed by the even more dramatic developments in the USSR, gave added significance to the SMP and the role and constitution of the EC in a changing world order. It was the combination of economic and political factors that shaped US responses and it is to those that we now turn.

The US response

US attitudes towards 1992 have to be seen against the backdrop of the long-term transatlantic relationship and the factors conditioning it.[12] Perhaps the key point to note in this context is the consistent support, on the one hand, for the ideals and objectives of European integration which have characterized American approaches to its post-1945 organizational manifestations. This has been balanced, on the other, by growing tensions as the EC acquired the capacity to challenge the USA, particularly in the economic sphere. Second, the relationship has always rested on the intersection of military–security and economic concerns, the balance between the two usually determining the state of the relationship at any given moment.

As is well known, this balance has changed over the past four decades or so. Despite the economic costs of supporting European integration in the late 1940s and 1950s, US economic hegemony combined with the onset of the Cold War ensured that the positive aspects were dominant. Since then, the pattern of relationships has become far more complex for several reasons. The changing character of East–West relations was part of the picture. Not only did the threat from the USSR appear less starkly drawn as the post-war years evolved, but Western European governments began to adopt positions on the nature of the conflict and the policies appropriate to their interests, which differed from those of Washington. Attitudes to the Vietnam War, to the possibilities of maintaining *détente* in the 1970s and to the Soviet policies of the early Reagan years symbolized these differences.

This reflected a second factor in the changing relationship, namely the emergence of a far more complex multipolar, interdependent international environment from which the transatlantic relationship could not be insulated. In particular, new centres of economic power, notably Japan, ensured that both the USA and Europe would be forced to view one another in a broader context and to adapt their policies to new realities. These developments underpinned a third contextual change: the relative economic 'decline' of the USA – or, put another way, the loss of its overwhelming economic power in the immediate post-1945 period. We shall return to this point later in the chapter.

Finally, there is the impact of generational change, particularly among the policy elite. The linkages created during and after the Second World War formed a major feature of US–European relations and helped to ease tensions at critical junctures. Certainly by the 1980s, a theme of commentaries on the relationship was the erosion of this fund of experience through death and retirement, together with the emergence of new preoccupations, notably the Asia-Pacific region. This was not an insignificant factor for understanding US responses to the SMP and subsequent developments on the path to further European integration.

Thus, by the late 1980s and the early 1990s, the disappearance of the military security imperatives provided by the East–West conflict were creating a new context for the already existing economic tensions between the countries of the West.[13] As the logic of geo-politics was transformed by that of geo-economics, an 'admixture of the logic of conflict with the methods of commerce' to employ Luttwak's terminology, so the processes of world politics, rather than being replaced by those of world business, interacted with them, and the instruments of conflict became increasingly economic in nature.[14]

This, combined with a greater equality in the distribution of economic power, has helped to elevate economic disputes to a new level of significance. Thus, for writers such as Garten and Thurow, the ideological battles of the Cold War have been replaced by an emerging polarity based on three variants of the victorious belief system of the post-war struggle, namely capitalism. The resultant 'Cold Peace' reflects fundamental differences between the three centres of economic power in the emerging order: the USA, Japan and Germany. Consequently, among the 'old assumptions' that require re-examination is that which portrayed the USA, Europe and Japan in close partnership as the post-Cold War era emerged.[15]

Rather than enhanced cooperation, a series of issues and events –

German unification, aid to the former Soviet Union, financial cooperation, the Gulf War, Third World debt forgiveness, the Uruguay Round of
GATT trade talks and the former Yugoslavia – each in its own way
illustrated the differing priorities preoccupying Washington, the EC and
Tokyo, in part a reflection of the growing salience of domestic
considerations.

Each set of problems reflected fundamental shifts in the priorities of
Americans, Europeans and Japanese as the 'overlay' that the Cold War
had imposed on the traditional European security structures began to
erode.[16] As it did so, it became increasingly clear that underneath these
tensions lay fundamental differences relating to social, economic and
political structures. Returning to a theme of the previous chapter, as the
demands of access became relatively more prominent compared with the
needs of control, so these differing systems became issues of contention in
their own right, regarded in some senses as attempts to secure and
perpetuate unfair advantages. Thus disputes with Japan over market
access issues became, effectively (as some US legislators and officials have
made clear on occasion), a debate about the very nature of Japanese
society and political culture.

Against this background the USA and the EC can be seen as both allies
and adversaries. This impinged on the military–security agenda as
represented by the long-running conflicts over burden-sharing, but it
was on the economic front that tensions were at their most marked. Thus,
by the time that the SMP attracted the attention of various US interests in
the latter 1980s, a pattern of linkages and conflict was well developed, if
shifting in its precise character. Europe was America's largest market for
exports, purchasing 24 per cent of US exports in 1988 as compared to the
22 per cent destined for Canada. But of even greater significance is the fact
that 45 per cent of US exports to Europe in that year were classified as
high-technology goods, compared with 29 per cent of US exports to
Japan.

Similarly, in terms of foreign investment, the US stake in Europe was
high, rising from about 18 per cent of total US overseas investment in 1960
to almost 40 per cent in 1988.[17] Furthermore, the EC was the only major
regional trading partner with which the USA enjoyed a trade surplus – a
fact which one industry spokesperson saw as 'the most significant aspect
of EC-92 for American foreign policy'.[18] However, these linkages in one
sense simply served to enhance US sensitivities to perceptions of what the
SMP might portend for its interests. In this light, responses to 1992 have to
be viewed against the doubts and uncertainties exemplified in reactions to
Paul Kennedy's book, *The Rise and Fall of the Great Powers*.[19]

Such preoccupations, of course, are by no means unique to the USA.
They reflect a more closely integrated global community embracing
complex networks of linkages, together with pressing global issues, not

least those presented by growing environmental challenges, and confront all national communities to a greater or lesser extent. But the central position of the USA within the international system, together with the scope of its global interests, ensures that it remains the object of external pressures related to a broad range of policy issues. Thus, whereas in the post-Cold War environment, the relative power of the USA appears to be underscored by its status as the sole claimant to superpower status, so the degree to which American society and the political processes are open to external influences is equally apparent.

At the economic level, the internationalization of the American economy, as represented by the growing contribution of foreign trade to GNP, was accompanied by a rapid growth in foreign direct investment attracted by the size and diversity of the US market and further stimulated in the late 1980s by the decline in the value of the dollar. Taken with the escalating trade and budget deficits produced by Reaganite macroeconomic policies (the US merchandise trade deficit rose from $26 billion in 1980 to $150 billion in 1987), the transformation of the country from a net creditor to a net debtor during the 1980s and a variety of other indices (such as the growing percentage of the US workforce employed by overseas firms), it was not surprising that both the public and political elites – not least Congress – should be alerted to the enhanced impact of international economic forces.[20]

These trends were to stimulate a debate regarding appropriate strategies which have underlain the evolution of trade policy over decades.[21] At the structural level, a dialogue developed regarding the extent to which US economic decline was linked to the international economic crises of the 1970s and 1980s. Hegemonic stability theorists argued that the diminution of American power had removed the key prerequisite for an open, liberal trading order, namely the leadership of a powerful state to underwrite that order.[22] In terms of practical politics, the administration's commitment to free trade became tempered with another theme in US trade policy, that of 'fair trade'.

Increasingly during the 1980s, the conviction grew – particularly in Congress – that the ballooning trade deficit was the result of unfair competition on the part of America's trading partners. Whereas the USA adhered to a 'level playing field' philosophy of international trade, ran the argument, applying the 'rules of the game' fairly, other countries did not. In particular, the accusatory finger was pointed at the Japanese, seen as the arch-perpetrators of 'mercantilist' policies designed to penetrate foreign markets while denying others access to their own. This set the scene for the adoption of strategic trade policy measures intended to counter what were regarded as displacements of the level playing field.[23] From the European perspective, given the views of influential figures in the new administration, the balance between commitment to free trade and to managed trade became particularly critical as President Clinton succeeded President Bush.[24]

The preoccupation with power and 'decline' that these phenomena encouraged extended beyond economic access, however, to a concern that the openness of the US political system was permitting foreign interests, particularly the Japanese, to gain access to the policy-making processes, even to the extent that they were excluding the legitimate expression of domestic interests. Consequently, rather than foreign interest lobbying being regarded as a natural outcome of the combined effects of an open political system and an increasingly internationalized economy, it was perceived as the political equivalent of the 'buying into America' concerns represented by the growth of foreign investment.[25]

Overall, these factors served to interact with and reinforce a growing sense of concern and disillusion with many aspects of American society: primary and secondary education, health care, civil rights and urban decay, to be reinforced by drug addiction and law and order. Although defined as 'domestic' issues demanding enhanced salience on the White House agenda, these were, in many of their manifestations, inherently international, in the sense that managing them demanded an international perspective and/or they conditioned the position of the USA in its international setting – not least in terms of its industrial competitiveness.

Issues

It was against this background that the specific US–EC trade tensions which helped to condition initial US responses to 1992 arose or re-asserted themselves. Some of these – such as steel and agriculture – reflected long-standing disputes rooted in the fact that both were competing for access to the same markets. Washington's concerns with the CAP and EC inroads into US markets for agricultural products were shadowed by European objections to the 1985 Export Enhancement Program, which Brussels challenged under the GATT Subsidies Code. Disputes over citrus fruits, rice and wheat flour, among other products, resulted in the imposition of, or the threat to impose, duties on a range of agricultural products. In the high-technology area, European subsidies to Airbus Industries, rivals to Boeing and McDonnell Douglas, and US access to the European telecommunications market were continuing issues on the trade agenda.[26]

The SMP had, therefore, a significant cognitive dimension to it. What did it represent in terms of European economic and political ambitions? Was it a further twist of the protectionist screw marking a reduced commitment by the EC to the Uruguay Round of GATT negotiations? Clearly, much of this was located in the realm of speculation, a fact reinforced by EC officials' tendency to respond on an *ad hoc* basis to matters relating to the external implications of the SMP. The answers to these questions revolved around general concerns regarding the implications of the SMP and a series of specific issues. At the more general level, as we have already suggested, 1992 posed potential problems for US influence. Not only might an economically (and politically) more powerful Europe challenge US firms in the global market place, it would have sufficient clout to shape the attitudes and policies of other actors. This would be of particular concern within the context of the GATT negotiations, as the Europeans acquired added leverage in the forum within which Washington hoped that many of the long-standing transatlantic trade disputes might be resolved. Noting that SMP rules and regulations could eventually apply to more than twenty countries, one analyst observed:

> The vast size of the EC alone would provide it with considerable leverage in negotiating with smaller countries or trading blocs. Moreover, the enhanced power of the EC as a trading bloc, combined with its single market liberalizing reforms, could be used to pressure other countries to make changes in their legal and regulatory systems.[27]

A second general issue, again linked to the introspection generated by the preoccupation with vulnerability and decline in a changing world order, related to the competitiveness of US firms and the role of government in export promotion activities. In this context, a growing awareness of the nature of the single market proposals was to draw attention to what appeared to be coherent trade strategies on the part of European states and their absence in the USA. Among its main trading partners, America comes last in expenditure on export promotion as a percentage of GNP.[28]

This reflects the historical truth that it is the interests of large firms rather than small and medium-sized enterprises (SMEs) that have governed the fashioning of federal trade policy. The ability of the Department of Commerce to oversee an effective export assistance strategy has been questioned. Hence one study, commenting on a US General Accounting Office report which revealed that ten federal agencies were engaged in export assistance, but without any overall strategy, questioned whether the federal government has 'either the will or the resources' to match the efforts of European countries in supporting SMEs.[29] Indeed, to the extent that the interests of exporters are being met, the initiative – as will be seen in Chapter 5 – has passed largely to the state level, which is closer to the concerns of SMEs.

Thus, at the organizational level, 1992 presented challenges in adapting to the new European economic arena and determining the appropriate roles for and relationships between government and business. Speaking in early 1995, the Under Secretary of Commerce for International Trade noted that government departments had not responded to the SEM, still adopting what he termed a 'compartmentalized' approach to the support of American business.[30]

Beyond these general concerns were to be found a series of more specific issues. Among them, of course, was the likely impact on US exports as a consequence of trade creation versus trade diversion. Conflicting trends were predicted. On the one hand, it was assumed that there would be some trade diversion from US exporters to European-based firms; on the other, assuming that predictions such as those contained in the Cecchini report were proved correct, then the internal market would enhance demand for goods and services, leading to trade creation, the benefits of which would be felt by US firms.[31]

Another issue of concern to the Americans was the degree to which the SMP foreshadowed enhancement of support to high-technology industries – such as those in the computer and information technology areas – through the use of subsidies (as in the case of Airbus) and a range of other practices, such as local content rules. This question, of course, was closely linked to the broad issues of US economic power and also to US–Japanese trade relations in particularly sensitive sectors. Would the internal market encourage trends which might make further inroads into the US share of high-technology exports to Europe; moreover, would it enhance challenges to US firms in other markets?

Further down the list of US concerns came a set of problems which were derivative of the general questions relating to the impact of 1992 on US firms in Europe, and US exporters to European and other-country markets. Among these stood the vexed issue of reciprocity and the definitions attached to the concept. At its most fundamental level, the problem focused on the demands that the Europeans might make on the USA in return for the right to operate in the unified European market. Probably the most celebrated case in this category occurred in the banking sector, with the reciprocity requirements of the first draft of the Second Banking Directive.[32] To the US authorities, this had represented a worrying departure on the part of the EC from the accepted 'national treatment' approach to reciprocity and a failure to appreciate the constraints that the American federal system, with its state-based regulatory structures, imposed on the federal government in trade negotiations.

Also of concern was the issue of national quotas, given the fact that these were clearly incompatible with a unified market. How would the 700 plus quantitative restrictions limiting third country suppliers (the majority relating to clothing and textiles within the framework of the Multifibre Arrangement) be phased out? Technical standards posed another potentially difficult issue. Under the 1992 programme, the method of handling the problem of differing national standards was to be the adoption of the 'mutual recognition' system whereby goods meeting the standards ruling in one member state would be regarded as saleable in the others. However, for a select group of products, notably in the areas of health, safety and the environment, minimum standards or harmonization were proposed. Views on the impact of these processes for US firms varied. On one side, there would be savings to be made since only one set of standards would have to be met; yet at the same time, concern was expressed that US firms would be shut out of the standards-setting processes, thus limiting their access to the European market.

A further contentious issue, one going back to the early 1970s, existed in the shape of government procurement, one of the case studies examined in Chapter 7. The EC has, traditionally, favoured national suppliers, particularly in key areas such as telecommunications. Between 1984 and 1988, the UK, France, the Netherlands and Portugal awarded 100 per cent of telecommunications contracts to national suppliers.[33] Thus, whereas Europe constitutes the largest export market for US telecommunications equipment (over twice the size of the Japanese market), it has the potential to be far larger. As Hufbauer noted in 1990, the abolition of preferential government procurement and national treatment of foreign firms would open up an enormous market for US suppliers of telecommunications goods and services.[34] Within the GATT framework, a Government Purchasing Agreement was agreed in 1979. However, it had little effect, partly because procurement barriers to market access are rarely set out in legislation and partly because it excluded a major dimension of the issue, namely preference operating at the levels of state and local government.[35]

A concern which intermingled with several of these issues was that of the prospect of 'forced investment' by US firms wishing to gain access to the single market. While the logic for firms to establish a presence within such a vast market seemed obvious, there was a fear voiced by some that European leaders had as a central objective the desire to force foreign firms to locate in the EC through the use of various rules such as rules of origin and local content regulations. This would have the effect of transferring valuable technology to Europe. But from the US perspective, it was far more desirable to export to than to invest in Europe, since this would result in increased production and employment and remove the likelihood of the export of highly skilled jobs, some of them touching on national security interests.[36]

It was the range and complexity of issues which the 1992 programme presented for the USA that helped to constitute its character as an example of the multilayered policy environment discussed in the previous chapter. Not only were a wide range of actors involved, but to complicate matters further, the cast of actors was likely to vary between problems and to cut across two axes: the national and subnational on one side, and the public and private realms of political and economic activity on the other.

At the national level (discussed in detail in the following chapter), the broad issues posed were those relating to substantive policy problems and, second, developing appropriate responses. This required nothing less than redefining the US–EC relationship in the context of the changing global architecture, a task undertaken by the Bush administration that resulted in a new institutional framework for the conduct of the relationship in the shape of the 1990 Transatlantic Declaration. In a broader context, as noted earlier, the impact of 1992 raised the issue of appropriate strategies within the Uruguay Round to achieve US trade policy goals, against the possibility that the SMP would enhance EC economic leverage within the Multilateral Trade Negotiations (MTN).[37] Furthermore, the emergence of the SMP encouraged the exploration of regional approaches to trade liberalization. The successful completion of the Canada–US Free Trade Agreement was to be followed in 1993 by the completion of the NAFTA agreement negotiations, embracing the USA, Canada and Mexico. The interaction between regionalism, the protracted negotiations within the Uruguay Round and US concerns over EC intentions were further reflected in the Clinton adminstration's approach to the Asia-Pacific Economic Cooperation forum during 1993 and the warnings directed to Europe that America had Pacific interests which might eclipse those linking it to Europe.[38]

Added to the policy problems presented by the SMP were those relating to the management of the US response, particularly in a context where it was essential to link government with business interests. Clearly, this reflected the broader dimensions of the US foreign economic policy-making environment, with its growing degree of fragmentation, discussed in Chapter 3.[39] But, as we shall see in Chapter 4, the capacity of the executive to manage foreign economic policy was dramatically lessened by the growing involvement of Congress in trade policy, partly a reflection of the diminishing economic status of the USA.

Congressional concern with the 1992 agenda underscored the fact that specific items would impact selectively on economic interests with a regional base and encourage the growing state interest in trade policy issues (see Chapter 5). But state and local governments were also a target for the EC in the shape of local 'Buy American' laws, which discriminate against foreign firms in the area of government procurement. Taken together, these two facts ensured that the patterns of US–EC interactions surrounding issues on the 1992 agenda would have a local/state dimension. The overall tensions in the conduct of trade policy created by these factors as the USA contemplated responses to the SMP were well expressed by Raymond Vernon:

Americans place a high value on the diffusion of bureaucratic power and on the participation of the public in policy-making. At the same time, they prefer an international economic environment that is open – and stable. American negotiators, in consequence, are supported by a fragmented decision-making structure that was never designed to shape and implement foreign economic policies.[40]

Cutting across the national–subnational divide are the varying relationships between government and business interests. Here, as Woolcock argues, it is important to note that these are significant in understanding transatlantic trade and investment relations. Whereas most US firms operate in the European theatre without great difficulty (as do the majority of European firms in the American) by adapting to a specific regulatory environment, at the political level economic relationships are marked by high levels of tension, symbolized by the often shrill language of declaratory diplomacy. Hence 'the interaction between the political and corporate planes will therefore determine EC–US trade relations'.[41] But the multilayered diplomatic environment is further enlivened by the differences of interest between US corporate players, and this is clearly reflected in attitudes towards the SMP.[42]

Given the fact that, over the past twenty years or so, the stock of US direct investment in the EC has risen at a far greater rate than have exports, it is not surprising that there should be differences of interest between large corporate actors with a European presence and smaller firms whose primary perspective on the single market is determined by its impact on exports. In certain sectors, of course, such as financial services, 'presence' in the European market place and policies affecting that presence assume far greater significance than do trading links. This is reflected in the capacity of large 'inside' firms to operate within the EC system, as indicated in a National Association of Manufacturers report on the SMP, which identified the following 'points of access' for US companies:

- specialists in appropriate directorates of the European Commission;
- member state trade and industry associations, as well as EC-wide bodies such as the employers' association UNICE;
- appropriate national ministries;
- permanent delegations to the EC;
- the European Parliament;
- EC member state legislatures.

The problem for the large firms with a European presence, it was suggested, would be in adapting to the new realities created by the SMP and developing pan-European strategies to exploit the opportunities it presented. At the other end of the scale, SMEs with little or no European interest might find their markets penetrated by aggressive European firms benefiting from the stimulus of an enlarged home market base. By the time that some US companies become aware of the danger, 'they are likely to find strategic alliances already formed, regulations established, market access closed, and powerful new competitors in place'.[43]

Thus the image of 'Fortress Europe' shutting out US exports was countered by the positive attitude of large firms with significant European operations and capacity to exercise influence in the EC, such as IBM and AT&T. The distinction between the interests of SMEs and large corporations was clearly reflected in the character of the US diplomatic effort and the relationships between business and governmental actors as the potential impact of 1992 assumed greater salience on the political agenda. This is discussed in Chapter 6.

Multilayered policy

Against the background of issues and interests generated by the SMP examined in this chapter, a complex policy environment emerged. To a considerable degree, the interactions that developed within it were shaped by the nature of the main political arenas involved: the EC on one side and the USA on the other. One of the challenges confronting both US governmental and non-governmental interests was that of operating in the challenging milieu presented by the EC. This was enhanced by the need to anticipate the impact of the changes implicit in the 1992 programme and associated measures. In one sense, the EC offers a political environment balancing openness and closedness. On the one hand, its neo-federal and multinational qualities combined with its openness to lobbying create an environment compatible with access. Yet, as Mazey and Richardson suggest, it also possesses features which make it a difficult arena in which to operate. Apart from the diffusion of policy-making power between national and community levels, the EC possesses a degree of instability which reflects the absence of the policy processes associated with national settings. This makes tracking policy both difficult and expensive in terms of effort.[44]

At the same time, the EC has undergone internal transformations – of which the Maastricht Treaty is one manifestation – which reinforce these characteristics. The debate about subsidiarity, the significance of regions and, in the German context, the trilateral tensions between Bonn, Brussels and the *Länder* are representative of them.[45] Moreover, the rapidly changing international environment has impacted on the EC as relationships with other actors, EFTA and the Eastern European countries, have developed. Interpreting the nature of the European enterprise, far less operating within its structures, has always proved testing for the USA, partly because its federalist aspirations for Europe have sometimes inclined it to place too much reliance on Brussels as a centre of influence, while, in other contexts, it has operated as if the EC were little more than a collectivity of independent national governments, each of which should be dealt with separately.[46]

The notion that the EC might be less than an imitation of the American federal system but more than an intergovernmental arrangement – an idea encapsulated in the term 'complex governance' – has often proved difficult to come to grips with.[47] But these changes have also resulted in an opening up of the EC as a diversity of external forces enter into its policy processes. The consequence is 'a Community policymaking process which is increasingly if somewhat unevenly penetrated, and which gives sources of leverage to new participants'.[48]

What this suggests is that complex governance is not constrained by boundaries, whether these be national or supranational, in its attempts to deliver goods and services to those under its aegis. Economic goals in particular demand patterns of coordination which extend beyond the EC into various forums, such as the GATT/WTO, OECD and G7, to name but three.[49] In short, the EC is itself a complex polity and one that has to operate in an increasingly intricate regional and global context. The implications of these factors for the analysis of US–EC interactions revolving around the SMP are that they create what we might term a 'reticulated' diplomatic milieu that fails to correspond to conventional notions of foreign policy and which accords much more closely to that of the multilayered policy environment discussed in the previous chapter. This implies a network of relationships embracing a wide range of actors, governmental and non-governmental, some located in the European, others within the American, 'space'.

A 'traditional' foreign policy perspective on US–EC relations would stress the linkages between the national governments and between the US federal government and the EC where the latter possesses external policy competences, as in the case of international trade. This basic model has to be supplemented to take into account the role of subnational actors, governmental and non-governmental, and the transnational relationships that can develop between them. Furthermore, the institutions of the EC need to be disaggregated in recognition of the distinctive roles of institutions such as the European Parliament, the Council of Ministers and the Commission, each of which can be the target of outside influence. Additionally, recognition must be accorded to the transgovernmental relationships that can develop between agencies of government in different national settings.

This is not to suggest that the resultant network has an even quality to it or that the disjunctures imposed by national boundaries are irrelevant or insignificant. Rather, it is marked by an unevenness which reflects these but is tempered by boundaries and linkages between actors at several levels. In this sense, the designation of actor roles in terms of their geographical 'home' becomes less significant than the interests they represent and the relationships which they have developed in the target geographical area – in this case the EC. An obvious example is the distinction between US firms with a presence in Europe ('insiders') and those without such a presence ('outsiders'). In terms of interests and strategic responses to elements of the SMP, it is clear that this distinction was at least of equal importance to the geographical 'home' of a US firm.

This leads us to note that one of the key features of the multilayered policy environment is the opportunity it offers, or the necessity that it imposes, to pursue a variety of strategies which link governmental and non-governmental actors in a variety of political settings. In this context, considerable attention has been devoted to Putnam's image of two-level games, characterized by the role of national policy-makers operating at the domestic and the international negotiating table simultaneously, and seeking domestic approval (or 'ratification') for their international actions.[50]

There is a temptation here to extrapolate from this (as do Smith and Ray) a more nuanced image which suits the EC policy environment.[51] To a degree, their notion of 'multilevel' games accords with the issues with which this study is concerned. However, the essence of Putnam's linkage of the domestic and the international policy environments, clearly central to our concerns, is that the national policy-maker is in a privileged and often controlling position, which resembles the traditional gatekeeper role enshrined in the classic foreign policy model. Indeed, in a later article he has argued that the future of US–EC relations in a more interdependent and equal environment will be determined by 'the skill and strength of our political leaders'.[52] One does not have to dispense with the proposition that national policy-makers can influence policy outcomes independent of domestic pressures to realize that the realities of *multilevel* as distinct from *two-level* games are so hard to describe, let alone convert into practical strategies, that this basic tenet of Putnam's analysis becomes vastly more difficult to operationalize in the complex political arena of US–EC relations.

Conclusion

In this chapter we have sought to flesh out the bones of the multilayered policy environment discussed in Chapter 1. In so doing, we have looked briefly at the ways in which the USA and the EC related to each other in the context of the SMP. More specifically, we have focused on the key issues that the 1992 agenda presented to US interests and their responses to them, thereby setting the scene for the analysis in the ensuing chapters.

Taking a broad overview, it is possible to detect three interlinked aspects to the US attitude to the SMP as it sought to respond to these events and to interpret them in terms of a balance between opportunities to be exploited and challenges to be diverted.

The first of the three assumed the form of a cognitive challenge, that of making sense of what 1992 actually meant and how it related to the concerns of the various stakeholders. In part, this was a problem of focusing on Europe during a period when the dominant issues on the trade agenda lay in other geographical areas. Once US interests were aware of the existence of the SMP, the problem became one of determining its likely impact and relating it to the broader trade agenda, particularly the multilateral trade negotiations within the GATT. In short, a learning process was involved in which a range of actors, including industry and its representative groups and Congress, were participants.

The dynamic character of this process would be illustrated by the relatively short-lived fears concerning 'Fortress Europe'. By 1989, the Commerce Department was discounting this as an alarmist vision, while, at the same time, pointing out that the USA needed to be vigilant regarding a number of 'strongholds' – or issues which endangered its interests.[53] Furthermore, given the dramatic international events which accompanied the development of the SMP in the late 1980s and early 1990s, there was a clear need for the federal government to re-examine its relationships with Europe and the means by which they were conducted. It was this realization which led to the Transatlantic Declaration.

The second challenge was at the level of institutions and their capacity to respond to these events. In part, this reflected a continuing concern with the problems of coordinating responses at the bureaucratic level in the face of the forces of internationalization, linked to domestic pressures. As we shall see in the following chapter, the SMP raised in a different context well rehearsed questions regarding who should do what within the federal bureaucracy. Added to this was the increasingly strident voice of Congress on matters relating to trade, something that could not be ignored. Nor could state governments be overlooked for two reasons: first, they were demanding a voice in trade policy, which they recognized was affecting their economic interests; second, they were themselves now an item on the international trade agenda by virtue of protectionist policies operated at the subnational level.

But the issues posed by 1992 could not be dealt with simply by coordination between various layers of government. Industry, in its various forms, was a key player. Certainly, there was an issue concerning the role of government in promoting SMEs in Europe, but industrial interests were broader, fragmented and uneven, reflecting the multiplicity of issues on which the internal market measures touched. Even on the standards question, as we shall suggest in Chapter 7, the patterns of interaction between the various actors depended on the precise character of the problem.

The third dimension to interpreting US responses to the SMP is to be found in its relationship to preoccupations at various levels of government and society with America's power and role on the world stage. This, of course, involves a heady mix of cultural, political and economic factors, which have to be seen in the context of the growing exposure of the US economy to international influences and the challenge to American firms presented by the Japanese in particular. Awareness of the SMP thus came at a time when political and economic attention had been directed elsewhere but in a climate conducive to the acceptance of the initial proposition that 1992 was another potential threat to US interests.

Added to this were the broader political uncertainties that the changing international picture presented, with its implications for the EC's political orientations and the transatlantic relationship as it had evolved during the Cold War era. In short, further integration in Europe twisted the screw of apprehension within the USA regarding its vulnerability in a world where the shifting nature of access and control posed fundamental questions regarding America's role and influence.

Notes and references

1　There is a large literature on the origins and character of the SMP, including the following, which cover the main issues: J. Lodge (ed.), *The European Community and the Challenge of the Future*, London, Pinter, 1989; D. Swann (ed.), *The Single European Market and Beyond: A Study of the Wider Implications of the Single European Act*, London, Routledge, 1992; J. Palmer, *1992 and Beyond*, Luxembourg, European Communities, 1989; P. Cecchini, *The European Challenge: 1992: The Benefits of a Single Market*, Aldershot, Wildwood House, 1988; D. L. Smith and J. L. Ray (eds), *The 1992 Project and the Future of Integration in Europe*, Armonk, NY, Sharpe, 1993; M. Calingaert, *European Integration Revisited: Progress, Prospects and US Interests*, Boulder, CO, Westview Press, 1996.

2　Again, there is a large literature, as indicated in the bibliography. For an overview of the relationship up to the early 1980s, see M. Smith, *Western Europe and the United States: The Uncertain Alliance*, London, George Allen and Unwin, 1984. For analyses covering the period dealt with in this book, see: R. H. Ginsberg, 'US–EC relations', in Lodge, *op. cit.*, pp. 256–78; the collection of essays in H. Haftendorn and C. Tuschhoff (eds), *America and Europe in an Era of Change*, Boulder, CO, Westview, 1993;

M. Smith and S. Woolcock, *The United States and the European Community in a Transformed World*, London, RIIA/Pinter, 1993; K. Featherstone and R. Ginsberg, *The United States and the European Community in the 1990s* (2nd edn), London, Macmillan, 1996; J. Peterson, *Europe and America: the Prospects for Partnership* (2nd edn), London, Routledge, 1996.

3   A. Moravcsik, 'Negotiating the Single European Act: national interests and conventional statecraft in the EC', *International Organization*, 45(1), 1991, pp. 19–56.

4   W. Sandholtz and J. Zysman, '1992: recasting the European Bargain', *World Politics*, 42(1), 1989, pp. 95–128.

5   D. Swann, 'The single market and beyond – an overview', and D. Allen, 'European union, the Single European Act and the 1992 programme', in Swann, *op. cit.*

6   The most influential depiction of this threat came from J. -J. Servan-Schreiber, *Le défi americain*, Paris, Denoel, 1967.

7   Sandholtz and Zysman, *op. cit.*, pp. 104–6.

8   D. Allen, 'European union', *op. cit.*, pp. 26–50.

9   Quoted in Palmer, *op. cit.*, p. 11.

10 J. Lodge, 'European political cooperation: towards the 1990s', in J. Lodge (ed.), *op. cit.*, p. 237.

11 *Ibid.*, p. 223.

12 Probably the most useful single source outlining US responses to 1992 can be found in the collection of essays contained in *Europe and the United States: Competition and Cooperation in the 1990s*, Study Papers submitted to the Subcommittee on International Policy and Trade and the Subcommittee on Europe and the Middle East of the Committee on Foreign Affairs, US House of Representatives, Washington, DC, US Government Printing Office, June 1992.

13 One view of the security implications of the SMP can be found in R. Hormats, 'Redefining Europe and the Atlantic link', *Foreign Affairs*, 68, Fall 1989, pp. 71–91; also Smith and Woolcock, *op. cit.*

14 E. N. Luttwak, 'From geopolitics to geoeconomics', *The National Interest*, 20, Summer 1990, pp. 17–24.

15 J. E. Garten, *A Cold Peace: America, Japan, Germany and the Struggle for Supremacy*, New York, Times Books, 1992, pp. 29–36.

16 B. Buzan *et al.*, *The European Security Order Recast: Scenarios for the Post-Cold War Era*, London, Pinter, 1990.

17 G. C. Hufbauer, 'An overview', in G. C. Hufbauer (ed.), *Europe 1992: An American Perspective*, Washington, DC, Brookings, 1990.

18 S. Cooney, 'The impact of Europe 1992 on the United States', *Proceedings of the Academy of Political Science*, 38(1), 1991, p. 105.

19 P. Kennedy, *The Rise and Fall of the Great Powers*, London, Unwin Hyman, 1988. A debate on the decline thesis ensued which can be

traced in, for example, J. Nye Jr, *Bound to Lead: The Changing Nature of American Power*, New York, Basic Books, 1990; and H. Nau, *The Myth of America's Decline*, New York, Oxford University Press, 1990. A close observer saw this debate as one of three major factors conditioning US responses to the SMP: see G. L. Bustin, *A US View of Fortress Europe*, an address given to the United Kingdom Association for European Law, King's College, London, 20 July 1990.

20 I. M. Destler, *American Trade Politics* (3rd edn), 1995, Chapter 4; R. S. Walters, 'US trade negotiation in perspective', in R. S. Walters (ed.), *Talking Trade: US Policy in International Perspective*, Boulder, CO., Westview, 1993, pp. 4–9.

21 On the importance of ideas in the shaping of US trade policy, see J. Goldstein, 'Ideas, institutions and American trade policy', *International Organization*, 42(1), 1988, pp. 179–217.

22 On this theme, see S. Krasner, 'State power and the structure of international trade', *World Politics*, 28, 1976, pp. 317–47.

23 There is a considerable literature on strategic trade policy, including J. Zysman and L. Tyson (eds), *American Industry in International Competition: Government Policies and Corporate Strategies*, Ithaca, NY, Cornell University Press, 1983; and C. Barfield and W. Schambra (eds), *The Politics of Industrial Policy*, Washington, DC, American Enterprise Institute, 1986.

24 In particular, the new Treasury Secretary, Lloyd Bentsen, as an architect of protectionist legislation, and Laura Tyson, head of the Council of Economic Advisers and a supporter of reciprocity, were looked upon with some concern in Europe. See L. Barber and N. Dunne, 'A meeting of suspicious minds', *Financial Times*, 11 February 1993.

25 An extensive literature developed around the foreign interest lobbying theme, often linked to inward foreign investment and focused on the Japanese. Among the most widely discussed examples are M. Tolchin and S. Tolchin, *Buying into America: How Foreign Money is Changing the Face of Our Nation*, New York, Berkeley, 1989; and P. Choate, *Agents of Influence: How Japan's Lobbyists in the United States Manipulate America's Political and Economic System*, New York, Knopf, 1990.

26 Ginsberg, *op. cit.*, pp. 270–6; Peterson, *op. cit.*, Chapter 5; S. Woolcock, *Market Access Issues in EC-US Relations: Trading Partners or Trading Blows?*, London, RIIA/Pinter, 1991.

27 R. J. Ahearn, *US Access to the EC Market: Opportunities, Concerns and Policy Challenges*, Washington, DC, Library of Congress, Congressional Research Service, 16 June 1992.

28 W. E. Nothdurft, *Going Global: How Europe Helps Small States Export*, Washington, DC, Brookings, 1992, p. 4.

29   *Ibid.*, pp. 88–9.

30   These comments were made in a speech to the American Council
      on Germany: J. E. Garten, *The United States and Europe: Towards
      the 21st Century*, American Council on Germany, 9 March 1995,
      p. 23.

31   See J. A. C. Conybeare, '1992, the Community, and the World: free
      trade or fortress Europe?', in Smith and Ray, *op. cit.*, pp. 143–63.
      One of the major governmental surveys on these issues came from
      the US International Trade Commission in the form of regularly
      updated reports. See United States International Trade Commission,
      *The Effects of Greater Economic Integration Within the European
      Community on the United States*, Report to the Committee on Ways
      and Means of the United States House of Representatives and the
      Committee of Finance of the United States Senate, Washington, DC,
      USITC publication 2204, July 1989. Various industry organizations
      produced their own guides, such as those from the US Chamber of
      Commerce: *Europe 1992: A Practical Guide for American Business*,
      Washington, DC, International Division, US Chamber of Com-
      merce, 1989 and subsequent updates. Also, S. Cooney, *EC-92 and US
      Industry*, Washington, DC, National Association of Manufacturers,
      February 1989.

32   Woolcock, *op. cit.*, Chapter 3.

33   Hufbauer, *op. cit.*, p. 42.

34   *Loc. cit.*

35   Woolcock, *op. cit.*, pp. 72–3.

36   Ahearn, *op. cit.*, pp. 10–12.

37   *Ibid.*, p. 18.

38   Warren Christopher in late 1993 suggested that one of the problems
      of US foreign policy was its Eurocentrism. An analysis of US–EC
      relations in the wake of these events and on the eve of President
      Clinton's first European visit can be found in J. Martin, 'Still
      chairman of the board', *Financial Times*, 8/9 January 1994.

39   For a trenchant critique of the management of US trade policy, see B.
      Stokes, 'Organizing to trade', *Foreign Policy*, 89, Winter 1992–3, pp.
      36–52.

40   R. Vernon, 'European Community 1992: can the US negotiate for
      trade equality?', *Proceedings of the Academy of Political Science*,
      37(4), 1990, p. 9.

41   Woolcock, *op. cit.*, p. 25.

42   For a summary of the potential impact of 1992 on different
      categories of US firms see J. F. Magee, '1992: moves Americans must
      make', *Harvard Business Review*, May–June 1989, pp. 78–84. There
      was a deluge of press articles on the fate of US business in the wake
      of 1992. See, for example: J. W. Tuthill, 'US–Europe after '92:

"cultural disdain", not trade barriers, biggest hurdle', *Christian Science Monitor*, 6 July 1989, p. 19; J. L. Dutt, 'Why US business will lose out in Europe', *Christian Science Monitor*, 2 May 1991, p. 19.

43 Magee, *op. cit.*, p. 84.

44 S. Mazey and J. Richardson, 'Environmental groups and the EC: challenges and opportunities', *Environmental Politics*, 1(4), 1992, pp. 109–17.

45 K. H. Goetz, 'National governance and European integration: intergovernmental relations in Germany', *Journal of Common Market Studies*, 33(1), 1995, pp. 91–116.

46 Writing on US approaches to Europe, a professional lobbyist has suggested that part of the problem lies in the failure to understand the lobbying processes operating in Brussels, consequently elevating trade disputes to intergovernmental battles. See the comments of J. N. Gardner, 'Lobbying, European style', *Europe*, 311, November 1991, p. 30. On this theme see the comments concerning US attempts to influence the Second Banking Directive in R. Hill, 'Lobbying Brussels: a view from within', in S. Mazey and J. Richardson (eds), *Lobbying in the European Community*, Oxford, Oxford University Press, 1993.

47 B. B. Hughes, 'Delivering the goods: the EC and the evolution of complex government', in Smith and Ray, *op. cit.*, pp. 45–69.

48 Smith and Woolcock, *op. cit.*, p. 28.

49 Hughes, *op. cit.*, pp. 57–8

50 R. D. Putnam, 'Diplomacy and domestic politics: the logic of two-level games', *International Organization*, 42(3), 1988, pp. 427–61.

51 D. L. Smith and J. L. Ray, 'The 1992 project', in Smith and Ray, *op. cit.*, pp. 6–10.

52 R. D. Putnam, 'Two-level games: the impact of domestic politics on transatlantic bargaining', in Haftendorn and Tuschhoff, *op. cit.*, p. 79.

53 T. J. Hauser, 'The European Community Single Market and US trade relations', *Business America*, 114(5), 1993, p. 3. The National Association of Manufacturers appeared to dispense with the fortress Europe image early on, as indicated in the remarks made by one of its officers to a Congressional hearing in April 1989: Statement by S. Cooney to Hearing before the Joint Economic Committee, Congress of the United States: *Europe 1992: Long-term Implications for the US Economy*, Washington, DC, US Government Printing Office, 26 April 1989, p. 9.

3

The executive

The questions raised in this chapter are about the extent to which and the ways in which the US executive was challenged by the SMP, and the ways in which it responded. In order to construct this analysis, it is important to remain aware of the ways in which the SMP related to other ongoing concerns of the executive, both in the economic and in the political/security fields. Not only this, but the analysis should be sensitive to the ways in which the SMP challenged existing assumptions about the boundaries between different domains of executive activity, and between the executive and other governmental and non-governmental bodies. One of the key issues here is the generation of variety, both in policy problems and in processes and outcomes. The SMP challenged not only the substance of US foreign economic policy as perceived by the executive, but also the 'rules of the game' in foreign economic policy-making (see Chapter 2). It thus expanded the range over which responses needed to be coordinated and strategies evolved, and demanded awareness of the linkages among a wide variety of policy areas.

The challenge of the SMP was simultaneously internal – to the ways in which US economic activity was organized and had developed within the USA – and external, to the ways in which the USA was conceived as functioning and as playing a distinctive role in the world economy. Thus this chapter will also pursue a set of questions relating to the climate of ideas and the broader policy context within which the US executive could respond to the multiple challenge of the SMP, and the ways in which this shaped its continuing role in the world political economy. In an interdependent and interpenetrated world, changes in national or regional economic structures and strategies will have broader effects on the climate of economic activity and on the 'rules of the game' at the global level. Whether these changes are unilateral, bilateral, plurilateral or multilateral in their focus, they cannot escape international constraint or international response.[1]

This said, it must be added that the development of the EC and the changing fortunes of the European integration process have always been a problem for the USA. There has never been a time since the 1950s at which the Americans have not been concerned with the consolidation of the EC, on the one hand because of its contribution to the political and economic stabilization of Cold War Europe and on the other hand because of the often damaging impact of the EC on specific areas of US economic life, such as agriculture or certain parts of traditional heavy industry. The SMP, though, focused the development of the USA within the world political economy in a very sharp and immediate fashion, interacting as it did with the broader processes already noted in Chapters 1 and 2.[2]

The challenge of the SMP not only took a number of forms in itself; it also interacted with other challenges to provide a case study in the ways in which the executive could respond to a changing world economy. One way of expressing this is in terms of the demand for and the supply of executive policy-making: the demand arose from the specific impact and broader implications of the SMP, while the supply was expressed in terms of the executive's capacity to respond both in terms of its own structure and policy processes and in terms of strategy. In both cases, the answers over the period 1987 to 1993 were as often unexpected and contradictory as they were coherent and predictable.

The executive and foreign economic policy

In discussion of foreign economic policy, the starting point is often the presumed primary – if not exclusive – role of the executive. In realist and neo-realist theories of international relations, and mercantilist or neo-mercantilist perspectives on foreign economic policy, the focus on national interests and their expression by top decision-makers is a central given: as many writers in this tradition have argued, state action is effectively action taken by those acting in the name of the state. More recent and nuanced statist theories of the generation and implementation of foreign economic policy do not deny a place to legislatures and to a range of non-governmental groupings; rather, they stress the strategic location and the active role of the state, its officials and its political leadership.[3] It is argued that the executive, as the guardian of state interests and as the recipient of important information and communications, holds the initiative in shaping the foreign economic priorities of the society it represents. Political leaders and officials are not merely representatives. In important respects they are guardians – of the rules, of the accumulated body of knowledge and understandings, and of agreements with significant actors in the world arena. In addition, as already noted, the state as represented by political leaders and officials has responsibilities for the regulation of relations between a given society and its international rivals or partners, based upon the assumption that it can aggregate and articulate the needs and interests of the whole society.

In contrast, the study of foreign economic policy from a multilayered policy-making perspective emphasizes not the central and strategic role of the executive, but the array of networks in which the executive may have a significant role, and in which it is also surrounded by a web of linkages and associated behaviour patterns (see Chapter 1). Government in this conception is disaggregated, and is often characterized by intense competition for 'voice' and the right to shape or to express policy. There is also the possibility not only of interaction between several levels of government and private activity, but also of almost continuous negotiation within and across levels, as complex webs of policy emerge. The emphasis here is thus not only on the variety of processes and participants, but also on the ways in which understandings about policy and its execution can evolve without definitive or determining action on the part of any one agency.[4]

This means that access and control are issues of importance within the executive as well as within the broader national and international arenas. It also means that there is both a tension and a dialogue between the different views of the state outlined in this chapter so far. The state is not lifeless, and government officials can gain a good deal of autonomy and span of control.[5] But in many issue areas, the state is surrounded by and often constrained by national and international networks which shape its actions even when they appear to express its essential freedom of action. It is within such a context that this chapter will explore the ways in which the SMP posed a challenge to the US executive, and the ways in which this led to a reshaping of government and strategies.

The Single Market Programme: a multiple challenge to the executive

An essential part of the analysis of foreign economic policy-making is analysis of the ways in which policy challenges emerge and make themselves felt. As already noted in Chapter 2, the SMP was elaborated at a time when US policy-makers were less than certain of their bearings in the world political economy. The combination of widely shared perceptions of decline with the specific and immediate problems of the 'hangover' from the Reagan boom in the mid-1980s created a very particular climate for the reception of the SMP, and this was underlined in crucial ways by the manner in which the SMP itself was handled within the EC.

Many Americans – including many in the administration itself – were only patchily aware of the changes taking place in the EC during the mid-1980s. The years of 'high Reaganism' had been occupied with transatlantic tensions about nuclear policy, and by the assertive 'domesticism' of many US policy initiatives.[6] Even when the SMP itself was announced in 1985, and then fully launched in 1987 after the ratification of the Single European Act, there was every reason for Americans to look the other way, given the intense debate in trade policy circles about the Omnibus Trade and Competitiveness Act of 1988. This act itself had demonstrated two important features of US policy: first, the attempt to constrain the freedom of the executive in making findings of unfair trade and initiating proceedings; second, the relative lack of concern for the reactions of outsiders, among whom the EC played an active role in attempting to moderate some of the more objectionable features of the legislation. The atmosphere in the USA was thus alert to issues of trade policy and of international competitiveness, so much so, that active attempts had been made to insert into the legislation provisions about the preservation of national economic security and the opening of overseas (and therefore implicitly protected) markets for such sectors as telecommunications.[7]

This being so, the SMP crept on to the scene as far as many Americans were concerned, surrounded with a good deal of ambiguity. Inasmuch as it promised further consolidation of the Community, Americans – both in the executive and elsewhere – could support it in the tradition of EC contributions to the stabilization and development of the continent. But the SMP itself was a very extensive and often highly technical exercise, which was likely to have differential impacts on many of the most sensitive areas of the US economy; therefore, it was unlikely to be received with complete acquiescence and at the same time it was likely that special interest groups would wish to latch on to it at every opportunity.

This ambiguity was compounded by the way in which the SMP was 'marketed' by the Europeans, and in particular the European Commission. One of the points most frequently made about the SMP, both by its supporters and by its detractors, is that in its early stages it took little or no account of its external impact or of possible external responses. Only during 1988 did the attention of the Commission turn to mollification of those who had read the worst into the lack of attention to the SMP's external dimension. In the USA, this onset of awareness about the SMP as an international issue also coincided with a presidential election year. In terms of both the economic cycle – and particularly of trade policy-making – and the political cycle, the SMP could not help but arouse some strong emotions. Despite the attempt at the Hanover European Council in July 1988 to reassure outsiders about the multilateral credentials of the SMP, the ground for recriminations and fears was fertile.

How did these fears and recriminations make themselves felt, and how was the executive placed in its attempts to deal with them? At one level, the challenge of the SMP was a challenge of ideas and values. Through the 1980s, US administrations had preached the protection of the multilateral system and the primacy of the GATT, but the Omnibus Trade and

Competitiveness Act had marked a further advance of those in Congress and outside who wished to wield the big stick in US trade policy. It had also extended the surveillance of policies into new areas, especially those of trade in services and various forms of regulatory policy. While the Reagan White House had asserted its opposition to this advance of 'fair trade' doctrines, it had not been able to resist them at much more than the rhetorical level. By 1988, the rise of 'new trade theory' and the demand for executive action to take strategic positions in sensitive trade sectors had created an atmosphere in which the White House and government agencies were at least on the defensive. In this context, the SMP seemed to confirm the rise of a new and formidable competitor, armed with some rather potent weapons in the form of regulatory and standards-setting powers, and decidedly unforthcoming about the ways in which it intended to wield them.

In many ways, therefore, the early perception of the SMP by the Reagan administration was strongly shaped by the prevailing atmosphere in the USA and by the lack of information about the programme itself. As such information emerged, it was not reassuring. The EC Commissioner for External Trade Relations, Willy de Clercq, made a series of speeches in the spring and summer of 1988 which were intended at one and the same time to reassure Americans about the EC's commitment to multilateralism and to flex the new-found muscle given by the SMP. In particular, de Clercq and other EC policy-makers were wont to stress the desirability of reciprocity in areas where the SMP would open up the EC market, including banking and financial services. As we shall see, this hit a very raw nerve in Washington, not least in the Department of the Treasury.

If reciprocity was one focus of attention for the executive in 1988, it was only given more cause for concern by the lack of transparency in EC policy processes. By its nature, the SMP was a highly technical exercise, but its handling through what US leaders saw as a byzantine web of committees and working groups with no representation from outside interests was guaranteed to arouse concerns about access and the ability to shape decisions. A prevalent notion in the administration during 1988 and early 1989 was that the EC would effectively express the SMP as a series of *faits accomplis* to which outsiders had little chance of responding effectively. Lack of information and effective access had a predictable effect, even among those who would consider themselves well informed; a mild paranoia spread, fuelled by the views of congressman and a number of business groupings (see Chapters 4 and 6). History also played its part: a number of administration officials could see parallels between the Europeans' obstinacy in disputes, such as that over the European Airbus or over the effects of enlargement in 1986, and their unwillingness to afford easy access to the workings of the SMP.

These suspicions at the level of ideas and concepts were further reinforced by the evidence that the SMP had targeted a number of important sectors. Some of these were linked to long-standing areas of dispute; for example, the role of phytosanitary regulations in the Single Market had important implications for the CAP and for the Americans' continued access to the European market, and their fears were borne out by the outbreak of a dispute occasioned by the EC's attempts to bar beef fed on certain types of hormones from the European market. Others were linked to broader concerns about the nature of 'fair trade'; for example, the implication that under the SMP quotas on the import of Japanese automobiles would be extended from the national to the EC level, and possibly made applicable to the products of Japanese 'transplant' factories in the USA.

More challenging still, though, were areas of the SMP which dealt with activities outside traditional trade in goods. Particularly important were the parts of the programme which focused on financial services, technical standards and public procurement. None of these areas was subject to effective and comprehensive international regulation, and the GATT Uruguay Round promised to subject at least some of them to international discipline. For the White House, the issue went to the heart of the administration's responsibility for promotion of the multilateral trading system; could the EC be allowed to pre-empt or to bypass the GATT, while at the same time proclaiming its adherence to the rules of the world trading system? A difficulty emerged at this point for the executive, since a number of these highly sensitive areas were not entirely within its control within the USA itself: such sectors as telecommunications, which featured large in the SMP, were organized on a largely decentralized and often private basis in the USA, with the federal authorities having little more than a background regulatory role. The same, or much the same, was true in standards and public procurement: while the EC was moving regulation from national to the Community level, in the USA there was no parallel state (or state-like) regulatory structure (see Chapter 7). The challenge to the executive on these 'behind the border' issues arose not only from the nature of the SMP but also from the diffusion of regulatory power in the USA itself, and this was clearly a potential problem in any international bargaining over such issues.

The issues raised for the executive by the SMP were thus those of substance and of institutions. Arguably, the institutional challenge was at least as sharp as the substantive one, and this was borne out in the early stages of the White House response. The SMP was a prime example of what has been termed 'cross-national–cross-departmental' policy, and as a result it posed an awkward challenge to the institutional framework in Washington. As Stephen Cohen noted in the early 1980s, international economic policies in Washington emerged in a fragmented and incremental way, thanks to the intervention of diverse actors in a set of policy networks or communities.[8] This process had become if anything more marked by the late 1980s, and the multidimensional challenge of the SMP did nothing to moderate it.[9] As will be seen later in the chapter, the difficulties of defining a coherent policy across as many as 25 agencies with a substantive concern in the SMP give considerable weight to arguments about the ways in which access and control become an issue within as well as between governmental systems. The Omnibus Trade and Competitiveness Act had in any case created new tensions between those parts of the executive charged with preservation and enhancement of the trade policy framework and those who saw their role as 'competitiveness policy-making' – in brief, between the Office of the United States Trade Representative (USTR) and Commerce. The SMP presented a package which challenged the status and authority of departments within the executive as well as the authority of the executive itself.

It was not surprising in this context that the executive faced difficulties of strategy in responding to the SMP. The response itself will be dealt with later in this chapter, but it is important here to note the ways in which the programme laid down a number of important markers for the making of policy in the US administration. Three such challenges can be discerned.

First, there was a challenge of *ideas*. We have already noted that the circulation of ideas in Washington had created an atmosphere in which both the multilateral system and the authority of the executive had come under pressure. The SMP accentuated this challenge, since it was itself not only a technical programme but also the expression of a position on the 'rules of the game'.[10] It thus played into all of the accumulated debate in the USA about the role of strategic trade policy, about the relationship of regulation to deregulation, about the relative merits of 'rules' as against 'results' in commercial policy and about the respective merits of reciprocity and national treatment as principles of market access. Not only this, but it posed a challenge of conceptualization, as pointed out by a number of commentators at the time: was the EC to be treated as a proto-state, as a complex set of functional networks or as a type of federal system in which the national member states were analogous to the American states?[11] On the answer to this question would depend in large measure the effectiveness of executive policies.

Second, there was a challenge relating to *policy instruments*. This was clearly related to the philosophical challenge – in many ways, it grew out of it. The 1988 Trade Act had expressed a particular view on the role of the executive, and had tried to limit this role in significant respects (although opinions differed on the extent to which it had succeeded). It had also tried to get to grips with the appropriate policy instruments for the handling of 'behind the border' issues, and a similar debate was in progress relating to North American free trade. The SMP, though, raised the issue in a very specific form, and did not allow for very much prevarication. Was the EC to be dealt with in the same way as Japan, through bilateral arm-twisting with a view to market-opening, or did the political and historical baggage accumulated over the years in EC–US relations demand different measures? Not only this, but could the executive deal at arm's-length with the EC, whose economy and society were heavily interpenetrated with the USA?

Third, there was a question of *diplomacy*, again flowing out of the questions attaching to philosophy and instruments. The responsibility for trade diplomacy lay squarely with the USTR as an executive office, but there were many other agencies with a legitimate interest in the management of US policy towards the SMP. The State Department had always had a proprietorial interest in the political and security aspects of the European integration process; Commerce had new-found operational responsibility for trade administration, and wished to flex its muscles on the competitiveness front; a range of other executive bodies and departments were sensitized to the SMP and ready to respond to the challenge if they could only work out what it was.

As a result, the SMP found the US administration uncertain about its response, but with a clear view that there must be a response to meet the demands both of a major development in its major export and investment market and of the domestic debate about the nature and effectiveness of international economic policy. As already noted, the responses can be sought in two areas: first, the impact of government structure; second, the evolution of strategy in the period 1988 to 1993.

Government structure

One of the key features of the policy process in international economic policy-making is the growth of complexity and of the linkages between issues. In turn, this characteristic of the policy environment has led to the growth of complexity in the formulation and coordination of policies; as Destler has put it, 'substantive complexity leads to organizational complexity'.[12] In this part of the chapter, the focus is on the implications of the policy challenges posed by the SMP to the executive policy-making process in the United States. One of the key arguments is that longer-term changes in the policy machinery were focused and in some cases catalysed by the SMP challenge. This is not the end of the story, though: the process of responding to the SMP, when combined with other events and trends encountered during the period 1988 to 1993, led to new directions in the development of the executive policy machinery, and this in its turn had major implications for strategy.

During the 1980s, the role of the executive in US foreign economic policy-making had come under considerable pressure. Not least was this the function of changing relationships between the executive and the Congress, which had been partly expressed in the debates over the 1988 Omnibus Trade and Competitiveness Act. From a situation in which the executive had been given a good deal of discretion over the negotiation of trade agreements and the imposition of sanctions against those seen as trading unfairly, there had emerged a number of constraints on the autonomy of the administration.[13] These constraints had also reflected the growth of regional, parochial or single-issue pressure groups who had found much to concern them in the increasing vulnerability of the USA to external economic competition (see Chapters 1 and 2).

The key concern here is not so much with the pressures exerted by Congress and non-governmental interests in the USA (these will be covered in subsequent chapters) as with what might be described as the changing map of the executive itself. It has already been noted that one of the challenges of the SMP was to the internal balance of the executive and to the claims made by different agencies. This was part of a broader picture of development, which had seen two central trends. First, the responsibility for trade negotiations and the trade policy framework had moved from the State Department to the USTR, which although part of the executive also had naturally close links with Congressional and business groupings. The USTR was and is a specialist agency, with a strong bias towards trade law and the operation of the multilateral trading system: in the late 1980s, this was increasingly supplemented by responsibility for oversight of fair and unfair trade, particularly through the application of section 301 and 'super 301' of the relevant trade acts. In addition to the shift from State to the USTR, the responsibility for operational trade policy had increasingly been taken up by Commerce, through a number of its many agencies including the International Trade Administration.

In its turn, this growth of responsibility in Commerce intersected with a second trend: the shift of attention from trade policy pure and simple to what might best be described as 'competitiveness policy'. During the late 1980s, as already noted, there was a tendency in both academic and political circles to ascribe US economic difficulties to a cluster of problems which expressed themselves in a loss of competitiveness, and in vulnerability to external competitors. Not only this, but larger and larger swathes of the US economy seemed to be vulnerable to takeover by the same external forces. In countering this trend, the executive was seen as having a strategic role, not only through the traditional instruments of trade policy but also through a raft of other initiatives in the industrial and commercial fields, many of which were the concern of Commerce. A focus on competitiveness also brought the Treasury and international financial policies into the picture, while, as will be seen in Chapters 4 and 5, there were new roles for both Congress and state governments.[14]

The US executive thus responded to the EC-92 challenge against the background of considerable debate about the role of government in international economic policy, and about the linkages between national and international economic policy. The SMP, as already noted, posed an immediate and sharp challenge on both of these fronts. In the first place, it focused precisely the question about substantive and organizational complexity already outlined. In early 1988, the SMP was a focus only for a limited range of specialists in a limited range of agencies: the over-whelming proportion of executive attention was focused on the passage of the 1988 Trade Act and the attendant struggle to preserve at least some executive discretion in the finding of unfair trade and the application of penalties. This was in turn closely linked to the continuing negotiations in the Uruguay Round, due to come to a head at the Montreal interim meeting in December 1988. During the spring and summer of 1988, interest in the SMP both spread and was institutionalized. Awareness within the executive grew, as did awareness of what the congress might do when its attention was finally grabbed by the SMP. Specifically, the de Clercq speech of August 1988, and earlier attempts by Lord Cockfield and others to reassure the Americans that they had nothing to worry about, led precisely to the perception that there was something to worry about.

As a result, by the late summer of 1988, there had been established a fully fledged inter-agency Task Force focused on the SMP and coordinated by the USTR. This was a fairly standard response to the perception of a wide-ranging trade policy problem. But the SMP was far from being a standard trade policy issue. This much was reflected in the increasing complexity of the organizational map for US policy-making on the SMP; by 1990, the Task Force had generated a wide range of sub-committees and working groups involving over twenty agencies, each of them with its own set of specialist interests and each with its own broader constituency in Congress and the country. Figure 3.1 gives an impression of the way in which this was presented by the Task Force itself in 1990.

The Task Force was one of the key reasons for judgements by some commentators that the executive had developed an effective mechanism for dealing with the SMP – by implication, more effective than Congress in particular.[15] It reported to the Economic Policy Council in the White House, which was chaired by the President himself, and had additional links to advisory groups linking the executive and private sector interests. It must be remembered, however, that this is in effect a 'Washington map', and that as such it omits some crucial aspects of executive engagement with the SMP. Two such omissions are particularly significant. First, the US Mission to the EC in Brussels plays a major role in generating information about the development of EC affairs, and in providing access to networks in Brussels. It is important to note that, as of 1988, this mission had no representation from the Department of Commerce, and was effectively dominated by State and the USTR; in

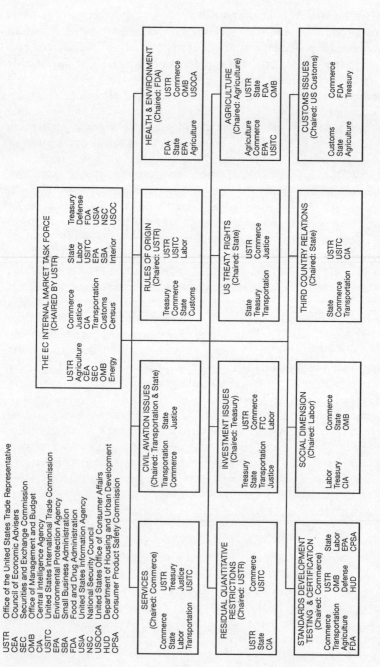

USTR Office of the United States Trade Representative
CEA   Council of Economic Advisers
SEC   Securities and Exchange Commission
OMB   Office of Management and Budget
CIA   Central Intelligence Agency
USITC United States International Trade Commission
EPA   Environmental Protection Agency
SBA   Small Business Administration
FDA   Food and Drug Administration
USIA United States Information Agency
NSC   National Security Council
USOCA United States Office of Consumer Affairs
HUD   Department of Housing and Urban Development
CPSA Consumer Product Safety Commission

THE EC INTERNAL MARKET TASK FORCE
(CHAIRED BY USTR)

USTR   Commerce   State   Treasury
Agriculture   Justice   Labor   Defense
CEA   CIA   USITC   FDA
SEC   Transportation EPA   USIA
OMB   Customs   SBA   NSC
Energy   Census   Interior   USOC

SERVICES
(Chaired: Commerce)

Commerce   USTR
State   Treasury
Labor   Justice
Transportation USITC

RESIDUAL QUANTITATIVE
RESTRICTIONS
(Chaired: USTR)

USTR   Commerce
State   USITC
CIA

STANDARDS DEVELOPMENT
TESTING & CERTIFICATION
(Chaired: Commerce)

Commerce   USTR   State
Transportation OMB   Labor
Agriculture   Defense   EPA
FDA   HUD   CPSA

CIVIL AVIATION ISSUES
(Chaired: Transportation & State)

Transportation State
Commerce   Justice

INVESTMENT ISSUES
(Chaired: Treasury)

Treasury   USTR
State   Commerce
Transportation FTC
Justice   Labor

SOCIAL DIMENSION
(Chaired: Labor)

Labor   Commerce
Treasury   State
CIA   OMB

RULES OF ORIGIN
(Chaired: USTR)

Treasury   USTR
Commerce   USITC
State   Labor
Customs

US TREATY RIGHTS
(Chaired: State)

State   USTR
Treasury   Commerce
Transportation Justice

THIRD COUNTRY RELATIONS
(Chaired: State)

State   USTR
Commerce   USITC
Transportation CIA

HEALTH & ENVIRONMENT
(Chaired: FDA)

FDA   USTR
State   Commerce
EPA   OMB
Agriculture   USOCA

AGRICULTURE
(Chaired: Agriculture)

Agriculture   USTR
Commerce   State
EPA   FDA
USITC   OMB

CUSTOMS ISSUES
(Chaired: US Customs)

Customs   Commerce
State   FDA
Agriculture Treasury

Figure 3.1 Organization of the US government for policy-making on the European Single Market Programme, 1990.
Source: United States Government Task Force on the EC International Market, *EC 1992*, Washington, DC, Office of the United States Trade Representative, May 1990.

other words, it reflected the traditional 'international trade' aspects of executive concern. The same was broadly true of the second key mission, that to the GATT in Geneva, which was dominated by the USTR, and which was naturally focused heavily on the progress of the Uruguay Round.

This in itself furnishes an insight into the range and quantity of interactions set up within the executive by the SMP. But this is only part of the story, since organizational maps on their own tell the observer relatively little about the quality of the interactions and the alignments between different agencies on different issues. On the basis of the earlier argument about the challenges posed by the SMP, we would expect that the executive would be faced with considerable problems of attention and coordination. We might also expect that as institutional learning occurred, this would be reflected in allocations of responsibility and the effectiveness of coordination itself. But we would not expect the adjustment to be either smooth or instantaneous.

In the autumn of 1988, it was apparent that the executive had made a decision to focus on the SMP, and to issue some warning notices to the EC. Partly, this arose out of the growing awareness that EC-92 would mean significant changes in the EC's international presence, and in the operating conditions for US firms, wherever they were based. Partly also, it arose out of the desire by the administration to be seen to be taking the issue seriously – or, as some put it, to pre-empt the possibly hostile reactions of Congress as it turned its attention to the SMP.[16] But the decision to pay attention to the SMP did not automatically mean that all executive agencies would pay the same sort of attention, or that they would coordinate their positions at the operational level. Seasoned observers identified the possibility of a fragmented and sub-optimal policy response at an early stage of the process:

> The role of the United States government will be to monitor the process closely to ensure that United States business interests are able to compete on an equal basis. The government has begun to turn its attention to 'Europe 1992'. However, it is essential that this effort be intensified, that greater resources be devoted to the task, that attention be focused on the issue at the highest levels, and – by no means least important – that a clear division of responsibility among the many, often competing, government agencies be established.[17]

The implications were that because of the complexity and diversity of the SMP, and because of the ways in which it intersected with the interests of many agencies, attention would be diffused and there would be a competition for 'voice' in the policy process. This had important resonances with the problems raised in the first part of this chapter about ideas, instruments and diplomatic strategy.

It was during the later part of 1988 and the first part of 1989 that the competition for attention and voice was most apparent within the executive. During the autumn of 1988, a series of speeches by administration figures acted as early markers both of US suspicions about the SMP and of the inter-agency tensions which were almost inevitable. The first to make a major impression was, somewhat surprisingly on the face of it, the Department of the Treasury. On 4 August 1988, Deputy Treasury Secretary Peter McPherson made a speech to the Institute for International Economics which first raised a number of fears which were to become familiar.[18] McPherson emphasized two dimensions of Treasury concern: for the international economy and for the United States. He saw the international economy as being at a 'critical juncture', with the multilateral system under pressure and a danger of mounting protectionism; in this context, he was anxious to point out to the Community that it should sustain the multilateral system, rather than contributing to the onset of new forms of protection. He also saw dangers that the EC would introduce measures that would be at odds with existing treaties between the USA and Community member states – in particular, the Treaties of Friendship, Commerce and Navigation.

Apart from these general concerns for the system and for the EC's role in it, McPherson listed an agenda of items on which the USA would want to see fair play. This list, with minor variations, was to become the standard menu for US policy-makers as they tried to assert their position *vis-à-vis* the SMP. On it were:

- The danger of discrimination in areas which were liberalized internally by the EC without full consideration of external interests. Among these were: the right of establishment (in McPherson's case, specifically that for banks threatened by the EC's Draft Second Banking Directive); competition policies (particularly merger controls); public procurement; subsidies; local content and rules of origin measures; standards and certification.
- The danger of the extension of GATT-illegal measures such as voluntary export restraints – which were still at the member state level – into Community-wide restrictions. The classic example was the establishment of a Community-level regime for imports of automobiles. In 1988, there were still twelve different regimes in the EC, ranging from free entry in West Germany to severe restrictions in Italy, and although almost all of these were targeted on Japanese producers, the Americans could see a danger that they would be generalized (for example, to include USA-produced cars manufactured by Japanese 'transplant' factories).
- The possibility that the EC would be so preoccupied by its own internal liberalization process (and its need for difficult compromises over the

costs of liberalization) that it would become an impossible negotiating partner in the GATT or other forums.

- The threat that the EC would impose requirements for reciprocity on those seeking access to the Single Market. Here again, the key measure in 1988 was the Draft Second Banking Directive, which appeared to threaten that access to the EC market would only be granted to those who could offer comparable access to EC banks. For the USA, where most banking was at state level rather than federal level, and where legislation kept securities and retail banking strictly separate, the danger was that the federal government could offer nothing comparable to what the SMP was in the process of establishing.

This litany of issues was accompanied by another overarching problem as the American saw it: the lack of transparency in the EC process, which would prevent the USA or US interests from being consulted at the appropriate juncture. Not just for the Treasury, but also for a range of other agencies and groupings, the threat of exclusion from the legislative process in the EC implied that decisions in which billions of dollars were at stake could be made without a US voice being raised. McPherson's speech was only the first of half a dozen designed to let the Europeans know that the US administration was watching and wished to be heard.

This said, it would be wrong to give the impression that the executive machine operated in complete harmony. From an early stage, it was apparent that different agencies wanted to add their specific gloss to the overall executive line, and to pursue their own strategies for gaining access and voice. This was facilitated by two factors. First, the coordination achieved in terms of general statements was precisely that: a statement of 'support in principle' for the SMP with a list of concerns to be considered, but with a great deal of latitude for interpretation by specific agencies. Second, the initial coordination was achieved at a time when the Reagan administration was on its last legs, and it fell foul of the transition to the Bush presidency, which had considerable difficulty in filling even third-ranking jobs in key agencies.

The result was that a policy vacuum and an inter-agency free for all could develop in late 1988 and early 1989. Perhaps predictably, the State Department was opposed to 'bludgeoning' tactics and wished to place the SMP within a broader political context. But alongside this, the Department of Commerce was interested in asserting its 'competitiveness' credentials, not just in relation to the EC but also in relation to its competitors within the administration. Meanwhile, the USTR adopted a legalistic line as it was almost forced to do by the 1988 Trade Act and its involvement in the Uruguay Round. Although McPherson's speech stood symbolically for the robust approach to the SMP, Treasury in many respects was a single-issue body, focused on the banking legislation. It was predicted that in the first year of a new presidency, the high level of domestic pressure and expectations would divert attention from the EC, except insofar as it could be seen either as a scapegoat or as a source of inter-agency leverage.[19]

This led to a period in governmental terms of 'broken play', with forays by individual agencies but little in the way of overall coordination. Symbolic of this was the attempt in early 1989 by Robert Mosbacher, the Secretary of Commerce, to establish a 'seat at the table' for the USA on SMP standards legislation (see Chapter 7). Equally, it was noted in discussion of the US Mission to the EC that there was no representation in Brussels of the Department of Commerce, and little presence from other 'economic' agencies.[20] It was apparent that the White House played little part – perhaps for obvious reasons – in the coordination of activity. This did not prevent progress, but in some ways this was a result of change in the EC position rather than of administration leverage (see below).

This scene was reminiscent of traditional 'turf battles' either over new areas of policy or over positions in a new administration. Here, in fact, both came together, with a challenging and complex new policy domain and a change of administration which proved to be fairly traumatic despite the apparent continuity between Reagan and Bush. There was a problem for agencies and their heads in establishing voice and credibility, and the SMP was one of the subjects which catalysed this process. The Reagan administration went out of office trying to establish that it meant business in respect of the SMP, but it was replaced by an administration whose chief business was establishing itself.

This impression persisted perhaps for longer than was merited. The Bush administration in this as in other areas took time to gather itself, but when it did it undertook a methodical and effective review of Single Market policy. Although a gap was sometimes visible between the high-level political input into the process and the positions adopted by specific agencies, the result was an increasingly coordinated position, informed as time went on by the perceptions not only of Carla Hills as USTR but also of the Secretary of State, James Baker.[21] This was crucial in terms of the coordination of government positions, given the closeness of Baker to the President as well as the assertive stance taken by Hills both in the GATT and in bilateral US–EC negotiations. During the spring and summer of 1989, there was a coming together of the political and the economic aspects of the US policy towards the SMP, and it could be argued that from the middle of 1989 onwards it was increasingly dominated at the top political level by the Bakerite perception of change in the wider Europe. This was reflected in important changes in strategy (see below). The net result was that by the beginning of 1990, as well as an elaborate policy coordination process at the working group level, there was also an important if not crucial commitment at the political level to resolving issues with the EC and in respect of the SMP.

The outcome thus appeared to be in the short term that government had adapted and had responded to the demands of the SMP. This was true at the political and at the operational level. It is not clear that this actually encapsulated a 'remaking' of government, in the sense that the SMP stimulated far-reaching changes in mechanisms and practices. What it did express was a series of shifts in the political context, which transmitted themselves both to the inter-agency level and to the administration more generally. By the end of 1990, this had also been supplemented with the negotiations for and the acceptance of the Transatlantic Declaration. If nothing else, this expressed the philosophy of the Bush administration *vis-à-vis* the EC: a strong political commitment, coupled with the beginnings of a working group structure which would act to complement the ways in which both the Europeans and the Americans had come to deal with the issues.

This is a crucial shift in the 'government' of EC–US relations and their mutual interests in the SMP. To put it simply, there was a shift in 1990 from a focus on access and voice to a focus on institutionalization, which expressed a perception on both sides that they were not as vulnerable to each other as had at first appeared. This is an important addition to a view of executive action which sees it as fighting a battle for access on behalf of the national society, or as safeguarding the national interest through strategic action. It appears that the later Bush administration moved from an initially rather disjointed assertion of the national desire for access and reduction of vulnerability through a process of learning and policy-sharing to the institutionalization of EC–US relations partly – but only partly – in relation to the SMP.[22]

This meant that by the time the Bush administration left the scene in early 1993, government at the national level had been supplemented by governance at the EC–US level as the means of assuring access and leverage in the transatlantic policy process. This had been underlined in mid-1992 by the adoption of a new US–EC understanding, which among other features instituted an 'early warning system' for EC–US economic issues.

The Clinton administration inherited this set of structures; but it also inherited a different set of demands and priorities, reflecting the development of economic problems at other than the transatlantic level. This increased rather than diminished the leverage of the executive in terms of policy-making within the USA. The need to bring to a conclusion both the NAFTA and the Uruguay Round, within the compass of a few weeks late in 1993, gave the White House an almost unparalleled responsibility for the conduct of trade relations, but not only traditional trade relations. The behind-the-border nature of both the NAFTA and the GATT talks gave added point to President Clinton's assertion that 'It's the economy, stupid' – the interesting point from the perspective of this study is that, for the US executive, it was far from clear which or whose economy 'it' was. Much has been made of the Clinton progression from being a domestic policy presidency to a foreign policy presidency; rather less has been made of the progression from being a President for the domestic economy to being a president for the world economy, a progression driven by the need to handle pressing trade negotiations.[23]

From the perspective of government, therefore, the SMP seems to have shaped but not to have created a set of debates and structural shifts in the executive. In much of what has been discussed in this section, the issue has not simply been one of government structure, however; the question of strategy and the playing out of initial positions has to be explored, together with its implications for market access and the making of foreign economic policy.

Government strategy

As noted above, it is very difficult in discussing US governmental responses to the SMP to avoid discussion of ideas and of the strategies which emerge from those initial orientations. More generally, it is important to the analysis of foreign economic policies to understand the ways in which orientations, institutions and strategies interact to produce actions and outcomes. In this connection, it is significant that from the outset the SMP was seen by many US policy-makers and commentators as a strategic challenge, to which a set of coordinated responses would be necessary. Joseph Greenwald, writing in one of the most substantial collections of essays produced at the time, was in no doubt that the test for the US administration was one of its ability to act coherently in response to a multidimensional negotiation challenge.[24] Similarly, Randall Henning, in another collection of essays indicated the dimensions of the strategy problem:

> The United States government will ... have to adapt to decentralized decisionmaking in Europe. When United States officials determine that American interests are engaged, they will have to mount a full-court press across all of the important decision centers in the Community. Second, the United States should firmly support international regimes and organizations that provide an open, multilateral, cooperative global context in which the new Europe will evolve. An hospitable global environment will favour those within the Commission advocating open trade, investment, sectoral, regulatory and macro-economic policies. Third, the United States should re-examine its own policymaking institutions with an eye to becoming more clearsighted and effective in pursuing its international economic goals.[25]

A first issue to be faced by the executive was thus that of defining the challenges and the parameters for US responses. As has already been seen, though, the challenges posed by the SMP were essentially cross-national and cross-departmental, and this greatly complicated the task of defining an initial standpoint. None the less, it is clear that the executive in late 1988 made a clear and coordinated decision of principle: that the SMP would be welcomed in general terms but that it would be up to the specific agencies involved to identify the issues faced in their sectors of activity.[26] As has been seen, this produced a certain amount of rhetorical uniformity, but a great deal of diversity at the agency level.

One aim of early US strategy was thus to create awareness in the EC that Washington was watching, and that the Europeans would not get away with anything. In a sense, this had immediate pay-off by persuading the European Council at its October 1988 meeting to agree a statement presenting the Community as a 'world partner' willing to use the SMP as the basis for further multilateral negotiations.[27] This did not totally reassure the Americans, and the executive still had to cope with the widespread impression that the EC was preoccupied with its own internal development at the potential expense of US interests and the broader multilateral system.[28] None the less, there is evidence that the US executive was able to get its message across and thereby to put itself on to the board in dealing with the SMP at this early stage. During 1989, this impression was confirmed when, for example, Robert Mosbacher was able to come to informal agreements with his opposite number, Martin Bangemann, about what could be done on the 'seat at the table' question in the handling of standards issues (see Chapter 7).

It was at this stage, though, that a far broader set of issues became relevant to the administration's strategy. During the second half of 1989, the accelerating pace of change in Central and Eastern Europe, and finally the breaching of the Berlin Wall in November, radically changed the political calculus surrounding the SMP. Although the issues of access and influence remained at the core of the context for several agencies, the events of later 1989 and beyond gave a different shape to the administration's strategy. No longer was the SMP either a technical issue or a matter of trade politics. Those remained important, but the SMP and US responses to it were now fundamentally shaped by American perceptions of the stakes in the 'new Europe'. The most public evidence of this came in a series of speeches by both Secretary of State Baker and the President, in which they talked about the EC's role in the 'new European architecture'.[29]

As many commentators have noted, these speeches were part of the approach to issues arising out of the 'new world order'. However vague and contradictory this notion was, and however much it faded into inconsequence in the events of the following years, it is important to register its salience in the atmosphere of 1990. In the case of EC–US relations, one of its most tangible results was the negotiation and then the acceptance of the Transatlantic Declaration of November 1990. Alongside this went a series of less public but equally important developments in areas of sectoral policy and of multilateral trade policy. These were not always positive – far from it, the attempts to make progress on the Uruguay Round during late 1990 threatened to derail the whole exercise[30] – but there was also a more positive attempt to develop an 'early warning system' for trade conflicts and other frictions. There was a new sense that policy and responsibility needed to be mutually adjusted and shared in the context of the emerging post-Cold War order, however much this was shaken by specific events.[31]

The policies of the executive had thus developed very rapidly along a number of interrelated but not always coordinated lines. Initial principled approval of the SMP had been accompanied by confusion at the agency level as different groupings manoeuvred for position on different sectoral issues and became concerned with problems of cross-national policy-making. At the same time, there had been an attempt to emphasize the GATT dimension as a way of exerting discipline on the SMP and on the Commission in particular (US policies tended to give the Commission a central place, and if anything rather to play down the role of the Council of Ministers, at least initially). During 1989, the impact of the Bush administration's inter-agency review of SMP strategy, and the increasing influence of the State Department in the policy-making process, tended to give a higher profile to strategy in the political domain, and to the role of the EC as a political interlocutor as well as an economic support in the 'new Europe':

> The American interest in having the EC reach out to Eastern Europe and become a magnet to draw the East European countries toward a democratic orientation gave the United States an incentive to cooperate effectively with Europe rather than to sharpen trade conflicts with it.[32]

This is an important interim conclusion in dealing with the issues arising from the SMP for US executive strategy. The landscape had shifted radically and surrounded the issues of access to the Single Market with a broader set of considerations. It had also, however temporarily, elevated the longer-term political meanings of the SMP over the shorter-term more technical or parochial matters which had been prominent in late 1988 and early 1989. By the end of 1990, even the fiasco of the Brussels GATT meeting was insufficient to destabilize the new EC–US dialogue.[33]

This did not mean that there were not continuing issues centring on matters of market access and leverage for the administration in the policy-making process. The administration had to respond to continuing pressure from Congress and other bodies on 'traditional' trade issues such as agriculture and the European airbus, and it adopted a robust attitude on both. In the first case, the United States Department of Agriculture (USDA) and USTR continued to press for movement on the reduction and tariffication of agricultural price supports in the context of the Uruguay Round, while, in the second, the USTR adopted a positively abrasive stance, often in advance of those favoured by aviation industry interests. On more specifically SMP issues, it was clear that during 1989 and 1990 there was a move towards what Reagan's last Commerce Secretary, William Verity, had called for in 1988 – a process based on public–private working groups, and one in which mutual learning was the key to progress on policy coordination.[34]

One implication of this policy elaboration was clear by 1991–2: that the rather undifferentiated view of the EC held in late 1988 had been replaced by a complex view of the EC, its member states and institutions and the strategies best suited to enhancing access to them. It is important here to note a distinction which is central to the nature of foreign economic policy in the 1990s: between institutional access and market access. The US executive during 1989 to 1992 made great strides in achieving more effective institutional access to EC policy-making, and thus being able to shape the outcomes of the policy debates in Brussels and elsewhere. This could be achieved by linkages to specific parts of the Commission, to specific member states or groups of members states or to specific institutions. On such measures as the Second Banking Directive or the standards-setting process, this differentiated strategy could be very effective. It was limited, however, by the evolving internal balance in the Commission and in the EC more generally, which was also given a twist by the events of 1989–90. Such increasingly effective institutional access did not necessarily guarantee more effective market access for US corporations, and this relationship will be explored more fully in Chapter 7.

It is thus possible to see a progression in US policy at the executive level. The initial response was shaped strongly by domestic and inter-agency forces, and, it has to be said, by ignorance of the SMP and its implications. Over the years 1989 to 1992, this was supplanted by awareness – not always uniform but always more developed than at the outset – of the internal variety of EC processes, of the availability of trade-offs and compromises and of the influence of broader forces of political change.[35] As a result, administration strategies were capable of adaptation and learning. At times, the internal ambivalence and the shifting balance of forces within the Community itself would play a part in confounding administration strategy, but this became less frequent as time went on. When this process of learning was supplemented by the radical shift in political incentives for learning to live with the SMP, it is clear that there was a reformulation of strategy at the top diplomatic level which buttressed the learning going on at the sectoral and agency level.

Apart from the shifting political landscape in Europe, another major role in the reshaping of administration strategy was played by the developing use of other channels, which supplemented the US–EC dialogue. The Transatlantic Declaration has already been noted, and it is important to note here that there were those who saw its uses not only in the enhancement of dialogue but also in the insulation of US–EC relations from the influence of parochialism and interest group politics in the USA.[36] Beyond this, though, there was a major role for the growing range of channels in the multilateral or the plurilateral arenas, and the US executive showed increasing flexibility in using them to discipline the EC or to make it aware of other possible avenues for US policy.[37]

During the period 1989 to 1993, it can thus be argued that the USA paid increasing attention at the executive level not only to the SMP itself but to the ways in which it fitted within the range of channels open to American policy. At one level, these channels were those of alternative regionalisms. First the NAFTA and then the Asia-Pacific Economic Cooperation forum (APEC) could be used by the Americans to stress the fact that they had policy options additional to those offered by the Community. Indeed, it appeared during the first year of the Clinton administration that such manoeuvring was a significant part of US policies.[38] At the same time, the Americans were able to put increasing pressure on the EC in the context of the Uruguay Round. In a number of areas, the Uruguay Round provided for action in areas central to the SMP, such as regulatory policy, trade in services, public procurement and standards. As the Round proceeded, and as it became clear that the EC was both potentially the largest gainer from it and the biggest obstacle to its conclusion, it became possible for the Americans to exert further leverage on the Community. This is not the place for a detailed study of the Uruguay Round 'endgame', but it is clear that the shifting balance between bilateral, plurilateral and multilateral economic forums could be and was used by the Americans to shape their strategy towards the SMP; for example, by using the emerging 'quad group' of the USA, the EC, Canada and Japan.[39]

Conclusion

Exploration of the strategies pursued by the successive US administrations towards the SMP adds a further dimension to analysis of executive policy-making and action in the face of a complex and evolving challenge. One important conclusion is that as time went on, a process of learning took place through which the executive developed a more complex hypothesis about the nature of the EC and its policy machinery.[40] This enabled intervention to be judged more effectively and targeted with greater precision. The original 'moving target' of the EC and the SMP was pinned down at least to some extent, and the US administrations were able to coordinate strategy not only at government level but also across the public–private divide. At the same time, over a period of three to four years, the political and economic landscape around US–EC relations was transformed. This transformation was most dramatic in the political/ security sphere, and the landslide of change in 1989–90 fundamentally reshaped US evaluations of the EC and its uses. In the world economy, the development of alternatives to US–EC relations as a focus for strategy and action gave US administrations greater freedom for manoeuvre and greater leverage, both institutionally and within specific policy sectors.

The reshaping and adaptation of strategy intersected with and was clearly influenced by the structural shifts identified earlier in this chapter. As was noted then, these shifts were by no means smooth or well coordinated, but they did produce over a period of months if not years a relatively effective executive response to the SMP. Given the range and diversity of the challenges posed by the EC-92 programme, it cannot be said that the US executive failed to adapt or to learn. This did not mean that the challenge of the SMP had been comprehensively met: it did mean, though, that the ability of the executive to shape and reshape policy, and thus to gain both institutional and market access leverage, was far from negligible. In this sense, the demand for policy from the executive had been matched, and a supply of initiatives and strategies had been forthcoming. We shall see in later chapters whether this is a sufficient explanation of the US approach to the SMP.

Notes and references

1   These arguments can be found for example in H. Nau, *The Myth of America's Decline: Leading the World Economy into the 1990s*, New York, Oxford University Press, 1990.

2   A good brief review of these issues is S. D. Cohen, J. R. Paul and R.A. Blecker, *Fundamentals of US Foreign Trade Policy: Economics, Politics, Laws, and Issues*, Boulder, CO, Westview Press, 1996, Chapter 10.

3   For example, see: P. F. Cowhey, ' "States" and "politics" in American foreign economic policy', in J. S. Odell and T. D. Willett (eds), *International Trade Policies: Gains from Exchange between Economics and Political Science*, Ann Arbor, University of Michigan Press, 1993, pp. 225–52; and G. J. Ikenberry, D. A. Lake and M. Mastanduno, 'Introduction: approaches to explaining American foreign economic policy', *International Organization*, 42(1), 1988, pp. 1–14.

4   See M. Smith, 'The United States and the Single European Market: federalism and diplomacy in a changing political economy', in

B. Hocking (ed.), *Foreign Relations in Federal States*, London: Leicester University Press, 1993, pp. 236–51.

5   See Ikenberry, Lake and Mastanduno, *op. cit.*

6   Nau, *Myth of America's Decline*, *op. cit.* See also M. Smith and S. Woolcock, *The United States and the European Community in a Transformed World*, London, Pinter for the Royal Institute of International Affairs, 1993, Chapters 1 and 2.

7   J. Spero, 'The mid-life crisis of American trade policy', *The World Today*, 45(1), 1989, pp. 10–14; P. Low, *Trading Free: the GATT and US Trade Policy*, New York, Twentieth Century Fund, 1993; *Europe*, Jan/Feb. 1988.

8   S. D. Cohen, *The Making of United States International Economic Policy: Principles, Problems, and Proposals for Reform*, (2nd edn), New York, Praeger, 1981.

9   For a discussion of these issues, see K. Featherstone and R. Ginsberg, *The United States and the European Union in the 1990s: Partners in Transition* (2nd edn), London, Macmillan, 1996, pp. 251ff.

10   This aspect is explored in, for example: S. Woolcock, *Market Access Issues in E.C.–U.S. Trade Relations: Trading Partners or Trading Blows?*, London, Pinter for the Royal Institute of International Affairs, 1991, Chapter 1; Smith and Woolcock, *The United States and the European Community in a Transformed World*, *op. cit.*, Chapter 4; W. Sandholtz and J. Zysman, 'Europe's emergence as a global protagonist', in W. Sandholtz *et al.*, *The Highest Stakes: Economic Foundations of the Next Security System*, New York, Oxford University Press, 1992, pp. 81–113.

11   See, for example: A. Sbragia, 'Introduction', in A. M. Sbragia (ed.), *Euro-politics: Institutions and Policy-making in the 'New' European Community*, Washington, DC, Brookings Institution, 1992, pp. 1–22; R. O. Keohane and S. Hoffmann, 'Institutional change in Europe in the 1980s', in R. O. Keohane and S. Hoffmann (eds), *The New European Community: Decisionmaking and Institutional Change*, Boulder, CO, Westview Press, 1991, pp. 1–40.

12   I. M. Destler, *Making Foreign Economic Policy*, Washington, DC, Brookings Institution, 1980, p. 6.

13   See I. M. Destler, *American Trade Politics: System under Stress* (2nd edn), Washington, DC, Institute for International Economics, 1992, esp. Part II; Low, *Trading Free*, *op. cit.*, Part II.

14   See Destler, *American Trade Politics*, Chapter 5; for general background to these developments, see Destler, *Making Foreign Economic Policy*, and Cohen, *The Making of United States International Economic Policy*.

15   K. Bonine, 'US 1992: how the US government is preparing for the Single Market', *Europe*, April 1990, pp. 14–17.

16 Interviews, Washington, DC, August–September 1988.
17 M. Calingaert, *The 1992 Challenge from Europe: Development of the European Community's Internal Market*, Washington, DC, National Planning Association, 1988, p. 130.
18 'The EC's Internal Market Program: an American perspective', Remarks by M. Peter McPherson, Deputy Secretary of the Treasury, to the Institute for International Economics, Washington, DC, 4 August 1988.
19 Interviews, Washington, DC, September 1988.
20 This argument was made particularly by Lloyd Bentsen in the Senate: see *Washington Post*, 7 April 1989, for reports.
21 See J. Peterson, *Europe and America in the 1990s: Prospects for Partnership* (1st edn), Aldershot, Edward Elgar, 1993; 2nd edn, London: Routledge, 1996, Chapter 2, pp. 50ff.
22 See Featherstone and Ginsberg, *The United States and the European Union in the 1990s*; Peterson, *Europe and America in the 1990s*.
23 See M. Smith and S. Woolcock, 'Learning to cooperate: the Clinton administration and the European Union', *International Affairs*, 70(3), 1994, pp. 459–76; M. Smith, 'Clinton and the EC: how much of a new agenda?' *The World Today*, April 1993, pp. 70–3.
24 See J. Greenwald, 'Negotiating strategy', in G. C. Hufbauer (ed.), *Europe 1992: An American Perspective*, Washington, DC, Brookings Institution, 1990, pp. 345–88.
25 C. R. Henning, 'Management of economic policy in the European Union', in US House of Representatives, Committee on Foreign Affairs, Subcommittee on International Economic Policy and Trade and Subcommittee on Europe and the Middle East, *Europe and the United States: Competition and Cooperation in the 1990s*, Washington, DC, US Government Printing Office, June 1992, pp. 28–9.
26 Interviews, Washington, DC, September 1988.
27 'Europe 1992: world partner', European Community Office of Press and Public Affairs, Washington, DC, 20 October 1988.
28 See Calingaert, *The 1992 Challenge from Europe*, pp. 92–5.
29 Peterson, *Europe and America in the 1990s*, pp. 51ff.
30 See R. Schwok, *US–EC Relations in the Post-Cold War Era: Conflict or Partnership?*, Boulder, CO, Westview Press, 1991, Chapter 9.
31 See Smith and Woolcock, 'Learning to cooperate'; for the broader institutional context, see R. O. Keohane, J. S. Nye and S. Hoffmann (eds), *After the Cold War: International Institutions and State Strategies in Europe, 1989–1991*. Cambridge, MA, Harvard University Press, 1993.
32 J. S. Nye and R. O. Keohane, 'The United States and international institutions in Europe after the Cold War', in Keohane, Nye and Hoffmann, *After the Cold War*, pp. 104–26, p. 123.

33   Low, *Trading Free*, Conclusions.

34   Smith and Woolcock, *The United States and the European Community in a Transformed World*, Chapter 5; Smith and Woolcock, 'Learning to Cooperate'.

35   See Sbragia, *Euro-Politics*, Introduction; Keohane and Hoffmann, *The New European Community*, Chapter 1.

36   This argument is made by Peterson, *Europe and America in the 1990s* (1st edn), Chapter 8.

37   For an important treatment of the institutional aspects of these developments, see M. Kahler, *International Institutions and the Political Economy of Integration*, Washington, DC, Brookings Institution, 1995. For an argument presenting this as a source of additional power for the executive, see C. Weiler, 'Free trade Agreements: a new federal partner', *Publius*, 24(3), 1994, pp. 113–34.

38   Smith, 'Clinton and the EC'; Smith and Woolcock, 'Learning to cooperate'.

39   Featherstone and Ginsberg, *The United States and the European Union in the 1990s*, Chapter 4.

40   Such a process was advocated by a number of commentators in the early stages of the SMP. See, for example, Sbragia, *Euro-Politics*; Keohane and Hoffmann, *The New European Community*; Greenwald, 'Negotiating strategy'.

4

Congress

The previous chapter analysed the development of federal government policy responses to the challenges – both substantive and process-related – which EC-92 presented. As we have seen, the key to those responses lay in a growing awareness of the increasingly complex environment of transatlantic relations, in which a juxtaposition of trade and security issues established new perspectives and priorities. In turn, this encouraged in Washington a more sophisticated awareness as to the means of influencing outcomes in the EC policy arena. But this has to be seen against the background of Congressional involvement and interest, particularly in trade policy. In constitutional terms, the primacy of the legislature is clearly spelt out, and although congressional power in this area has been delegated to the executive, the latter is well aware that this is subject to continuing scrutiny and the formal processes of renewal.

Congress is therefore closely intertwined with the allocation of roles, coordination of responsibilities and political-bureaucratic tensions associated with trade policy. And, not unexpectedly, it often possesses a different set of perspectives on the goals of foreign economic policy, deriving from the interests which it represents, frequently resulting in conflict with the executive – and certain agencies in particular. However, the patterns of relationships between Capitol Hill and the executive in the trade policy area are complex, as recent studies suggest.[1] Carter, for example, identifies four possible models for evaluating the congressional role in trade policy.[2] Furthermore, the image of a 'protectionist' Congress confronting a 'free trade' executive oversimplifies the picture and has been subject to qualification.[3]

These points need to be borne in mind as we seek to identify the roles that Capitol Hill played as US responses to the SMP developed. We have already argued that the development of the multilayered policy environment demands a re-evaluation of the roles that institutions play and where they fit into the stages of the policy cycle.[4] In the case of legislative bodies, this changing environment alters fundamentally the bases for evaluating their scope for action in international policy. In particular, the shift in the balance between the twin concerns of access and control towards the former poses questions regarding the significance of secrecy as a prime objective – a reason usually cited for limiting the democratic input into external policy processes. While restrictions on the flows of information are obviously relevant in certain contexts, in many aspects of foreign economic policy, the problem is one of gaining access to knowledge and to transnational actors who influence policy outcomes.

This raises the key issue regarding the functions of legislatures in the complex policy milieu with which we are dealing. A focus on policy-making activities has discouraged evaluation of their broader roles. For example, it has been argued that Congress's representative functions in the sphere of foreign policy have received relatively little attention.[5] The same might be said of its functions as channel of communication, consensus-builder and educator.[6] Yet these may be critical to the conduct of US trade policy, where success in achieving goals – in the NAFTA negotiations, for example – often depends on the management of a highly politicized environment.

The congressional oversight function in particular has been neglected in terms of inputs into the conduct of international policy, but is a potentially significant mode of influencing executive and bureaucratic behaviour. Part of the problem lies in the definition of oversight as an activity and the expectations generated by varying conceptions of this dimension of legislative activity.[7] As we shall see later in the chapter, this is particularly relevant to congressional input into US responses to EC-92, given the fact that, unlike the NAFTA agreement, there was no treaty requiring legislative approval.

It is equally important to an understanding of its role in the trade – as in other – policy areas to view Congress as more than a set of institutionalized processes. Rather, it occupies a crucial place in the complex network of relationships which are characteristic of the multilayered policy environment. These may span national boundaries and can become significant channels for the projection of extranational forces on domestic policy, discussed in Chapter 6. This provides part of the context for the frequently heated debate on foreign interest lobbying on Capitol Hill – particularly notable in the area of trade politics.[8] Moreover, the 'legislature' becomes more than its elected members, embracing, for example, committee and other ancillary support staff who can themselves become significant actors in the development of policy. Thus the oversight function has been defined as 'behaviour by legislators and their staffs, individually or collectively, which results in an impact, intended or not, on bureaucratic behaviour'.[9] This 'broader' image of Congress as an actor is significant to an appreciation of its role in trade policy generally and to US–EC relations more specifically.

Congress and foreign economic policy

One of the key features of the US foreign economic policy environment is the different approaches towards it adopted by Congress and the executive. While we must bear in mind the dangers of oversimplification noted at the start of the chapter, the latter has placed greater emphasis on the value of trade liberalization while the former has been far more receptive to the arguments of domestic constituencies affected by its consequences. Similarly, the executive has shown a greater inclination to view trade policy in the context of broader foreign policy priorities.[10] Clearly, this basic orientation is crucial to understanding the interplay between the actors on any given issue such as EC-92, but the relationship between Capitol Hill and successive administrations has changed in response to the developments noted in Chapter 2. Greater congressional assertiveness in trade policy during the 1970s and 1980s was due in considerable part to the enhanced sense of vulnerability reinforced by the internationalization of the US economy. Escalating trade and budget deficits, growing foreign direct investment and a more complex trade policy agenda, as negotiations shifted from tariff reductions to politically sensitive non-tariff barriers, served to undermine the relative insulation of Congress from trade policy which developed during the Roosevelt era.

Those firms and workers most vulnerable to foreign imports not unnaturally pressured their congressional representatives to act on their behalf and reinforced the persistent disquiet on Capitol Hill regarding the management of US trade policy and the belief that the growing trade deficit was the result of unfair competition on the part of America's trading partners – not least the Japanese. When combined with internal changes, such as the decentralization of power within Congress and the growth of resources as Congressional staff increased, its insulation from the domestic pressures of trade politics lessened, protectionist sentiment increased while its capacity to act grew.[11]

In responding to this changing environment, Capitol Hill has developed three main means by which it can affect the conduct of trade policy.[12] The first is by setting out the rules which determine the way in which both it and the executive deal with such policy. A major example of this has been the evolution of the 'fast-track' authority first given to the President in 1974 and intended to speed the conclusion of trade agreements and insulate them from political pressures within Congress. This delegation of authority to the President was limited in the 1988 Omnibus Trade and Competitiveness Act and it became the centre of the growing battle over the NAFTA during 1992 and 1993.

Second, Congress has regularly modified legislation directed towards remedying situations deemed as constituting 'unfair trade'. The best known example of this is section 301 of the 1974 Trade Act, intended to provide the President with the powers to take action against such transgressions as discriminatory rules of origin and public procurement practices. The 1988 Act strengthened section 301 considerably by specifying in some detail procedures to be followed in specific cases and by moving responsibility for its adminstration from the President to the Office of the US Trade Representative.

The latter point reflects the third impact of Congress in the trade policy sphere; namely on the institutional arrangements surrounding its conduct. Hence the 1974 Act also required that members of Congress be included in delegations to trade negotiations and that private sector advisory committees be established to inform the trade policy process. Although the developments throughout the 1970s and 1980s on the trade policy front were more incremental and *ad hoc* than surveys sometimes suggest, their effect was to underscore the role of Congress as a significant partner in the shaping of US trade policy.

The effect of this on the executive could be viewed from two perspectives. On the one hand, it increased the burden of conducting trade policy as the administration was required to expend considerable effort in playing legislative trade politics. Trade Representative Robert Strauss recalled that he spent as much time negotiating with Congress during the Tokyo Round as he did with foreign governments.[13] Clayton Yeutter was confronted with a similar need during the negotiation of the Canada–US Free Trade negotiations. Carla Hills, President Bush's Trade Representative, occupied this key position during a highly critical phase in trade policy-making, which included the mid-to-late phase of the EC-92 issue and was regarded by many as the most competent holder of the post, highly skilled in playing the legislative game.

The second perspective is more positive from the executive viewpoint and rests on the knowledge that Congressional involvement in trade policy might be exploited to Washington's advantage in trade negotiations. Certainly, EC policy-makers are well aware of the significance of Congress – although their ability to deal effectively with it has been questioned by Washington observers, as we shall see below. But perhaps the most critical point in this respect is the fact that the USTR was created by Congress and that its behaviour as a bureaucratic entity in trade negotiations reflects that fact. In practice, this ensures that the USTR will be sensitive to the domestic interests frequently articulated through Capitol Hill, and that trade partners can thus expect Congress to have a vicarious 'presence' in trade discussions. At least potentially, this presence can act as a weapon in the US trade armoury, tempering the negotiating stance of trade partners aware that deals have to be 'sold' to Congress members and the interests they represent.

Congress and EC-92

Timing was a significant factor in the role played by Congress as the Single Market issue entered the US political agenda. As noted above, the hundredth Congress had been dominated by trade issues, particularly the negotiation of the Canada–US Free Trade Agreement (CUSFTA) and the passage of the Omnibus Trade Act. Legislative attention was now moving on to other issues against a background of improving US trade performance. During 1992 and 1993, attention was focused on the concluding stage of the Uruguay Round and the intense politics generated by the NAFTA negotiations. While there were linkages between the GATT and the SMP agendas, NAFTA – following George Bush's eager adoption of President Salinas's 1990 proposal for a free trade agreement between the USA and Mexico – represented a very different type of issue in terms of congressional politics.

While it is true that EC-92 issues resonated with protectionist sentiments and market access concerns which the 1988 Trade Act reflected, the patterns of Congressional response were conditioned by their specific character. These had to be viewed in the broader context of the transatlantic relationship and the place of Congress within it. Taking the broad historical view, the dominant sentiment on Capitol Hill has been that the objectives of European integration are worthy of support and have accorded with US interests. Indeed, Congress has been at times a significant external actor in the development of European integration. But at the same time, it has been a strident critic of aspects of EC trade policy. Moreover, as we have already seen, the relationship was subject to a re-evaluation in the light of the changing international context, not always to the Europeans' favour, as reflected in responses to EC responses to the Gulf War and in the former Yugoslavia.[14] No appreciation of Congressional responses to the emergence of the SMP can therefore ignore the overall texture of transatlantic relations.

It was therefore almost inevitable that attitudes within Congress would reflect sentiments grounded in recent, post-1945 history, the changing context of East–West relations and the trading environment. In one sense, as we shall suggest later in this chapter, one of the key roles of Congress as EC-92 developed was to act as a focus of debate and deliberation, principally through various committee hearings, on the meaning and implications of this new phase in economic integration.

On the one hand, the implications of enhanced integration for the security architecture of Europe, the unification of Germany, the future of NATO and the US role within it were issues of central concern on Capitol Hill as elsewhere in Washington, and could not be dissociated from the narrower trade agenda.[15] Moreover, the SMP emerged at a critical phase in the debate over the future of the international trading system. On the multilateral side, the Uruguay Round negotiations were in progress. But the SMP reinforced the impression, sustained by CUSFTA and the prospect of NAFTA, together with discussions on Asia-Pacific economic cooperation enlivened by the appearance of the APEC, that a world of trading blocs stood ready to replace the GATT regime. Given Congress's legislative involvement in CUSFTA, NAFTA and the GATT, it was inevitable that linkages would be made between them and EC-92.

Alongside these broader contextual concerns have to be placed the running trade and investment disputes which have marked transatlantic economic relations. Disagreements during the 1980s over steel, US farm exports to Portugal and Spain following their accession to the EC and the ongoing dispute over hormone-treated beef are but three examples of issues which have raised the political temperature on Capitol Hill. But there is a qualititative difference between the character of these disputes and those between the USA and Japan. As Hufbauer points out, while transatlantic relations can be stormy, the characteristic pattern has been 'a history of issues getting resolved'.[16] This is markedly different from US–Japanese trade relations, which have not simply generated considerable acrimony in Congress but have often remained unresolved. Furthermore, there is a difference in the nature of the agendas around which the relationships have developed. In the case of the EC, US concern has focused on a diverse range of market access issues in the context of what US policy-makers have regarded as a relatively open trade regime. This is not the case with Japan, where the very nature of the social, economic and political systems has been called into question and offered far more visible targets for Congressional attack. Consequently, the atmosphere surrounding trade disputes is different in the two instances.

This fact contributed to one of the central problems for Congress as it became aware of the SMP: namely, what role could it perform and how might that role be discharged? The nature of the SMP was a central conditioning factor here. Unlike CUSFTA or NAFTA, there would be no agreement to ratify and therefore weapons of influence over internal and external parties, such as the fast-track procedure, were irrelevant. While legislative powers stood in reserve to strengthen the administration's hand should it require them, it was unlikely that they would assume a central dimension of Congress's involvement in EC-92. Second, Congress could only respond to directives as they became available for scrutiny. Third, many of these directives, particularly in the areas of local content and rules of origin, were extremely complex. Fourth, Congress was highly dependent on US firms in defining its role on EC-92. All this meant that the Congressional presence would be reactive rather than proactive and that Congress was more likely to act in the role of a mediating rather than a primary actor in the EC-92 arena. It also meant that, as already noted, the main Congressional function appropriate to the situation was that of oversight.

One study of the US trade policy processes has suggested that just as the inter-agency forum constitutes the focal point of executive trade policy-making, so the standing committees assume a similar role for the legislature.[17] Indeed, one feature of Congress's work in the oversight of trade policy is the diversity of committees which become involved in specific issues. The conference committee which deliberated over the final text of the 1988 Trade Act comprised 199 members from 14 House and nine Senate committees. Some observers have described this as representing a 'balkanization' of committee activity, producing delay and duplication of effort and have argued for the creation of a trade policy committee.[18] Whether or not one regards this multiplication of effort as an inevitable consequence of the way in which most trade issues impinge on a variety of interests, it was certainly true that EC-92 generated a spate of Congressional committee oversight hearings. By mid-1990, some five committees in both the House and the Senate had conducted hearings.

Thus it became clear that the Congressional input would be likely to focus on the twin roles of ensuring that the administration was alert to US trade concerns as they were affected by the SMP, keeping a watching brief on the strategies adopted, and where possible exerting pressure on the EC to take note of those interests. In terms of functions relevant to these roles, these could be defined as:

- agenda clarification – identifying the nature of the SMP and the issues involved, and helping to determine strategies;
- acting as a central locus of information exchange in the policy network;
- providing a point of access for the articulation of interests by industry and other parties, including European interests;
- providing a policy resource for the administration in its dealings with Brussels, while overseeing the federal government's response;
- acting as a legitimizing agent for the SMP itself and the US response to it.

Agenda clarification: issues, strategies and organization

One of the themes of this book is the complexity of the agenda-setting processes in US foreign economic policy and the extent to which this reflects an interaction between domestic and extranational pressures. Given the range of interests focusing on the SMP, Congress's role could be more accurately portrayed as one of contributing to a broad process of agenda identification and clarification rather than agenda setting in the strict sense of that term. Hence the first impact of EC-92 was to generate what might be termed 'the what's it all about?' phase of Congressional involvement, which spanned 1988 and 1989. Congressional staff reported a 'scramble for information' during this period, which reflected the emergence of an 'EC-92 industry' in the private sector as consultancy firms fell over each other to run conferences and briefing sessions.

The main agenda item was the prospect that EC-92, either by intent or as a by-product of specific directives, would create the feared 'Fortress Europe'. Here, as in other areas of trade policy debate, it is difficult to separate the rhetoric (directed to both domestic and international interests) from the reality of perceptions on Capitol Hill. Certainly, the phrase 'Fortress Europe' was common coinage during 1988 and early 1989, although there was plenty of available opinion which cast doubt on its accuracy – and public pronouncements by leading Congressional figures such as Lee H. Hamilton were careful to balance this image with the positive features of EC-92. From the Brussels side, however, Congress was seen as allied with those elements of the bureaucracy, particularly in Commerce, who were unconvinced that enhanced European integration was in US interests.[19]

Perhaps one of the notable features of discussion within Congress was the linking of the emergence of the SMP with the broader transformations in world politics as the Cold War era drew to a close. In this sense, developments in European integration encouraged reflection on the nature of the transatlantic relationship generally, the future of the Western Alliance and the implications of events in Germany and Eastern Europe.

Testimony given to various Congressional committees argued at the minimum that there was much in the SMP that was of advantage to the USA. We shall return to this below when discussing the interactions between business interests and Congress, but it is worth noting in passing that the dominant view both in contemporary comment and from those interviewed during the course of this study is that the negative images came primarily from a series of speeches made by EC Commissioner for External Trade Relations Willy de Clercq during 1988, which focused on the sensitive issue of reciprocity. By 1989–90, this phase had moved into a more detailed review of specific areas covered by SMP directives – such as public procurement and standards, discussed in Chapter 7.

Both the general and the more specific sets of concerns were clearly reflected in the 1989 report of the House Foreign Affairs Subcommittee on International Economic Policy and Trade chaired by Sam Gejdenson.[20] The report of the subcommittee, having noted the potential advantages for US firms of a European single market, went on to identify the three issues of standards, local content and rule of origin restrictions and reciprocity as key areas of potential concern. There was, of course, nothing new in this, since similar opinions were being voiced by a range of policy practitioners and academics. But the fact that these concerns were voiced by Congressional committees helped to reinforce their significance, particularly on the administration's agenda.

However, it was in the areas of strategy and governmental organization to achieve policy objectives, discussed in Chapter 3, that Congressional pressures were of greatest significance. This turned on decisions to be made on the appropriate channels for dealing with issues posed by EC-92. The administration's chosen route appeared to be to solve SMP-related problems through the GATT negotiations where possible, while tackling specific problems – such as those presented by the draft Second Banking Directive – through direct bilateral diplomacy. This twin-track approach appeared to cause some concern on Capitol Hill, in the sense that the multilateral trade negotiations option might not be sufficiently focused on US interests and sectoral issues and that the quest for multilateral free trade goals might fail to protect these interests. In short, this reflected the more general difference in perspective on trade policy between executive and Congress noted above. Capitol Hill was alert to the issues presented by the SMP and determined that these should be actively addressed and not ignored. As one Congressional insider put it in 1990:

> There is a feeling in Congress that we lost the trade war with Japan precisely because we did not act more decisively against the individual, sector-specific trade barriers which create a significant portion of the US–Japan bilateral trade deficit. Many in Congress would argue that the long-term health of the US–EC relationship is dependent upon actively negotiating each protectionist element of Europe 1992, not pretending these elements are non-existent.[21]

The belief that executive departments were not performing adequately or were deficient in organizational terms was hardly a new theme in trade policy, but echoed through the deliberations of Congressional committees, particularly the House Foreign Affairs Subcommittee and the Senate Finance Committee. Thus the issues raised in the 'remaking of government' context discussed in Chapter 3 were regularly aired in committee hearings and reports. Of particular concern were the relationships between the various departments and agencies involved in the negotiations, both in Washington and on the ground in Brussels and Geneva.

Testimony given to the House Foreign Affairs Subcommittee between March and May 1989 indicated considerable expertise within the trade bureaucracy but the absence of a clear strategy as to how to proceed.[22] This was reinforced by the fact that President Bush had made no major speech addressing EC-92 issues – in part a reflection of timing. As noted above, the lack of transparency in, and access to, the European standards-setting processes were major issues of concern to the subcommittee. But almost immediately after its report appeared, the agreement between Secretary of Commerce Mosbacher and Commissioner Bangemann on this very subject was announced, defusing to some degree one of Congress's concerns.

However, the broad thrust of Congressional worries remained. While acknowledging that much of the initiative in dealing with SMP issues must come from the private sector, the subcommittee argued that there was a clear role for government and that a far higher profile needed to be given to EC-92 in US trade strategy, which it described as reactive rather than proactive:

> A more aggressive US strategy may allow for success in the Uruguay Round on the concerns identified in this report The Administration should establish a firm timetable for the immediate commencement of bilateral negotiations if the Uruguay Round is unsuccessful in resolving US problems with EC-92. This plan must clearly identify US leverage to respond to any unfair and protectionist elements of the European Economic integration plan.[23]

Turning to intra-departmental relations, the subcommittee argued for closer cooperation between departments (as in the case of the USTR, Commerce and Defense over defence procurement). Furthermore, it pressed for an enhancement of staffing levels at the US Mission to the EC, with the reassignment of personnel from other US embassies in Europe as an interim measure. It also suggested that Commerce should produce more complete and up-to-date analyses of the consequences of EC directives for US trade interests.

The issue of Commerce–State Department responsibilities in the area also came to the attention of the Senate Finance Committee, chaired by Senator Lloyd Bentsen. This reflected the long-standing perception on Capitol Hill that Commerce is far more sympathetic to US industries challenged by unfair foreign trade practices than is the State Department, usually regarded as anxious to subordinate such concerns to broader foreign policy objectives. Both Bentsen's committee and the House Foreign Affairs Subcommittee were keen to see the US Mission in Brussels strengthened by expertise from the Commerce Department. However, as we have seen in the previous chapter, this aroused resistance from the State Department, which viewed such a move as an infringement of its territory. During Senate Finance Committee hearings in May 1989, Bentsen expressed his concern over the apparent conflict and the US Trade Representative, Carla Hills, was questioned on the subject.[24]

Information exchange and articulation of interests

As noted earlier, one of the problems presented by the SMP was the gathering and transmission of timely information on what EC-92 meant for specific US interests. Given its involvement in trade issues and the links between members and senators and their domestic constituencies,

Congress was well placed to act as a focus for information gathering and the projection of key interests on specific aspects of the programme. This it did in part, as we have already seen, through hearings conducted by a number of House and Senate committees.[25] In addition, a considerable number of papers were prepared either for Congress in general or for specific committees by the Congressional Research Service.[26] Overall, this constituted a considerable body of information on the nature and implications of EC-92.

Congress also contributed to the process of information gathering and exchange by commissioning a number of reports from government agencies. Thus Senator Max Baucus, on behalf of the Subcommittee on International Trade of the Senate Finance Committee, requested the Government Accounting Office (GAO) to conduct an enquiry into how EC-92 might affect US small and medium-sized merchandise exporters. As the GAO report indicates, extensive fieldwork was undertaken in Washington and in Europe focusing on both the private sector and the key government departments and agencies.[27] However, the most extensive monitoring work was that undertaken by the US International Trade Commission (USITC) following a request from the Senate Finance Committee and the House Ways and Means Committee for a study on the effects of the SMP. This resulted in a series of reports based on research in both the USA and Europe by USITC industry specialists.[28] The special quality of this work and its contribution to the debate was described to us in the following terms by a senior USITC official:

> The role of ITC in EC-92 could be described as conducting a publicity campaign, alerting industry to specific issues. Much of the work was of a fairly general nature but we also tracked specific issues by focusing on EC directives (for example on standards). No other agency did this. In the process, ITC helped to correct the view of 'fortress Europe' – never one subscribed to by the Commission.[29]

In addition to the congressional committee activities, Senators Baucus (Democrat, Montana) and Roth (Republican, Delaware) established a Senate Task Force on EC-92 comprising some thirty senators, which acted as a switchboard aimed at 'ensuring a constructive dialogue between the EC and the Congress'.[30] Task Force meetings provided an opportunity for representatives of industry from senators' home states to be briefed on issues of concern to them. The information network thereby created helped to link the local and the national – a theme to which we shall return in the next chapter. By way of illustration, Senator Roth served on his state's Governor's Trade Council, and Representative Thomas J. Downey (Democrat, New York) chaired a conference in October 1989 which brought together businesspeople and government representatives to discuss the implications of the SMP.[31] At a more general level, prominent members of Congress, such as Lee H. Hamilton (chair of the Subcommittee on Europe and the Middle East of the House Foreign Affairs Committee), contributed articles on EC-92 to the press.[32]

But as we shall see in Chapter 6, the industrial and commercial interests concerned to gain a voice on Capitol Hill were diverse, ranging from large corporations with an established presence in Europe to small and medium business enterprises whose knowledge of the SMP was limited and whose fears of its consequences greater. Given the nature of their domestic constituencies and the roots of their political support, members of Congress are usually more likely to reflect the concerns of SMEs in specific sectors, and, as Chapter 5 suggests, this often creates a different 'local' perspective on such issues from that articulated by state governors. It is also obviously true that EC-92 was not an issue (for reasons set out in this and earlier chapters) likely to generate the kind of intense, highly politicized lobbying that the NAFTA agreement witnessed during 1992 and 1993.

Thus much of the thrust of Congressional activity was to focus on the needs of SMEs in gaining access to the emerging single market and to press the Commerce Department to provide maximum assistance in achieving this. In the process, some of the concerns regarding the implications of EC-92 were undoubtedly defused. At the same time, Congress acted as a warning bell for big business, including the 'insiders' with a presence in Europe. Here it has been suggested that the large corporations were engaged in a dual strategy focused on Congress, intended to alert the US trade policy community and, in so doing, to exert pressure on the EC to take heed of American interests.[33]

Certainly, US financial interests used the spectre of 'Fortress Europe' to generate a groundswell of opposition to the draft Second Banking Directive (DSBD). This posed in stark form one of the key issues exercising Congress, namely that of the principle of reciprocity and its impact on market access. In essence, the DSBD as it originally appeared in February 1988 would have denied access to third-country banks unless reciprocal access was given to European banks operating in the USA. Since legislation governing US banking operations imposes restrictions on inter-state banking (McFadden Act) as well as the services which banks can provide (Glass–Steagall Act), reciprocity could be viewed as a justification for discriminating against non-European financial services on the basis of legitimate national regulatory regimes. It was this Directive which generated some of the most intensive lobbying on Capitol Hill until in May 1989 the proposal was amended and the reciprocity requirement replaced by a more flexible provision based on national – or comparable – treatment.

Yet the picture was more complex than this account suggests, and provides a clear example of the interactions between actors and issues in different arenas characteristic of the multilayered policy environment.

While it is true that the financial industries were concerned about the principle of reciprocity, there was a parallel concern about the nature of the US regulatory regime and the impact of legislation such as Glass–Steagall on the ability of US banks to compete in the global financial market place. Thus there was a major debate within Congress on the regulation of the financial services industries to which the DSBD contributed. The case for congressional action was clearly put by the president of the Federal Reserve Bank of Atlanta: 'The prospect of limited access to the European market because of our inability to reciprocate has created a focus for discussion ... I hope this debate will prod Congress toward taking proactive steps to bring this country's depository institutions into the global mainstream.'[34] However, such a move was resisted by bodies representing the insurance industry keen to keep the banks out of their territory. Thus, spokespersons for the Bankers Association for Foreign Trade and the Independent Insurance Agents of America were delivering differing messages to Congress, in a debate on global competitiveness to which EC-92 was a major contributor. Indeed, the chair of the House Banking Committee predicted that the DSBD could be the determining factor in the outcome of the Glass–Steagall debate.[35] (The Senate had already voted to repeal Glass–Steagall by a large margin in March 1988.) As sentiment for repeal grew, the insurance industry began to modify its opposition. A statement from the Securities Industry Association announcing new proposals for reform suggested that the EC factor had been influential in this change of view.[36] The decision by the EC to replace reciprocity with national treatment, however, removed this key stimulus to amend the Glass–Steagall Act.

More generally, Woolcock has argued that the deliberate strategy of 'planting the seed' of Fortress Europe by insider lobbies helped to generate disquiet and unease regarding the EC-92 project among business 'outsiders' and on Capitol Hill. These concerns, he suggests, were reinforced by interests – such as beef exporters – locked in trade disputes with Europe. The telecommunications industry, for example, worried by its lack of bargaining power over market access following deregulation, had pressed Congress to include reciprocity provisions in the 1988 Omnibus Trade Act empowering the President to act against countries that do not provide 'mutually advantageous market opportunities for trade in telecommunications products and services'.[37] Concerned with the consequences for US–EC relations of using such powers, the administration had been reluctant to act. Whipping up Fortress Europe hysteria, the argument goes, goaded the federal government into adopting a more definite stance.

Interviews conducted during the course of this study suggest that however valid this image might be in specific cases, it provides only a partial picture of Congressional perceptions and the development of the

EC-92 saga between 1988 and 1990. It is true, for example, that representatives of the semiconductor industry complained to Congress that changes in the EC rule of origin that determines whether a chip is regarded as foreign or European had cost two US firms some $500,000 in lost sales.[38] But as those tracking these events at the time pointed out, it was hardly necessary for the insider lobbies to devise stratagems to get the SMP on the Congressional agenda, since de Clercq's 1988 speeches had already set the alarm bells ringing there. Moreover, industry groups such as the National Association of Manufacturers (NAM) were consistent in the evidence that they gave to Congressional committees, to the effect that the ultimate goals of EC-92 were not directed to denying access to US industry and were of potential benefit to it. Thus, one senior officer of the NAM saw Fortress Europe as a construct of the media and certain parts of the bureaucracy, particularly within the Commerce Department, which hearings before Congressional committees helped to defuse.

On the whole, the message that leading congressional figures such as Gejdenson received from industry at these sessions was that Congress should do nothing about EC-92 other than keep a watching brief, and that the dangers of precipitate action greatly outweighed any advantages that might accrue from it. Certainly, large players such as IBM, Du Pont and Ford saw themselves better placed to exploit the opportunities created by the SEM than many of their European competitors. From their perspective, there was a very real danger that action on Capitol Hill could generate responses from Europe unhelpful to their interests. Evidence given to the Senate Finance Committee in May 1989 by industry groups such as the US Chamber of Commerce tended to focus more on the administration's capacity to monitor what was happening and to develop coherent objectives. Such views, as we have seen, accorded with Congress's long-running concern with the conduct of US trade policy.

A further potential role for Congress in the evolving US response to the SMP was as a focus for EC lobbying efforts. Brussels appeared to be caught off-guard by initial US responses and the emergence of the Fortress Europe idea. In particular, the experience of the DSBD, where Congressional oversight was used to some effect, galvanized the EC into action. But that action seemed directed towards the administration rather than to Capitol Hill. In the view of one close observer, this was a reflection of a continuing failure on the part of Brussels to give sufficient weight to the role of Congress and to view it in terms more appropriate to the role and functions of the European Parliament. On a purely practical level, there was a real question (applicable to diplomatic missions other than the EC Delegation) as to whether the single delegation official responsible for tracking Congress was adequate for the task. To another, the European response to Congressional criticisms was both hasty and ill-conceived:

the EC tried to label any Congressman or Senator having a legitimate problem with Europe 1992 as part of the 'fortress Europe' crowd. This crowd, according to the EC, was ignorant of the European Community's trade and economic policies, and completely ignored Europe 1992's positive side. To this day, some EC officials find it easier to simply dismiss congressional critics of the EC's trade policies than to deal with the substance of their charges.[39]

To some degree, the potential damage that such attitudes may have created could be defused by the 'back-channel' diplomacy provided by inter-parliamentary links. Thus the twice-yearly Interparliamentary Meeting of Delegations from the US Congress and the European Parliament provided an opportunity to discuss EC-92 issues. At a more informal level, the American European Community Association, comprising legislators and businesspeople from both sides of the Atlantic, offered another forum for discussion.[40] But these, of course, are only part of the intensive formal and informal transatlantic linkages in which members of Congress are involved.

Congress as diplomatic resource

We have already noted that in the trade policy sphere the involvement of Congress stands as a potential weapon for an administration seeking concessions from negotiating partners. In some contexts, this relates to the need for congressional ratification of trade agreements, as in the case of NAFTA and the Uruguay Round. But whether or not the threat of non-ratification is relevant – and it was not in the case of EC-92 – the influence of Congress as a player in the trade policy process has to be taken into account.

Although it was the investigative role that underpinned Congress's involvement in the SMP, the possibility of legislative action lingered in the background. The April 1989 broadcasting directive, for example, with its local content requirements for television programmes, attracted considerable hostility from the US film industry – the major outside supplier – which viewed it not as a defence of European cultures but as a deliberate move to restrict its access to the European market. Washington threatened to take the issue to the GATT, although there was doubt as to whether its rules were applicable in such a case.[41] Sensitized to the issue, and with the intention of strengthening the US position in bilateral dealings with Europe, the House passed a resolution condemning the directive. In the standards and testing and certification area, Gejdenson introduced a package of legislation requiring European companies to have their products tested in the USA rather than Europe, pending agreement to open up European testing and certification procedures. This stood as a backcloth to ongoing negotiations on the subject.

However appropriate European reactions to Congress (and as we have suggested, there were many in Washington who were critical of them), there could be little doubt in Brussels and national capitals of EC member states as to its significance as a trade policy actor. On the one hand, this reflected the role of the legislature as a voice for sectoral interests. The fact that these were complex in their nature, however, meant that Congress was subject to conflicting messages, which helped to lessen the force of any legislative attack. At another level, however, the emergence of the SMP strengthened the arm of those on Capitol Hill who believed that the tide of economic and political events was moving against the transatlantic relationship, and that the primary focus for the USA lay westwards, towards the Asia-Pacific region.

This provided some support for the Clinton administration's moves towards APEC in 1992, with accompanying warnings to the Europeans that US international policy might be moving in a different geographical direction. That it was generally viewed as a shot across the Europeans' bows in the slow-moving GATT negotiations reinforced the linkages between progress on the Uruguay Round and responses to the EC-92 agenda which many on Capitol Hill appeared keen to stress during 1989–90. In the words of one study of the US trade policy processes, while supporting the outcome of the Uruguay Round, Congress 'provided a credible "bad cop" to bolster the adminstration's negotiating leverage with foreign governments'.[42] The Congressional presence in the US delegation to the unsuccessful December 1990 ministerial meeting in Brussels provided one occasion on which legislative influence was not lost on the Europeans. Here the key issue was agriculture, and Carla Hills's firm response to European reluctance to compromise reflected Congressional pressure on her to reject a 'bad' agreement in order to achieve a 'good' one later.[43] Although not part of the EC-92 agenda, the linkages between the various elements of the trade agenda in US–EC relations were apparent and the role of Congress in reinforcing those linkages was apparent.

As always, then, from the administration's perspective congressional involvement was a two-edged sword. The 1988 Trade Act provided all the support and bargaining strength that it needed. The problem was resisting congressional pressures to use the available powers where negotiators (and private sector interests) deemed these to be counterproductive. The proliferation of committee activity created a further dimension to the difficulties of policy management discussed in the previous chapter. As Greenwald noted when setting out the negotiating and organizational tasks confronting Washington, it was not simply a matter of keeping Congress informed, but deciding which government agency should handle relations with which Congressional committee.[44]

Congress as legitimizing agent

One of the key features in 'selling' trade agreements is to gain the approval of those domestic constituencies most affected by their outcome. We have seen that EC-92 differed from the Uruguay Round and NAFTA in that there was no formal agreement to ratify. However, ratification in the broader sense of legitimizing official policy was a role that Congress performed as the SMP proposals gained the attention of key interests. Congressional involvement, through the activities outlined above, contributed to an understanding and acceptance on the part of these interests of the concept of EC-92. In part this focused on the demystification of the Fortress Europe concept as Congressional hearings proceeded. Both by means of formal committee hearings and through their representative and educative roles, members of Congress were significant contributors to the debate over the broader implications of the SMP for the emerging international order as well as its implications for SMEs in specific sectors. In this way they were part of the learning process through which US public and private sector interests adjusted to the implications of the EC-92 agenda. This was of benefit to Brussels, in the sense that Congress was one mode of access to US decision-making – albeit one to which, as we have seen, Washington observers did not feel it had paid sufficient attention.

More specifically, Congress helped to legitimize the EC-92 agenda within the USA by contributing to the continuing debate over concepts and language in trade policy. In most cases this process was diffuse, given the complexity of the issues and the inevitably reactive response of Washington to a set of events driven by the logic of EC-92. But in others, as with the confused area of reciprocity, the debate focused on particular proposals. During the 1980s, Congress had succeeded in redefining reciprocity in terms of mirror image treatment in specific sectors, as distinct from the exchange of equivalent concessions. Because of this, US officials assumed that it was the mirror image definition that underpinned SMP initiatives, as with the DSBD. As noted earlier, Congressional participation in the dialogue on this issue became a key element in the processes by which national treatment was substituted for reciprocity. Furthermore, congressional acquiescence in the administration's approach on specific issues, such as standards and certification, helped to legitimize the overall US negotiating strategy on EC-92.

Conclusion

As an instance of legislative involvement in trade politics, EC-92 had none of the excitement that punctuated the NAFTA and Uruguay Round negotiations. This reflected the character of the US–EC relationship in general and the high level of support for the broad goal of European integration which, despite trade conflicts with Europe, exists on Capitol Hill. Certainly Congress was concerned with a number of aspects of the SMP agenda, but these issues were usually complex and reflected the heterogeneous nature of US–EC trade disputes. This gives transatlantic trade battles over market access issues a very different quality from those between the USA and Japan.

The technical nature of such issues as standards and testing and certification, moreover, offered little opportunity for the development of the extensive lobbying that accompanied the later stages of NAFTA. When combined with the fact that there was no agreement demanding legislative approval, this gave the Congressional role a more diffuse and subtle form. It was none the less significant for that. As we have argued, trade policy requires a continuous process of ratification through which affected domestic interests are reconciled to the outcomes of negotiations. Less and less often can this be achieved by formal processes such as legislative approval of a 'done deal'. Rather, international negotiations have to be accompanied by parallel domestic consultative processes. In the case of EC-92, the investigative function of Congress, undertaken by a number of committees, was the chief means by which this was discharged.

It was no easy task. The SMP appeared relatively suddenly to a Congress which had been sated with trade issues, not least, of course, the 1988 Trade Act. Problems such as testing and certification were specialist in nature and, in the case of the DSBD, touched on a major domestic debate regarding the regulatory regime for the financial services industries. Responses from industry were diverse (see Chapter 6), and the messages flowing into Capitol Hill, while usually cautiously supportive of EC-92 as a general exercise, were often contradictory in terms of responses to specifics. Congressional attitudes were also characterized by the recognition of the broader significance of these events in a rapidly changing international arena. Not only were the consequences of growing economic regionalism for the international trading regime debated, so were the implications of enhanced European integration for the future of the changing military-security environment. The emergence of EC-92 thus offered an opportunity for a degree of introspection, which ranged from the implications of enhanced globalization for US political and economic structures to the future of the Western Alliance.

Committee hearings provided the forum in which these issues could be aired. For industry associations such as NAM, they provided an opportunity to deliver messages to several audiences, within the administration and the EC, simultaneously. Whether these voices where calling for a 'hands-off' approach from Washington, as advocated by US firms with a European presence, or for intercession on behalf of their interests, as in the case of some smaller firms fearful of a new European challenge, the effect was to contribute to the learning processes central to the evolution of trade policy.

The message for the administration reflected the continuing Congressional concern with the management of trade policy and the belief that the key agencies were not sufficiently alert to the challenges represented by the SMP. The aim was to press the administration into action while indicating to the EC what aspects of the EC-92 proposals were unacceptable. Equally critical was the choice of forum within which disputes should be addressed. The initial European view that the GATT negotiations offered a suitable opportunity to resolve such problems was rejected by Congress, which pressed the administration to tackle them through direct bilateral negotiations.

Overall, then, the role of Congress was significant but somewhat at variance with that frequently assigned to it in this policy area. As some observers have pointed out, Congressional involvement in trade policy over the past half-century has not been marked by attempts to return to the protectionism of the 1930s but, rather, has sought to follow a pragmatic middle path between protectionist sectoral pressures and advocates of free trade.[45] This appears to be true of the responses to EC-92 on Capitol Hill. In the words of one observer, 'Congress simply wants to ensure that critical American industries do not get left in the dust as Europe rushes toward a unified economy.'[46] Congress could be seen as sharing, and helping to promote, the learning process which the previous chapter has suggested was a central feature of the federal government's response. Thus, although there were tensions between it and federal agencies on specific issues and differences of view as to the appropriate strategies to be pursued towards the EC, overall Congressional involvement accorded more with the 'joint partnership' model of Congressional–executive relations in trade policy than with either that of Presidential or Congressional dominance.[47]

Notes and references

1   See, for example, the essays in R. B. Ripley and J. M. Lindsay (eds), *Congress Resurgent: Foreign and Defense Policy on Capitol Hill*, Ann Arbor, University of Michigan Press, 1993; and T. E. Mann (ed.), *A Question of Balance: The President, Congress and Foreign Policy*, Washington, DC, Brookings Institution, 1990. Also B. Hinckley, *Less than Meets the Eye: Foreign Policy Making and the Myth of the Assertive Congress*, Chicago, University of Chicago Press/Twentieth Century Fund, 1994.

2   R. G. Carter, 'Congressional trade politics in the post-Cold War

era', paper presented at the International Studies Association Convention, San Diego, 16–20 April 1996.

3   L. E. Santos, 'Trade politics of the American Congress', *Journal of World Trade*, 29(6), 1995; pp. 73–8.

4   On this theme see H. M. Ingram and S. L. Fiederlein, 'Traversing boundaries: a public policy approach to the analysis of foreign policy', *Western Political Quarterly*, 41(4), 1988, pp. 725–47.

5   B. Cohen, *The Public's Impact on Foreign Policy*, Boston, Little, Brown, 1973, p. 113.

6   J. W. Fulbright, 'The legislator as educator', *Foreign Affairs*, 57, Spring 1979, pp. 719–32.

7   P. Falconer, 'US congressional oversight as a victim of over-expectation: a review article', *Politics*, 12(1), 1992, p. 9.

8   P. Choate, *Agents of Influence: How Japan's Lobbyists in the United States Manipulate America's Political and Economic System*, New York, Knopf, 1990.

9   M. S. Ogul, *Congress Oversees the Bureaucracy: Studies in Legislative Supervision*, Pittsburgh, University of Pittsburgh Press, 1976. Quoted in Falconer, *op. cit.*, p. 9.

10   S. D. Cohen, J. R. Paul and R. A. Blecker, *Fundamentals of US Foreign Trade Policy: Economics, Politics, Laws and Issues*, Boulder, CO, Westview, 1996, p. 15.

11   I. M. Destler, *American Trade Politics* (3rd edn), Washington, DC, Institute for International Economics and The Twentieth Century Fund, 1995, Chapter 4.

12   P. Low, *Trading Free: the GATT and US Trade Policy*, New York, Twentieth Century Fund, 1993, pp. 130–4.

13   J. E. Twiggs, *The Tokyo Round of Multilateral Trade Negotiations: A Case Study in Building Domestic Support for Diplomacy*, Lanham, MD, University Press of America, 1987, p. vii.

14   J. Peterson, *Europe and America: the Prospects for Partnership* (2nd edn), London, Routledge, 1996, p. 100.

15   G. C. Hufbauer, 'An overview', in G. C. Hufbauer, *Europe 1992: An American Perspective*, Washington, DC, Brookings, 1990, pp. 16–20.

16   *Op. cit.*, p. 44.

17   Cohen, Paul and Blecker, *op. cit.*, p. 116.

18   D. M. Snow, and E. Brown, *Puzzle Palaces and Foggy Bottom: US Foreign and Defense Policy-making in the 1990s*, New York, St Martin's Press, 1994, p. 27.

19   Peterson, *op. cit.*, p. 80.

20   See the executive summary in US House of Representatives: Subcommittee on International Economic Policy and Trade of the Committee on Foreign Affairs, 'European Community's 1992 Economic Integration Plan', 31 May 1989, pp. 1–4.

21 P. Yeo, 'Congressional response to European economic integration', London, Royal Institute of International Affairs discussion paper (mimeo), May 1990, p. 5.

22 C. H. Farnsworth, 'Panel sees trade threat from Europe', *New York Times*, 1 June 1989.

23 US House of Representatives Subcommittee, *op. cit.*, p. 65.

24 R. Scherer, 'US debates policy on Europe in 1992', *Christian Science Monitor*, 18 May 1989.

25 See, for example, the hearings conducted by the Joint Economic Committee. On 26 April 1989 representatives of the National Association of Manufacturers and the US Chamber of Commerce appeared before the Committee. Congress of the United States, Hearing Before the Joint Economic Committee, *Europe 1992: Long-term Implications for the US Economy*, 26 April 1989.

26 Among these are the following Congressional Research Service Reports for Congress: G. J. Harrison, *The European Community's 1992 Plan: An Overview of the Proposed 'Single Market'*, 21 September 1988; G. J. Harrison (coordinator), *EC-92 and the United States*, 29 August 1989; R. J. Ahearn, *US Access to the EC Market: Opportunities, Concerns and Policy Challenges*, 16 June 1992.

27 US General Accounting Office, National Security and Affairs Division, *European Single Market: Issues of Concern to US Exporters*, Report to the Chairman, Subcommittee on International Trade, Committee on Finance, US Senate, Washington, DC, February 1990, pp. 12–13.

28 United States International Trade Commission, *The Effects of Greater Economic Integration Within the European Community on the United States*, USITC publication 2204, Washington, DC, July 1989. The sixth follow-on report was published in 1994.

29 Interview, USITC, Washington, DC, November 1995.

30 K. Bonine, 'US 1992: how the US government is preparing for the Single Market', *Europe*, 295, April 1990, p. 17.

31 *Ibid.*, pp. 14 and 17.

32 Lee H. Hamilton, 'Will the US fit the new map of Europe?', *The Christian Science Monitor*, 28 September 1989.

33 S. Woolcock, *Market Access Issues in EC–US Relations: Trading Partners or Trading Blows?*, London, Royal Institute of International Affairs/Pinter, 1991, pp. 13–14.

34 R. P. Forrestal, 'Europe's economic integration in 1992: implications for the United States', *Vital Speeches of the Day*, 55(20), 1989, p. 634.

35 R. M. Garsson, '1992 countdown: fear and longing in the US', *American Banker*, 25 July 1989, p. 15.

36 C. H. Golembe and D. S. Holland, 'Banking and securities', in Hufbauer, *op. cit.*, p. 93.

37   G. J. Harrison, *The European Community's 1992 Plan: An Overview of the Proposed 'Single Market'*, Washington, DC, Congressional Research Service, 21 September 1988, p. 26 (the quotation comes from the Telecommunications Trade Act of 1988); Woolcock, *ibid.*, p. 15.

38   K. Flamm, 'Semiconductors', in Hufbauer, *op. cit.*, pp. 225–92; S. Auerbach, 'Europe 1992: land of opportunity beckons', *Washington Post*, 20 March 1989.

39   Yeo, *op. cit.*, p. 4.

40   Bonine, *op. cit.*, p. 17.

41   J. Greenwald, 'Negotiating strategy', in Hufbauer, *op. cit.*, pp. 365–7.

42   Cohen, Paul and Blecker, *op. cit.*, p. 273.

43   Destler, *op. cit.*, p. 135.

44   *Ibid.*, p. 379.

45   Santos, *op. cit.*, pp. 73–8.

46   Yeo, *op. cit.*, p. 5.

47   Carter, *op. cit.*

5

The states

EC '92 is a clarion call for the states. It signifies the growing interdependence of the
world economy or, in essence, the unity of the international economy. State governments, with their unique degree of flexibility, creativity and accountability, are best
poised to answer this call and serve the needs of our public now and into the
future.[1]

This statement, made by the former governor of Virginia, Gerald Baliles –
among the most active state governors on the international scene – at one
of the many EC-92 conferences and seminars held around the USA, casts a
shaft of light on state approaches to the SMP. It reflects the growing
awareness of states, cities and localities that their well being is
increasingly determined by events outside their national settings. This is
not a new development. A recognition of the impact of international
economic forces and the need to respond to them at local and regional
levels has been a recurrent theme in US foreign economic policy since the
1970s. In this sense, the SMP was one milestone, albeit a significant one, in
a process which has also been strengthened by the CUSFTA, Uruguay
Round and NAFTA negotiations.

Beyond the growing recognition at both federal and state levels that US
competitiveness in the global market place demands action in areas where
the states are best suited to operate, the burgeoning trade agenda of the
1980s began to pose fundamental challenges to the management of US
trade policy and, even more, to the character of the federal system and its
balance of powers and responsibilities. In part this is because economic
policies adopted by state governments in areas such as public procurement
and subsidies were now firmly on the agenda of trade negotiations.
Moreover, key provisions of the NAFTA and GATT deals raised the
politically sensitive issue as to the federal government's obligations to
assume responsibility for ensuring that state actions do not contravene US
trade commitments and how that responsibility might be discharged
without impinging on state powers. In other words, the growing
internationalization of the US economy began to pose fundamental
questions regarding the very nature of the US political system.

Thus, in this chapter we are concerned with a further dimension of the multilayered policy environment, one that transcends the assumption that it is central governments that are the sole points of interface between national communities and their international environments.[2] The erosion of this boundary in the conduct of foreign economic policy has become part of a more complex pattern of policy-making which is increasingly the subject of attention in Europe as well as the USA. It is reinforced by a dual breakdown in the distinction between the 'high' agenda of military–security and the 'low' agenda of social and economic issues. The constituent elements from each category become less differentiated and jostle for policy-makers' attention as subnational actors become empowered to act in areas which traditional assumptions regarding the conduct of foreign policy reserve to national government.

That this process is recognizable on both sides of the Atlantic, allowing for significant differences reflecting the character of the respective politico-economic spaces, adds a significant dimension to the environment in which US responses to the SMP developed. Having considered briefly the background to the growing internationalization of states and localities, we shall move on to discuss their role in US responses to EC-92 in terms of trade and investment promotion, the trade policy processes and the broader questions of governance that developments on the trade agenda are posing.

Internationalizing states and localities

Several elements have interacted to promote a growing international involvement on the part of US states and localities. On one side, these are reflections of the enhanced internationalization of the US economy, combined with the need for states to assume an increasingly active role in export promotion in the face of diminishing federal activity in the area. International events of the 1970s and 1980s had a clear but selective impact on US regions. For the Northeast, the centre of traditional industries and old infrastructure, economic trends in the 1970s and 1980s presented obvious challenges. Indicative of such change is the fact that the port of New York, which once handled more than 60 per cent of US trade, now handles less than the port of Houston. A determined policy of promoting New York state on the international scene was rewarded by an influx of foreign investors and financiers into Manhattan.

The Southeast sought to profit from the problems of its neighbouring region by trying to attract industry from the declining areas while pursuing a vigorous international policy. Atlanta, in particular, has sought to stake its claim as an international city and as the business centre of the new South, while Florida has promoted itself as a key gateway to Latin America and the Caribbean. In the Southwest, Texas, the beneficiary of the energy crisis of the 1970s, found itself the victim of the mid-1980s decline in oil prices, and attempted to diversify its economy and to seek new markets for its products. The Pacific Northwest has long had close links with Western Canada and its geographical location has lent it a specific international orientation with the growth of the Pacific Rim as a focus of international economic activity.[3]

Internationalization, however, is a reflection of social and political as well as economic factors. The growth of social activism, often manifesting a belief in the need to transcend traditional patterns of politics, has increasingly employed state and local strategies based on 'think globally, act locally' principles.[4] Frequent ineffectiveness on the part of central government in addressing such concerns has often combined with a sense of alienation from specific elements of external policy, on the part of locally based interests.

Thus, disenchantment with the Reagan administration's policies on arms control, on Central America and on South Africa were major factors in the growth of what has been termed 'citizen diplomacy'.[5] The Reaganite policy of 'constructive engagement' with South Africa was widely opposed at state and city levels, eventually leading Congress to pass the Comprehensive Anti-Apartheid Act in the teeth of a Presidential veto. In Iowa, opposition to a perceived increase in the reliance on force in US foreign policy was a stimulant to the creation of a bipartisan group of businesspeople – Business for Peace – and the decision of the Iowa state legislature in 1986 to vote money in support of the Iowa Peace Institute.[6] Political and demographic changes have reinforced these trends, as African-American involvement in local and state politics has grown since the 1960s and new patterns of immigration help to change the attitudes and interests of regions. It is estimated, for example, that the growth of the Hispanic population in Southern California will result in it constituting 40 per cent of the population by 2000.

The trade and politico-social agendas do not, however, exist in separate boxes, but feed off one another, creating added pressures in the management of public policy at the centre. This was clearly demonstrated in the context of the NAFTA negotiations, as states bordering Mexico (and cities in close proximity to the USA–Mexico border) expressed their concerns regarding the impact of an agreement on immigration from south of the border. This results in a growing diffuseness in the domestic environment within which international policy has to be conducted. To a not inconsiderable degree, it becomes less realistic to speak of a single international environment in which such policy has to be shaped and implemented than to speak of a multiplicity of environments regionally focused and encapsulating discrete interests. At the same time, it would be misleading to suggest that specific regions are exclusively focused on one area of the international environment. This is clearly important in appreciating the responses of subnational government to EC-92.

First of all, the nature of state responses reflects a number of factors, not least size, economic strength and geographical location. California, for example, given its status as the world's eighth largest economy, clearly has special needs and interests:

> California is so big, and its problems so immense, that it needs its own foreign policy. In an era when economics commands foreign relations, this does not mean embassies and armies, but it does mean more trade offices and state agents in foreign countries, its own relations with foreign nations and a governor and legislature willing to represent the state's interests independently of Washington.[7]

A coherence of approach to its international environment which size and geography endow is not replicated in the Midwest, for example. But, at the same time, the factors determining external orientations are complex. California is part of the Pacific Rim, but European markets are significant for sales of many of its products. Moreover, Europe (specifically the UK) remains its single most important source of foreign direct investment.

The Midwest has a strong European heritage, reflecting its demographic profile: ethnic factors led Midwestern governors to establish their first European offices in Germany. Although New York state has been characterized by a predominantly Atlantic orientation, it has increasingly sought to develop its Asia-Pacific and Latin America links. The crucial point here is that the rise of a global economy demands global strategies. Both business and local economic development agencies have come to recognize that success demands a capacity to exploit opportunities wherever they might arise, not simply in one region. For this reason alone, the image of the USA as a country moving to a dominantly Asia-Pacific rather than a European orientation – as portrayed by Warren Christopher in 1992–3 – appears less than convincing.

The states as trade policy actors

In trying to locate the states within the multilayered trade policy environment, it is important to recognize their qualities as hybrid actors in diplomatic processes which span the domestic–international divide. Within the context of the US political fabric, they are polities in their own right, within which regional interests develop and pursue their interests at various levels of political activity.[8] Consequently, their complexity, combined with their constitutional and political characteristics, means that they do not fit easily into conventional typologies of international actor: 'transnational' and 'transgovernmental', for example.

This complexity is reflected in the range of actors involved in state/

local responses to EC-92. Alongside state development agencies (SDAs), linked to local business, local government and the export promotion resources of the Department of Commerce, are the national organizations which project state interests at the national level. These include the National Governors' Association (NGA), increasingly active in developing states' responses to the internationalization of their economies; the Council of State Governments (CSG); and the National Council of State Legislatures (NCSL). Each of these played a part in developing state attitudes towards the SMP, in the case of the NCSL and CSG, through running conferences and seminars and producing reports.[9]

The NGA has become increasingly significant in the shaping of trade policy – as distinct from the pursuit of exports and inward foreign investment – and brings to bear on the process a different set of views and priorities from those of Congress. A study of governors' views on NAFTA, for example, contrasts the high level of support for the agreement (40 out of 50 governors) with the considerable opposition on Capitol Hill.[10] This, it is suggested, reflects the closer links that Congress members have with sectional economic interests, as contrasted to the governors' responsibilities for general economic development and the national orientation of lobbying activities. This difference of constituencies and audiences may also help to explain the apparently higher degree of pessimism over the impact of EC-92 that Oneal discovered in her survey of SDAs' responses to the SMP, when contrasted to the more upbeat attitudes reflected in the public utterances of the governors.[11]

The states and EC-92

These general developments provide the context for the response of local and state governments to the emergence of EC-92. Not surprisingly, this was regarded as both a challenge to be confronted and an opportunity to be exploited.[12] Furthermore, it heightened the awareness, particularly on the part of state governors, of the significance of pursuing a vigorous foreign economic policy in an increasingly harsh climate. As we shall see later, this awareness dovetailed neatly with a growing concern at federal level over US competitiveness in world markets and a dawning realization that this could only be enhanced by policies delivered at local level. But, at the same time, the interest of the EC in local policies, often associated with this drive for competitive edge, posed a problem for Washington in terms of its ability, constitutionally and politically, to meet obligations entered into under trade agreements.

Beyond the concern with competitiveness – to which we shall return shortly – the issues posed by the SMP for the states were, of course, little different in substance from those confronting national policy-makers.

Product standards, public procurement, local content rules, rules of origin and reciprocity were the issues addressed by state and local seminars and publications, including those of the state organizations, such as the NGA. But state administrations confronted the realities of the changing global economic environment of which EC-92 was part, not least because of their close interaction with business and their regional economic development responsibilities. In this context, the implications of closer European integration for patterns of foreign investment were critical.

The principal perceived danger here was the likelihood that US firms would need to invest in Europe to gain access to the single market, thereby exporting jobs from the USA. Beyond this, however, there was a clear recognition that the globalization of economic activity represented a fundamental shift in the character of local economies, with major economic and political implications. Echoing Robert Reich's thesis concerning the demise of national economies, the Secretary of the Pennsylvania Department of Commerce was quoted as predicting the integration of local economies into the global economy, with the result that the distinction between 'local' and 'foreign' companies would be hard to make.[13]

There was one vital respect in which the state perspective on EC-92 was very different from that of Washington, however. Along with the NAFTA and Uruguay Round agendas, it posed major questions regarding state powers and the possibility that internationalization of the US economy would lead to a redrawing of the constitutional map. As we have already seen in earlier chapters, the draft Second Banking Directive focused attention on the regulatory powers of state governments. But this was only a part of the broader issues posed by the demands of trade reciprocity and national treatment as they touched on areas of state responsibility. And where these related to state policies, as in the case of local 'buy-American' policies in the sphere of public procurement (see Chapter 7), the problems were thrown into sharp relief.

The general point to be made, then, is that state and local responses to EC-92 developed in an increasingly complex policy milieu focused on debates over the need for enhanced competitiveness in a global market place, the nature and shaping of trade policy and the implications of both of these for US constitutional structures and processes. In these areas the states have been instrumental in transcending two of the policy boundaries which we have discussed in earlier chapters: that between the public and private sectors and that which assigns to national government sole responsibility for external policy. Let us now examine in a little more detail each of the points raised above.

Competing in a global economy

A key feature in US responses to EC-92 reflects a growing concern with the differences between the USA and Europe in terms of export assistance services offered to small and medium business enterprises. The SMP has acted as a stimulant to a question which has gained increasing attention: why is the USA relatively backward in offering its firms the kind of assistance common to the European states?[14] When compared with its major trading partners, the USA is at the bottom of the league in terms of expenditure on export promotion: France was spending $6.19 per capita in the late 1980s and the US $1.20.[15] The consequent imbalance of export support activities was pointed up in the following terms by the Undersecretary for International Trade in testimony to Congress during 1991: 'In the fast-developing markets of Europe resulting from the EC 1992 process, the United States has three officers in Milan; the French thirty-eight.'[16]

A critical issue in this debate has been whether the federal government has either the will or the capacity to deliver a programme of the kind deemed necessary if the USA is to replicate the European patterns of export assistance to SMEs. Among the charges levelled at it are lack of coordination and overall strategy. This is not to say that the Department of Commerce (DOC) has been inactive in attempts to build close relationships with SDAs and local development agencies. The DOC and the United States and Foreign Commercial Service (USFCS) have placed considerable emphasis on the development of state and local partnerships through their Public and Private Programs Office and District Export Councils.[17] Rather, the question posed by critics such as Nothdurft is how successful these efforts have been. A 1992 report from the US General Accounting Office revealed that some $2.7 billion had been spent on export promotion, but without any guiding strategy or set of priorities.[18]

Against this background, the states (and local government) have assumed a major role, reflecting their growing significance in the field of economic development.[19] During the 1980s, state international trade programmes began to shift from investment attraction to trade promotion activities, including seminars/conferences, market studies, trade data dissemination, export credit insurance and trade missions/fairs, supported by an increasing number of foreign offices. Expenditure on these activities doubled every two years during the 1980s, and by 1992 the states were spending $97 million on international trade promotion, a sum comparable to that expended by the federal government.

The context of this activity has, however, changed, with a growing recognition of the nature of competitive advantage in a global economy wherein companies' allegiance to territorial jurisdictions, whether national or subnational, is weakening. A successful strategy in this environment demands an awareness that competitive edge means more than assisting individual businesses in the export drive. Thus the NCSL report on the implications of EC-92 stressed that its key lesson for the states was the need to create a coherent economic development strategy, into which a variety of elements – education, workforce training and basic and specialized infrastructure – are woven together.[20] In short, there is little point in promoting trade if there is no infrastructure to support it. The recognition of this reality has resulted in an emphasis on a range of activities, such as improving state educational systems, as one means of meeting the challenges at what an NGA report terms the 'international frontier'.[21]

In the EC-92 context, Oneal's survey (of 22 states) found that 86 per cent of SDAs had launched new initiatives or adapted existing programmes.[22] The range of activities is typical of those used in export promotion work:

- new information service (7);
- new research effort (7);
- conference (11);
- new unit within department (1).

But, as already suggested, these activities reflected the increasing emphasis on federal–state and public–private sector cooperative efforts. A few 'snapshots' help to illustrate the point.

The Division of International Trade of the New Jersey Department of Commerce and Economic Development, in cooperation with KPMG Peat Marwick, produced a guide to the SMP for New Jersey business.[23] As with others of its kind (the California World Trade Commission produced a similar guide in cooperation with KPMG), this provides a guide to the SMP, its likely impact on New Jersey businesses, the nature of the EC legislative processes and how to influence them. Beyond this, it provides a checklist for companies wishing to gain a presence in the European market place. Along with a number of other states, California and Maryland both developed initiatives focused on EC-92. 'Maryland Opportunity '92' incorporated three dimensions: trade development, business assistance and education.[24] In Tennessee, the Tennessee–European Economic Alliance, a public–private sector joint venture, sought to build public awareness of the significance of the SMP and the possibilities that it presented for business in the state. In common with SDAs and chambers of commerce across the country, it staged a conference on this theme in 1991.

In Indiana, the Vice President of the Indiana Chamber of Commerce, commenting on the number of trade seminars held in the state, observed: 'if there is a company in Indiana that wanted to go to a seminar about EC

1992 and didn't, it is living under a rock'.[25] Alongside the state's large companies, such as Eli Lilley and the automotive supply giant, Arvin Industries, both of whom had well developed European strategies, smaller businesses profited from partnerships between the private sector and various levels of government. The Columbus Enterprise Development Corporation, for example, put together a network of six small businesses, which exchanged information and machinery in a bid to enter the European market. The project – funded by state and federal grants, local businesses and the City of Columbus – included a quality programme to enable the firms to comply with European certification requirements.[26]

In Pennsylvania, one of the developing models of partnership sponsored by USFCS has developed in the form of the Western Pennsylvania Export Partnership. This links a variety of private sector interests and public bodies, including the Western Pennsylvania District Council, the Pittsburgh USFCS office, the Service Corps of Retired Executives, the Pennsylvania State Office of International Development, four Pennsylvania Local Development Districts and the Greater Pittsburgh World Trade Association. An 11 county organization aimed at helping businesses located in the rural areas of central Pennsylvania, SEDACOG, found its export promotion activities greatly strengthened by growing media attention on EC-92. A further dimension to the state-level response came from Ball State University, with its decision to focus the 1992 academic year on the changing European scene with its 'Bringing Europe to the Midwest' programme.

Virginia, with 50 per cent of its exports going to Europe, has a clear interest in the European market, as reflected in the fact that its former governor, Gerald Baliles, was one of the most active governors on the international trade mission scene. (Indeed, the level of expenditure on international trade promotion became a political issue, and Baliles's successor, Governor Wilder, abolished the World Trade Department in 1990.) As the major export agency for the state, the Economic Development Department, in cooperation with Peat Marwick and the Center for European Community Studies at George Mason University, published a business guide to the EC. In the private sector, the former director of the disbanded World Trade Department and a number of his staff set up a trade management consultancy, which has advised companies wishing to gain access to the EC.[27]

The states in Europe

As already noted, a considerable part of the states' growing international effort has focused on the establishment of an overseas presence by means of foreign offices. With a particularly rapid growth during the 1980s, when the number doubled, by 1992 there were 156 offices in 22 countries.[28] Some of these are staffed by full-time personnel, others are operated by contractors or consultants. State governments have regularly reviewed their overseas representation, closing and opening offices in response to domestic political and economic pressures and perceptions as to where it is profitable to locate in response to the changing international economy. Not surprisingly, Tokyo was the main focus for growth during the 1980s, and remains the city with the largest number of state offices (37 states were represented there in 1992). In the European theatre, Germany has become the most favoured target country (16 offices, 11 of them in Frankfurt). The SMP helped to stimulate a growing awareness of the significance of the EC, encouraging states to open offices in Brussels (13 were operating in 1992). Interviews with state officials revealed some uncertainty as to the precise reasons for locating in Brussels, apart from a feeling that this is a major decision-making centre demanding a presence.[29] However, there has been a minor relocation of offices from Brussels to centres of industrial activity. In the words of a California trade official, 'being in Brussels is like locating in Sacramento'. Levine's survey of state European offices reinforces this impression: 'Office directors in Brussels cited the fact that it is the capital of Europe because it is the headquarters city for the European Community and NATO. The directors acknowledged, however, that they have little contact with the Community and none with NATO.'[30] Rather, the focus of the state offices is on trade promotion and investment attraction, with the emphasis moving decidedly in favour of the former as the cost and efficacy of the battle for foreign direct investment has come under increasing scrutiny.[31] In this sense, they form part of an access network, gathering intelligence, identifying trade opportunities and feeding these to the home state, usually on to computer databases. The offices are also linked into more proactive programmes intended to identify firms which might become exporters to the European market.

The emergence of EC-92 helped to stimulate a debate concerning the effectiveness of this trade promotion activity. First, the level of cooperation between USFCS (with its 45 European offices) has been described as limited and reduced in scope rather than enhanced since the mid-1980s. Second, cooperative trade promotion activities among the states, underpinned by the Council of American States in Europe (CASE), which organizes trade shows and investment conferences, while appreciated by some states as providing an infrastructure within which even small companies can promote their products, have been criticized as using ineffective techniques and as receiving uneven support from US embassies. Third, inadequacies in the relationships between home departments and the offices have been identified, resulting in a lack of direction and a failure to devise means by which their activities can be evaluated.[32]

In part, this debate has to be seen in the light of what might be regarded as the reverse flow of subnational international trade and investment activity, symbolized by the enhanced presence of European regional authorities in the USA. (In 1992 some 38 offices or consultancy representatives were operating.) These are regarded as object lessons in at least two senses: (a) in terms of their flexibility of approach to export promotion activities which create 'niche' programmes tailored to the specific needs of SMEs, rather than the traditional 'blanket' approach symbolized by trade shows; (b) as examples of successful cooperative ventures between regional and national authorities and the public and private sectors. Among these, the Regional Mission for the Coordination of International Trade with Brittany (MIRCEB), with US offices in Seattle and Minneapolis, has been seen as a highly effective public–private partnership providing customized services for its clients on a fee-for-service basis.[33]

A concern with efficiency, effectiveness and, not least, cost in the face of developments such as EC-92 has opened up a debate about the nature of state and local trade promotion activity and its relations with the federal government and private sector. During the 1980s, Minnesota attempted to build an enhanced international presence by creating partnerships between the state and local companies, including multi-national corporations, banks and law firms, whereby executives of these firms located overseas acted as volunteer representatives. The use of shared foreign representation has been considered, made more viable by a shift in the nature of the offices from investment attraction work (highly competitive) to trade promotion, where cooperation can be profitable. The first such experiment came with the decision by the Great Lakes states to open a joint trade promotion office in Canada. Moreover, the office was located in the US Consulate General in Toronto, thereby reinforcing the federal–state link. In 1994 it was reported that this experiment would be replicated in Singapore or Saudi Arabia, but it had not been attempted in Europe at the time of writing.

Perhaps the most considered response to EC-92 and its implications for the regionalization of state overseas trade activities was to come from the Western Governors' Association (WGA).[34] Conscious of the growing internationalization of the West, the WGA commissioned a report on the possibilities of responding to the challenges which this presented on a regional as opposed to a state-by-state basis. Noting that Western overseas representation had increased from eight offices in 1986 to 29 in 1989, the report argued that this activity was unbalanced and failed to take into account such developments as EC-92. Thus there were 24 offices in Asia and only four in Europe, despite the fact that in such key sectors as transportation equipment, electrical and electronic manufactures and instruments, exports to Europe are greater in volume than those to East

Asia.[35] Part of the problem here, it was argued, was the need to overcome old and stereotyped thinking and to recognize the implications of Europe as a single market rather than as individual countries. Looked at in this light, the EC as a whole imported double the amount of goods that Japan did. The suggested solution was to rationalize offices in Tokyo and Taipei into single export offices and to set up a European Trade Task Force with a similar objective in view.

EC-92 also generated responses in terms of alternative modes of European initiative at the local government level. Of course, sister-city twinning arrangements are nothing novel, but the need to gain access to new markets has encouraged city authorities to look to the creation of strategic economic alliances as distinct from the cultural rationale for such relationships. Encouraged by the SMP and the recognition that, despite California's focus on the Pacific Rim, the EC is its second largest trading partner, the city of San Jose sought to establish a series of partnerships with five European cities: Dublin, Barcelona, Rouen, Stuttgart and Milan. The overall aim was to enable the six linked cities to develop more successfully than they could do individually. Through the agreement signed with Dublin, for example, in addition to exchanging information on investment opportunities, San Jose offered help to several Irish companies wishing to establish links with firms in Silicon Valley, and to place a number of Irish business students in internships with local companies. The Irish Development Agency, in exchange, offered assistance in educating local businesspeople about the nature of the SMP.[36]

The states and trade policy

One of the central lessons of the past decade regarding state involvement in US trade policy has been that if they are to respond to the challenges which the global economy presents them with, then the states need to gain a voice in the shaping of trade policy. In part, this is a reflection of the growing awareness, as indicated above, that competitiveness demands much more than merely tracking trade and investment opportunities. Rather, it requires, among other qualities, an ability to monitor and influence the trade policy agenda internationally and nationally. This is particularly true given the fact that this agenda is increasingly impacting on the economic development area, through its concern with subsidies, for example.

The second incentive is linked to the first: namely, the growing significance of non-tariff barriers (NTBs) to trade diplomacy, a development beginning with the Tokyo Round of GATT negotiations and given increased impetus through CUSFTA, NAFTA and the Uruguay Round. The point here is that (as we shall see in Chapter 7 in the context of public procurement) state powers in a variety of areas are brought into the international trade arena, posing problems regarding the relationship between the federal and state governments and the international environments in which they operate. Various forms of 'buy-American' state legislation have been at issue with America's trading partners for some years, not least with the EC.[37] But the problem is expanding as trade intersects with an ever larger part of the policy agenda, including services such as banking, insurance and advertising, each of which is subject to state regulation. This trend can also be seen in the sanitary and phytosanitary areas, where concern has been expressed concerning the impact of the GATT and NAFTA agreements on the ability of the states to maintain their own food safety standards where these exceed agreed international standards.[38] We shall return to this later in the chapter in the context of the impact of trade agreements on the operation of the federal system.

Just as the states are, as a consequence of the developments set out in this book, becoming sensitive to the internationalization of their economies and policy environments, so, equally, are foreign governments and business interests. One of the first events to underscore this was the so-called 'beer case' brought to a GATT panel by Canada. The issue turned in part on state regulations giving preference to home-produced over imported alcoholic drinks, and followed a similar challenge brought by the EC against the Canadian provinces in the late 1980s.[39] In both instances, the panels ruled against the subnational regulations as being in violation of GATT provisions on non-discrimination against trade. As in the earlier Canadian case, the US federal authorities have had to engage in a round of domestic diplomacy with the aim of removing the offending practices.

Another area of state regulatory practice which has aroused the interest of both business and governments alike has been that affecting the investment climate. Some states have long operated laws which determine the nature and extent of foreign investment, in real estate, for example, and in the banking and insurance industries.[40] However, these are relatively few in number. More significant is the broader regulatory climate affecting foreign investment, as in the area of taxation. The best example here has been the long-running saga focused on the attempts by a number of states (most significantly California) to impose a mode of corporate taxation, commonly referred to as 'unitary taxation', whereby companies operating in a state jurisdiction are taxed on a percentage of their global profits, not simply those derived from their local operations.[41] From the early 1980s until 1994, a coalition of UK-led business and financial interests, supported by such bodies as the EC and OECD, pursued an active campaign by political and legal means at both the state and federal levels.

Quite clearly, issues such as these touch on the fundamental character of the federal constitution and the balance of powers between the federal and state governments. Moreover, as a report from the Advisory Commission on Intergovernmental Relations has noted, it is one which will grow as the impact of globalization in such areas as drug trafficking, human rights, immigration and global warming – all areas where state and local government have interests and responsibilities – encourages states to seek a voice in the treaty-making processes.[42] In the trade and investment sphere the danger from the state perspective is that international pressures, whether from governments or the private sector, for uniform treatment may lend added impetus to federal pre-emption of state powers.

This presents the federal government with a set of problems even more testing than the issues discussed in Chapters 3 and 4. What is involved here is the nature of the political system itself, as opposed to administrative structures and processes for managing trade policy. As we shall see below, the addition of a subnational dimension makes the latter far more problematic, but the evolving character of the economic agenda, of which EC-92 is one manifestation, means that they assume a highly political hue. One example of this is to be found in Congressional resistance to change in the US financial services regulatory environment in the face of the challenges posed by the draft Second Banking Directive, discussed in earlier chapters. As Woolcock has noted, one of the major differences between the USA and the EC in terms of commercial relations has been that, in the face of state policies restricting access to the US market, Congress has been reluctant to act for political rather than constitutional reasons.[43]

This combination of external and internal pressures presents challenges to both levels of government. On the one hand, Washington is discovering that it needs to be able to integrate subnational state and local government into the trade policy processes. A failure to do so will not only present it with embarrassing situations as it finds itself involved in international trade disputes which focus on subnational level policies, but also detract from its negotiating strength in bilateral and multilateral trade diplomacy. Ultimately, the failure to engage in adequate communication with affected subnational interests will be the collapse of domestic consensus, on which so much diplomacy of this kind rests. But it is not only at the centre that a challenge presents itself. The states are confronted by the problem of developing a capacity to respond to these internationally generated pressures. Taken together, these issues create a mutual interest in consultation and coordination and the creation of 'linkage mechanisms' through which communications can be channelled.

State–federal communications: the national level

Broadly speaking, there are two overlapping modes of influence open to the states in seeking to gain an input into the trade policy processes. The first is the political channel directed towards Congress and the administration; the second is by means of consultative mechanisms established within the trade policy machinery. On the political front, as we have seen, the governors have become very active on the international trade and investment front, not least in projecting their individual and collective interests at national level. The states are supported in this respect by their Washington offices, together with three national organizations, the NGA, NCSL and CSG.

When the EC-92 issue appeared on the US agenda, the only state maintaining a dedicated trade representative (an ex-USTR official) in Washington was California. During 1989, he found that the SMP and the Uruguay Round were the two issues of main concern and described his role as threefold: (a) to push federal policy in a direction reflecting California's free trade interests; (b) to 'organize the California Congressional delegation'; and (c) to alert the California business community to the issues posed by EC-92 and thus increase political pressure on trade policy at the centre.[44]

Particularly for the states without the resources to focus so intensively on trade issues, it is the national state representative organizations which offer the route to influence at the centre. Given their different remits and constituencies, the NGA, NCSL and CSG were all active on EC-92. The CSG defines itself as a more research-oriented organization, promoting interstate coordination on responses to significant problems. Its perspective on the single market tended to focus on the broader issue of the impact of globalization on the federal system, and the consequent dangers of federal pre-emption of state powers. One of its main functions appears to have been as a facilitator in developing linkages between the EC and the states. Officials reported that they had close links with the EC delegation in Washington and that ambassadors Denman and Van Agt had done a good deal of information work for them at state level. Furthermore, they had hosted a delegation of members of the European Parliament (who were very concerned with state procurement policies) and organized two state delegations, comprising governors, legislators and businesspeople, to Europe. During 1992–3 they were also planning a major conference on the implications of the SMP for US–EC relations.[45]

Of the two more politically oriented bodies, the NGA has made much of the running on the issue of state involvement in the trade policy processes. On one level, of course, this is done through political channels, but, as was noted earlier in the chapter, the governors often take a different view on key trade issues from that adopted by Congress – even by their own state delegations. Thus the governors were on the whole much more sympathetic than Congress to the pressures coming from the US Special Trade Representative, Micky Kantor, to resolve the problems posed by state preference legislation (see Chapter 7). But the NGA has also been instrumental in developing the state input into trade negotiations at USTR level.

Machinery for state and local consultation has existed for some years in the form of the Intergovernmental Policy Advisory Committee (IGPAC), established under the 1974 Trade Act. Comprising some thirty-five state and local representatives, its purpose is to advise the USTR on items on the trade agenda that have implications for subnational interests. Apart from its two formal meetings per year with the Trade Representative, the IGPAC process functions through continual contact between state officials and organizations such as the NGA and NCSL. However, the expanding number and scope of trade agreements during the 1980s prompted the NGA to press for a more formalized set of trade policy links. In a working paper commissioned by the NGA's Committee on International Trade and Foreign Relations, it was argued that the existing arrangements: 'cannot serve the nation in the future. The central element of a new partnership must be increased capacity for communications and coordination between state governments and the federal trade policy system centered in the Office of the United States Trade Representative'.[46] The paper argued for the continuation of the IGPAC system but suggested that the valuable work performed by USTR in liaising with state and local governments should be strengthened by the creation of a new section dedicated to this function. Subsequently, an Intergovernmental Affairs section was established in late 1992, overseeing IGPAC and providing a central point of contact with the USTR for states and local authorities.

The impression gained through interviews with NGA and state trade policy officials is that although the system is overloaded (with about 170 staff, the USTR is regarded as heavily overburdened with coordination activities), the system works reasonably well. However, as one official located in his state's Washington office noted, the real test will come when an issue affecting the states as a collectivity (in the taxation area, for example) arises in the context of trade dispute settlement procedures under NAFTA or the new World Trade Organization (WTO).

Looked at from the USTR end, the problems appear to be somewhat different. Noting that the states had seized on certain aspects of EC-92, a staff member of the USTR had found that 'issues are grabbed at but not really understood'. The problem here is not so much unwelcome interference, but one of encouraging an informed interest and involvement in trade policy issues as they impinge on local interests. This, in part, as he noted, is determined by the capacity of the states to respond to such issues: 'State interest in trade policy is patchy, depends on bureaucratic resources and the character of the issue. States quickly grasped the issues that affected them in the case of the Canada–US free trade negotiations but it is much more difficult to get them involved in EC-92 or the MTN'.[47] The point is clearly a critical one. As we have seen, the EC-92 agenda posed a number of issues affecting, actually or potentially, state interests. This creates as much of a 'capacity to coordinate and respond' problem as confronts the federal government.

One of the features of this dimension of the policy network generated by the multilayered trade policy environment is the replication at local level of the horizontal fragmentation between agencies of government which exists at the national level. Just as the diffusion of issues on the international agenda poses problems of coordination between departments and agencies of central government, in federal systems such as that of the USA, so it does at the state level. Since the states have only recently come to grapple with trade policy issues, they face a steep learning curve. One of the problems confronting the USTR in the beer case filed by Canada with the GATT was discovering which agency it should liaise with. In some instances this proved to be the agency responsible for regulating the sale of alcohol, in others the attorney general's office or the governor's office. Consequently, when the GATT decision was handed down some governors were unaware of the case.

Not surprisingly, then, the NGA working paper referred to earlier identified the appointment of a trade policy coordinator in each state as the logical accompaniment of an enhanced USTR state consultative facility. Arguing that this was of sufficient concern to US interests to make it worth the federal government's while to fund such a post, the paper argued:

> if states are unprepared to effectively participate in trade policy discussions, it is the nation as a whole that will pay the price of lost market opportunities. In the event that state practices are found in violation of trade agreements, it is the federal government ... that may be obligated to compensate the aggrieved trading partner.[48]

Influencing trade policy in Europe

Given their international presence, both in the form of the growing number of governors' overseas missions and, particularly, through a far more extensive network of foreign offices than existed a decade ago, the question arises as to whether growing state involvement in trade policy nationally is being replicated in the international arena. The prospect of some measure of 'paradiplomacy' or 'microdiplomacy' – to use two terms employed to describe such activity as academic interest in the phenomenon developed, seems logical given the changing trade policy agenda.[49] Moreover, the issue of state involvement in the dispute settlement procedures of WTO and NAFTA raises the issue in another guise and presents a practical problem for the federal government.

Looked at in its broader dimension, this is one facet of the problem of balancing the oft competing goals of access and control which form a central theme in this book. On the one hand, the federal government has a clear desire to control the channels of communication with its trading partners as best it can. Not to do so offers the prospect of, at best, confusion in the conduct of foreign economic policy and, at worst, a weakening of negotiating stances. But at the same time, state access to the international arena has become a reality, is likely to grow as trade partners focus on US state policies and, as we have seen, has become essential in the quest for global competitiveness.

Equally, operating internationally is not without costs for the states. In part this is financially true – offices are expensive – but more tellingly, it opens the states to enhanced international pressures on issues which they may prefer to see diverted to Washington. In the case of the unitary tax issue referred to above, for example, California became a focus of political pressure from foreign governments as well as business interests. Thus the sovereignty-derived rules which dictate that non-central governments have no diplomatic status or standing in international law are being dissolved by the changing character of domestic and international politics and, at the same time, both levels of government have practical reasons for appealing to them.

In the context of US–EC trade relations, the conflicting pressures at work are well illustrated in the case of the long-running dispute over the European ban on the import of hormone-treated beef. The US position has been that in the absence of clear scientific evidence that hormones pose any danger to human health, EC policy is in contravention of trade rules. However, the Texas Agricultural Commission offered to certify independently that Texas beef shipments were hormone-free, thus undermining the official federal position.

Regarding the SMP agenda, however, the evidence suggests that the primary policy influencing attempts of the governors were through IGPAC and the informal channels of influence directed to the USTR and Congress. This reflected the primary perception that the best route for dealing with such issues lay in the Uruguay Round negotiations. That is not to say that the governors on their missions to Europe (by 1993, Germany had replaced Japan as the favourite destination) were insensitive to the issues, or that their hosts forsook the opportunity to direct some criticism towards state practices affecting international trade. Thus, one governor on a trade and investment mission was informed by a European leader that his state's desire to expand its European trading links stood uneasily alongside the protectionist record of its Congressional delegation! During the late 1980s and early 1990s, governors – either singly or in delegations – visited various European locations, including Brussels. In June 1989, for example, nine governors met EC officials to discuss EC-92 issues, particularly banking, telecommunications and standards.[50]

From the other major international arm of the states' trade effort, their overseas offices, all the available evidence suggests that their policy role is negligible and that a direct EC–state linkage has not formed a significant element in the interactions generated by the SMP. Interviews conducted at state offices reinforce Levine's findings from his survey of the European offices: namely, that their interaction with EC officials, or even European businesspeople, was relatively slight. Noting that EC contacts 'are inevitable and when they arise are fostered: but they are not organized or relied on', one office cited affordability of office space, a pool of skilled, multilingual staff and the concentration of US European corporate headquarters as the major reasons for locating in Brussels. Another responded: 'we have no diplomatic status nor are we here in any sense as representatives to the EC – nor is that the reason for having chosen Brussels'.[51]

Looked at in a more positive light, another state representative painted a picture of what might be termed a passive brand of quasi-diplomacy: 'As a sub-federal entity, we do not interfere in EC policy-making processes. However, we monitor them, directly and through the US Mission, as well as through the numerous socio-economic groups operating offices in Brussels.'

Two modes of lobbying activity appeared to be common to the state offices. The first route is through the US Mission in Brussels and other US European embassies back to Washington. In all cases this was seen as a major route. The other consisted of a more 'political' route, best illustrated in the following statement:

> Should our office discover EC activities which may appear detrimental to the state's interests, we would normally alert the [state] Department of Economic and Employment Development ... which, in turn, will pick up the matter with the governor's liaison office in Washington. The latter will, alone, or at NASDA or NGA level, pick up the matter with Congress and/or Senate.

The general view is that these patterns of interaction, focusing on the US Mission in Brussels, provide a satisfactory system based on complementary rather than conflictual or overlapping activities. As one respondent put it, 'they work on a macroeconomic basis, we on a microeconomic level with individual company/business projects'.

The same image of minimal policy-related communication between the EC and the states is reinforced from the Commission side. Here, two positions were expressed by officials: first, that there were issues of diplomatic protocol at stake and that the US Mission was the appropriate point of access to the US authorities; second, a recognition that, despite the fact that communication with the states was virtually non-existent, there was a need to open up links given the nature of many issues on the trade agenda.

This recognition of a need for a political presence in Brussels has been echoed by some of the states, particularly the WGA, which has considered the need for a 'listening post' directed towards the specific needs of the Western states – perhaps in the form of an office within the US Mission. The argument advanced in support of this proposal is the need to gain first-hand information on issues affecting Western interests and the claim that these interests 'are not always well served by a federal government establishment focused on Washington'.[52] Among others, such an office might perform the following functions:

- developing a WGA position on European and multilateral trade issues;
- contacting federal government authorities in Washington, Brussels and Geneva to advocate Western views;
- contacting European official bodies to advocate Western positions and influence policy-making.

To date, however, no such post has been established.

Conclusions

Incorporating the subnational governmental level into the densely configured texture of foreign economic policy underscores its growing complexity and adds a significant 'layer' to the multilayered policy environment with which we are concerned. As we have seen, the growing awareness of states and localities concerning the impact of international trends on their economic well being has been both gradual and uneven. Given their constitutional concerns and powers, together with differences of interest, this comes as no surprise. Nevertheless, the recognition at both federal and state levels that a changing environment demands adaptation in the policy processes has become an entrenched feature of the foreign economic policy landscape, and one that presents both opportunities and costs to all parties.

In terms of responses to EC-92, the issues as presented to the states by bodies such as the NGA, their governors and officials in SDAs was, in one sense, little different from those which have preoccupied the federal authorities. Reciprocity and national treatment, public procurement policies, services and technical barriers were as much the agenda at state level as they were in Washington. But in at least three ways, the SMP assumed a somewhat different perspective at grassroots level. First of all, and most generally, it underscored in a more focused way what were perceived as dramatic changes in the global economy carrying clear implications for states and localities. As the NCSL report noted, these lessons were not contingent on the relative significance of the European market in US trade relations: 'The process of EC-92 and what it represents, however, does deserve attention. In essence, the greatest value of EC-92 lies in its very visible and audible "ringing-in" of a new global economic order.'[53] Second, the states and local government agencies brought to the issues posed by the SMP the immediacy of the concerns felt by SMEs, the natural constituencies of SDAs and local development bodies. Third, several of the issues on the EC-92 agenda presented more than an economic challenge to the states. Partly because they themselves were an issue by virtue of the implications for the international trade agenda of certain of their own policies (those relating to public procurement being the clearest example), the states were finding themselves moving centre-stage in trade diplomacy. Pressures from the EC stood alongside that emanating from the MTN and NAFTA negotiations, in posing the issue of ensuring US compliance with international trade obligations where these related to policy issues under state jurisdiction. In short, the relative powers of federal and state levels of government were being raised as a consequence of international pressures.

Pursuing these broad themes in a little more depth, we can see from what has gone before that one impact of EC-92 was to underscore the need to modify assumptions regarding the appropriate strategies for an era of global competition. Traditional practices in assisting businesses to identify and follow up trade leads were being replaced by a recognition that competitiveness in a global economy begins at home. In other words, the best strategy available to state governments in assisting business is to pursue policies, in such areas as education, tax and regulatory regimes and public infrastructure, directed towards reinforcing the competitive edge of local economies. Furthermore, state governments have come to be seen as having a key educative role at the point of interface where the local economy meets the global. In this context, perhaps the most significant role of subnational government has been to assist SMEs to confront the challenges that EC-92 together with other major developments on the trade horizon presented to them. None of this could be done, as we have seen, without the capacity to build alliances with the private sector. Additionally, linkages had to be developed with the federal government, particulary with the Department of Commerce and USFCS. And to underscore the implications of global competitiveness strategies, transnational economic alliances linking localities across the Atlantic have developed, as in the case of San Jose cited earlier.

Inevitably, these developments have led to a growing concern with the policies which underpin economic competitiveness. Consequently, one of the major issues for trade policy managers has become the need to integrate state and local interests into the trade policy processes. This is stimulated by mutual needs at central and regional/local levels. For Washington, the capacity to pursue an effective trade policy depends to an increasing extent on conducting a congruent diplomacy with affected, and diverse, domestic constituencies. To fail in this respect is to weaken US foreign economic policy. For the states, the issue is partly one of gaining a presence in the framing of policies which determine the economic well-being of local economies and partly one of defending the integrity of their powers against internationally driven federal pre-emption. The tasks involved are no easy ones to accomplish, since they impose significant burdens on both levels of government.

Washington, long used to the problems of horizontal coordination between sometimes competing agencies in the management of foreign economic policy (see Chapter 3), now has the added problem of developing the means for a vertical pattern of coordination with the states as the latters' policies feature ever more centrally on the trade agenda. In part this demands a process of education, alerting the subnational level to the implications of international events whose relevance to its interests might not be at once apparent. This links to the burdens imposed on the state level. If the problems of bureaucratic fragmentation in the conduct of international policies at the centre are well understood, they are even more marked at state level, where the demands of responding to such policies are, for good reason, less clearly appreciated. Thus to the difficulties of adapting the machinery at the centre is added the sub-central problem of identifying a means of responding to national and international demands, where responsibility for an issue may lie either in the governor's office or in any of several state government departments.

Against this background, it would be easy and tempting to draw a picture of ruptured boundaries and unremitting conflict as subnational, national and international levels grated against one another in patterns marked by tension and, even, open conflict. But the evidence of US–EC relations in the context of EC-92 does not seem to sustain such an image. Certainly, there are tensions between federal government and the states, as the former seeks to limit the impact that fragmentation may have on the conduct of trade policy. But often it is the imperfections in federal–state cooperative structures, rather than the desire on the part of the states to plough their own trade policy furrow, that constitute the real problem. Indeed, one of the interesting lessons of the state development of a European presence is how little that presence appears to assume a policy-influencing form independent of the channels provided by the US Mission in Brussels.

Of course, there is a well developed tradition of intergovernmental cooperation in the USA, as in other federal systems. What lends the foreign economic policy agenda an aura of apparent exoticness in this respect is the intersection of international with domestic policy and the assumptions, built on constitutional foundations, that it is the federal government that has the sole right to 'act internationally'. What is occurring, then, is nothing less than the adaptation of the federal system to an environment where its boundaries are no longer purely national but are international in scope. That is not to imply that such adaptation is easy. Responding to the pressures from European and other trading partners, whether bilaterally or within the framework of NAFTA or the WTO, as can be seen in the context of the Second Banking Directive, poses fundamental issues regarding the nature of the American federal system and the rules and practices which it has generated.

In terms of US–EC relations, as Kline has noted in the context of investment policy, we are confronted by two federal economic models 'that differ in tradition and political decision making at a time when both parties are experiencing different centralizing versus decentralizing tendencies'.[54] To a degree, this is reflected in the recognition by some states, such as those represented in the WGA, that redefining their relationships in the context of a regional response to global economic challenges makes considerable sense. In the longer term, then, it may be the conclusions which are drawn by policy-makers at federal and state levels regarding the implications of EC-92 for the nature of the US federal system itself that prove to be its most telling influence.

Notes and references

1   Quoted in B. Roberts, *Competition Across the Atlantic: The States Face Europe '92*, Denver, CO, National Council of State Legislatures, 1991, p. 1.

2   B. Hocking, *Localizing Foreign Policy, Non-central Governments and Multilayered Diplomacy*, London/New York, Macmillan/St Martin's Press, 1993.

3   The Stanley Foundation, *The Changing Face of American Foreign Policy: The New Role of State and Local Actors*, Report of a New American Global Dialogue Conference, Warrenton, VA, 27–29 October 1994.

4   C. F. Alger, 'Perceiving, analysing and coping with the local–global nexus', *International Social Science Journal*, 117, August 1988, pp. 321–40.

5   The growth of local activism in the 1980s is described in H. H. Hobbs, *City Hall Goes Abroad: The Foreign Policy of Local Politics*,

Thousand Oaks, CA, Sage, 1994. See also M. H. Shuman, 'Dateline Main Street: courts v. local foreign policies', *Foreign Policy*, 86, Spring 1992, pp. 158–78.

6   D. R. Ryerson, 'Looking homeward: regional views of foreign policy: from Des Moines', *Foreign Policy*, 88, Fall 1992, pp. 49–51.

7   J. O. Goldsborough, 'California's foreign policy', *Foreign Affairs*, Spring 1993, p. 89.

8   D. J. Elazar, 'States as polities in the federal system', *National Civic Review*, 70(2), 1981, pp. 77–82.

9   See National Governors' Association, *America in Transition: the International Frontier: Report of the Task Force on Foreign Markets*, Washington, DC, 1989; Roberts, *Competition Across the Atlantic*, *op. cit.*; and B. Roberts, *Investment Across the Atlantic: New Competition and Challenges for States*, Denver, CO, National Conference of State Legislatures, 1992.

10   D. Seay and W. Smith, 'Free trade's forgotten amigos: why governors want NAFTA', *Policy Review*, 65, Summer 1993, pp. 57–64.

11   F. H. Oneal, 'US state government responses to EC-1992: a survey of state development agencies', in D. L. Smith and J. L. Ray (eds), *The 1992 Project and the Future of Integration in Europe*, Armonk, NY, Sharpe, 1993.

12   P. Lemov, 'Europe and the states: free trade but no free lunch', *Governing*, January 1991, pp. 49–52; B. Roberts, 'EC 1992: opportunities and challenges for state and local governments', *Government Finance Review*, December 1990, pp. 11–14.

13   Roberts, 'EC 1992: opportunities and challenges' *op. cit.*, p. 13.

14   This issue is discussed in W. E. Nothdurft, *Going Global: How Europe Helps Small Firms Export*, Washington, DC, Brookings, 1992. These concerns underpinned the creation at federal level of the National Export Strategy: see Trade Promotion Coordinating Committee, *The National Export Strategy: Third Annual Report to the United States Congress*, October 1995.

15   Nothdurft, *op. cit.*, p. 4.

16   *Ibid.* He goes on to point out that the USA has eight commercial officers in Canada against Canada's 112 in the USA.

17   D. E. Burke, 'Export promotion partnerships: working together to help exporters', *Business America*, 113(23), 1992, pp. 2–4; and S. Schwab, 'Building a national export development alliance', *Intergovernmental Perspective*, 16(2), 1990, pp. 57–64.

18   Nothdurft, *op. cit.*, p. 89.

19   R. S. Fosler, *The New Economic Role of American States: Strategies in a Competitive World Economy*, New York, Oxford University Press, 1988.

20   Roberts, *Competition Across the Atlantic*, *op. cit.*, pp. 37–8. See also P. R. Piccigallo, 'In search of exports: the states' new agenda', *USA Today*, supplement, September 1989, pp. 20–2; and R. M. Grubel, 'Foreign trade policies in the American states: innovation in times of budgetary stress', 34th Annual Convention of the International Studies Association, Acapulco, Mexico, 23–27 March 1993.
21   National Governors' Association, *America in Transition, op. cit.*
22   Oneal, *op. cit.*, p. 170.
23   *Europe in the 1990s: Implications and Strategies for New Jersey Businesses*, Newark, NJ, 1990.
24   Roberts, 'EC 1992: opportunities and challenges', *op. cit.*, p. 13.
25   S. J. Guyett, 'Indiana: state profile', *Europe*, 307, June 1991, p. 17.
26   *Ibid.*, p. 19.
27   C. Click, 'Virginia: state profile', *Europe*, 310, October 1991, pp. 29–30.
28   National Governors' Association, *Going Global: A Governors' Guide to International Trade*, Washington, DC, 1992, p. 7.
29   Much of the following information is based on interviews conducted between 1989 and 1995 at state offices located in Europe and in the 'home' government departments or agencies to which they are responsible.
30   J. Levine, 'American state offices in Europe: activities and connections', *Intergovernmental Perspective*, 20(1), 1993–4, p. 44.
31   On this theme see N. J. Glickman and D. P. Woodward, *The New Competitors: How Foreign Investors Are Changing the US Economy*, New York, Basic Books, 1988.
32   Levine, *op. cit.*, pp. 45–6.
33   Nothdurft, *op. cit.*, pp. 60–4 and Roberts, *Competition Across the Atlantic, op. cit.*, p. 30.
34   The WGA is described as: 'an independent, nonpartisan organization of governors from 17 states, two territories and a commonwealth. It is based on the need for regional leadership as the West becomes an important force nationally and internationally. It identifies key issues, assists in developing strategies, forms regional coalitions, serves as a research resource, and assists in the communication and advocacy of western issues.' J. Levine, *Going Global: A Strategy for Regional Cooperation*, Denver, CO, Western Governors' Association, 1989, p. 1.
35   *Ibid.*, pp. 49–50.
36   J. Eckhouse, 'San Jose looks to Europe for business alliances', *San Francisco Chronicle*, 9 September 1989.
37   See the sections on state level policies in European Commission, *Report on United States Trade and Investment Barriers 1993*, Brussels, Services of the Commission of the European Communities, April 1993.

38   M. Schaefer and T. Singer, 'Multilateral trade agreements and US States: an analysis of potential GATT Uruguay Round agreements', *Journal of World Trade*, 26(6), 1992, pp. 31–59; and C. Weiler, 'Free trade agreements: a new federal partner?', *Publius*, 24(3), 1994, pp. 113–34.

39   Weiler, *op. cit.*, pp. 122–3; Hocking, *op. cit.*, pp. 93–5.

40   B. Roberts, *Investment Across the Atlantic, op. cit.*, pp. 40–3.

41   Hocking, *op. cit.*, Chapter 5.

42   Advisory Commission on Intergovernmental Relations, 'State and local governments in international affairs: ACIR findings and recommendations', *Intergovernmental Perspectives*, 20(1), 1993/4, p. 35.

43   S. Woolcock, *Market Access Issues in EC–US Relations: Trading Partners or Trading Blows?*, London, Royal Institute of International Affairs/Pinter, 1991, p. 113.

44   Interviews at California State Office, Washington, DC, May 1989, July 1990.

45   Information gathered during interviews at Council of State Governments, Washington, DC, July 1993.

46   C. S. Colgan, *Forging a New Partnership in Trade Policy Between the Federal and State Governments*, Washington, DC, National Governors' Association, 1992, p. 2.

47   Interviews conducted at the USTR in July 1990 and July 1993.

48   Colgan, *op. cit.*, p. 9.

49   I. D. Duchacek, *The Territorial Dimension of Politics: Within, Among and Across Nations*, Boulder, CO, Westview, 1986.

50   National Governors' Association, *Governors' Weekly Bulletin*, 23(25), 23 June 1989, p. 1.

51   This and other information cited in this section was gathered from interviews conducted in state European offices between 1990 and 1993.

52   Levine, *Going Global, op. cit.*, p. 82.

53   Roberts, *Competition Across the Atlantic, op. cit.*, p. 3.

54   C. D. Wallace and J. M. Kline, *EC 92 and Changing Global Investment Patterns: Implications for the US–EC Relationship*, Washington, DC, Center for Strategic and International Studies, 1992, p. 28.

6

Firms

US business and industry have a vital stake in the evolution of the Single European Market. By the end of the 1980s, total accumulated foreign direct investment (FDI) by American companies in the EC approached $175 billion (by the same token, investment by EC companies in the USA was even higher). US exports to the EC in 1987 were approximately $70 billion, with particular areas of strength in high-technology industries as well as the perennial bone of contention, agriculture. Tellingly, though, at the same time the sales of the affiliates of US corporations in the EC approached $500 billion; a phenomenon clearly closely linked with the levels of FDI already noted. US firms operating in the EC were estimated to have created nearly two and a half million jobs.[1]

It is clear even from this sketchy evidence that US companies formed a major presence in the SEM and that thereby they had a major stake in its evolution and success. A number of other observations can be made at this very general level, many of them carrying important implications for the study of the USA and the Single Market. In the first place, the stake held by US firms in the SEM meant that they had a major interest in both the conditions of access to the market and the operating conditions within the market itself. The production of both goods and services by American companies in the European theatre goes far beyond the traditional image of exporters knocking at the door of a distinct EC market, with the Community acting as a kind of gatekeeper.[2]

Another implication of the positions held by US firms is that they are themselves significant 'European' actors. They exist in a triangular relationship with the US government and the EC, rather like that described by John Stopford and Susan Strange in their major works on 'states, firms and diplomacy'.[3] In this relationship, it is not to be taken for granted that the US and EC 'governments' hold the automatic right of precedence, or that they can determine outcomes in areas where firms have intense interests and strategic positions. The result is likely to be a complex interaction of the three sides of the triangle, moving a very long way from mercantilist views of the dominant state and the subordination of commerce to national interests. In some respects, indeed, the situation outlined here goes beyond the rather stylized view of 'triangular diplomacy', implying as it does the development of policy networks existing largely beyond the reach of governments, sustained both by contacts between firms themselves and by the shaping influence of European institutions.

A third implication of the intense interpenetration represented by the activities of US firms in the SEM is that it can be extremely difficult to identify separate or separable national interests. To quote the Clinton administration's Secretary for Labor, it is impossible in an intensely interpentrated world to determine 'who is us', and this impossibility has important consequences for strategy at both national and at firm level.[4] This problem is closely associated with other phenomena, such as the idea of 'global shift' in terms of production structures and the so-called 'borderless world' identified by Ohmae and others.[5]

From these implications of intense interpenetration and internationalization if not globalization arise a number of very significant questions in the context of this study. If there is a growing focus not only on traditional matters of commerce but also on 'behind the border' issues of regulation and operating conditions; if there is a complex interaction between the concerns and the strategies of government and business; and if there is difficulty in identifying the 'us' and the 'them' implied by notions of foreign economic policy, then the roles of government and business are central to the exploration of multilevel policy-making and implementation. Matters of business strategy and competitiveness at the firm level are difficult to separate from issues of strategy and competitiveness at the national or continental levels. The need is thus for an analytical approach which can cater for the complexity and for the policy consequences.

One element of such an approach is to view business as a set of networks, generating interactions and outcomes as a consequence both of positions held within the networks and of adaptations to the changing demands of communication and exchange. This has been explicated partly by Graeme Thompson and his collaborators in their drawing of distinctions between markets, hierarchies and networks,[6] which enable distinctions to be made between the operation of power hierarchies such as those represented in traditional views of statehood, the decentralized mechanisms of production and exchange represented by free markets and the networks of communication and regulation set up by firms and governing authorities in an attempt to deal with the consequences of complexity.

The use of an approach based on networks, exchange and regulation clearly has a lot to offer in dealing with the roles of US firms in the SEM. But in order to pursue the approach, a number of other factors should be taken into account. First, it is clear that even where firms are taken to be central to the generation and operation of networks, there is still a role for government; the analytical challenge is to identify the ways in which firms and government interact, and the resulting 'rules of the game'. Second, it is evident that to talk of 'firms' is to generalize unacceptably: there is a need to differentiate between the positions, interests and strategies of different types of firm operating in different sectors, at different locations and with different organizational structures. Finally, it is clear that as the result of this variety, no one model of the firm or its interests and strategies is likely to be all-encompassing; it is necessary to use what John Dunning has termed an 'eclectic' model both of firms' strategies and of their relationships with other significant actors.[7]

It is thus important to have a differentiated view not only of firms and their strategies but also of their relationships to government authorities. On this basis, it could be argued, for example, that the typical concerns of firms are sectoral in nature, focused on their particular areas of activity and on the problems encountered therein. Government concerns, on the other hand, are likely to be broader in nature, encompassing the framework of rules and institutions more generally. When firms think strategically, they are doing so in relation to their operational concerns in a given area of the economy; where governments think this way, they will have a more comprehensive perspective. It could similarly be argued that firms and governments approach questions of international integration in very different ways: for firms, the issues are those of corporate integration and the ways in which operations can be managed on a cross-national basis; for governments, the issues are those of political authority in relation to the market and to structures of regulation.[8]

Ultimately, many of these questions come down to a very simple enquiry: in dealing with an issue such as the SEM, what are the respective needs of government for firms and of firms for governments? In dealing with problems of market access, there is clearly a complicated interaction between the interests, needs and strategies of firms and the interests, needs and strategies of government. This study has so far indicated that the notion of 'government' itself needs to be questioned when we study such a phenomenon as the SMP; the purpose of this chapter is to enquire more closely into the relationship between government and business, in the light of EC policy developments which were bound to have important impacts on the prospects and performance of US firms.

US business and the Single Market: challenges and opportunities

It can convincingly be argued that one of the key aspects of the SMP was its hoped-for impact on the behaviour of firms.[9] In this sense, the programme was a 'confidence' trick, designed to enhance the confidence of firms and other actors in the institutions of the Single Market, and thereby to affect their strategies. It has already been noted that US firms had a stake second to none in the operation and development of the Single Market, and thus it can be inferred that the programme would be bound to have major implications for their expectations and behaviour. The fact that the architects of the SMP were primarily trying to galvanize what they would describe as 'European' firms meant that there was an inherent tension in the programme; were the dynamic effects of greater integration to be treated as an excludable good, with the benefits denied to non-Europeans? Could they be treated this way in a highly interpenetrated world?

It is clear that at the earliest stages of the SMP, US firms (and particularly those with long-standing involvement in the EC) identified the potential risks of the programme.[10] The most obvious at first glance was the possibility of exclusion; not necessarily literal exclusion from the Single Market, but rather exclusion from important benefits through discriminatory treatment by EC institutions and the rules they made. The example of financial services and the Second Banking Directive has been referred to at several points in earlier chapters; other perceived threats of discrimination included the potential impact of standards set within the EC, and the exclusion of US firms from a 'level playing field' in the bidding for public contracts (see Chapter 7).

Alongside the threat of exclusion and discrimination went the threat of increased competition from EC companies. This could be taken to be part of the normal commercial game, and the revitalization of EC companies through their exposure to competition and the removal of national restrictions was central to the SMP. It is only a short step, though, from the likelihood of increased competition as the natural consequence of the SMP to fears of collusion between EC firms and the EC authorities; a number of American companies, and parts of the US government, certainly perceived a possibility of less-than-equal treatment at the hands of those who wished to promote 'European champions'. The example of the European Airbus and its competition with Boeing and McDonnell-Douglas was not only fresh in the minds of US corporations, it was still being fought over.[11]

It was thus easy for US firms to see the SMP as the signal for an intensification of competition, both fair and unfair, in the world economy. *Business Week* summed it up in suitably apocalyptic terms:

A steadily growing giant whose companies often lack global fighting power, the new Europe is a tempting market for Japanese and American companies. And as the world's last such industrial market up for grabs, Europe is likely to become the fulcrum of the world's economic power balance for the new century. It's a booming base from which multinationals will consolidate the financial strength and the economies of scale essential to compete around the world. As a result, a three-way fight is now shaping up among Americans, Japanese and the Europeans themselves to determine who will reap these benefits.[12]

This kind of response epitomizes the view that the Single Market was effectively a stake in a global contest, and that the contest could end up with a clear-cut set of winners and losers. The challenge was clear, and it was accentuated by the programmatic nature of the SMP itself. The focus of the programme on large-scale regulatory policy-making, combined with the assumed vast benefits of its realization, heightened the awareness of US firms that they needed to assert their interests early and persistently. In this respect, as a major US government study pointed out, it was different from earlier and unsuccessful efforts at an EC 'industrial policy'.[13] It was both comprehensive and pervasive in its effects, and it relied on legislation rather than financial support or specific trade measures. A final aspect of the strategic challenge set up by the SMP was that it coincided for US business – as it did for the US government – with the challenge of other institutional changes in the world economy. In particular, the SMP ran alongside the Uruguay Round of talks in the GATT, and the negotiation of the Canada–US Free Trade Agreement, later to lead to the NAFTA.

The combination of a programmatic challenge demanding a clear sense of priorities and of high stakes was thus bound to sharpen the need for US firms to respond actively and early. The focus of the SMP on regulatory policy and 'behind the border' issues further increased the need for enhanced market intelligence and an active strategy. American corporations could not just 'wait and see' if they were to reap the full benefits or escape the most dire losses; they had to be out in the field making things happen. On the one hand, they needed to monitor the development of the SMP at the systemic level, analysing the ways in which the structures and institutions of the EC were changing and how they might affect corporate activities. On the other hand, individual firms were faced with the need to respond at the sectoral level, dealing with the very specific implications of the SMP for the development of markets in relation to particular goods, services and production processes. As an example of the ways in which this posed challenges for US firms, Table 6.1 was produced for a major study of the SMP and multinational corporations.[14]

Table 6.1 also highlights what has already been noted about the variety of firms and problems characteristic of the SMP; US corporations, as the largest single group of investors in the EC and as the longest established of multinational corporations in the Single Market, were to experience every one of the problems and issues noted. But the variety of US interests and involvements meant that these would be experienced in very different ways by different firms or groups of firms.[15] Again, the notion of the 'US firm' comes under attack.

Table 6.1 Effects of 1992 programme on foreign direct investment/collaboration – influencing variables

		Effect on cost/return/risk profile of potential investor collaborator[b]
Aggregate effects	Strategic and dynamic gains through economies of scale and learning, reduction in X-inefficiency, stimulus to innovation and competition ('virtuous circle')[a]	Market size and projected market growth stimulated
Specific effects		
Country of origin	External relations programme regarding reciprocity, treatment of foreign subsidiaries in the community, local content and anti-dumping rules	Protectionism (actual or threatened) increases risks to non-investors/collaborators mainly from Japan and Pacific Rim
Sector		Sector-specific effects:
Financial services	Common market for services	*Positive* impacts relate to improved access to public contracts, removal of administrative barriers, emergence of common standards and regulations, removal of trade obstacles. *Negative* impacts relate to increased competition, restructuring, reductions in price levels.
Low-tech products	Reductions of greater surveillance of state aids; ending of discriminatory public procurement	
Medium-tech products	Removal of barriers associated with standards, regulations, testing	

High-tech products	Removal of barriers associated with standards, regulations, testing; ending of discriminatory public procurement, state aids *plus* deregulation of public monopolies	Uncertain, and sectoral differences
Firm	Components of 1992 programme as above *plus* removal of fiscal barriers policies for transborder collaboration more active competition policy stronger regional policy, but possibly reductions as investment incentives	Improved competitive position of EC producers Acquisition possibilities reduced Lower subsidies to inward investors

[a]But the Cecchini Report, e.g. did not allow for possibilities of restructuring acting to diminish competitive pressures; and external relations issues were virtually ignored.

[b]Cost factors include costs of labour, capital, raw materials and services; transport costs; productivity; government policies, i.e. taxes, incentives, performance requirements, trade policies; foreign exchange considerations. Return factors include market size, projected market growth, competitive factors, foreign exchange considerations. Risk factors include political and economic stability; transparency and predictability of government policies; flexibility to close down or relocate. See Kay, N. M. (1989) *Corporate Strategies, Technological Change and 1992*, Working Paper Series, Standing Commission on the Scottish Economy, Glasgow, April.

From the evidence so far examined, a picture emerges of a large-scale and programmatic challenge to US firms, but also one distinguished by the ways in which it underlined the differentiation between firms and groupings. Whatever the characteristics of firms and groupings, though, they needed to adapt to and learn within a relatively uncertain and rapidly changing EC environment. The initial need was thus for reliable information about the development of the SMP, and preparation for its impact.[16] In this cause, a number of possible sources were available. For the largest and longest established multinationals inside the SEM, the experience of dealing with the EC and its institutions, along with highly developed public affairs functions in the European context, could be used. But not every US firm affected by the SMP was in this happy position. For those less privileged, there were effectively three information and preparation strategies available. First, they could 'piggy-back' on the large and experienced, either because they were suppliers to them or because they had some other sort of prior association. Second, they could use the trade associations and more general-interest groupings which had grown up, especially in Brussels during the evolution of the EC; the most highly developed of these was the EC Committee of the American Chamber of Commerce, but this catered largely for the large multi-nationals. As a result, other trade associations, such as the National Association of Manufacturers in the USA itself, were led to develop large-scale analysis of the SMP and of its effects for a wide range of US firms. Some sectors, such as the pharmaceutical or electronics industries, already had well established international and EC lobbying operations, and were able to bend these to the service of the SMP.

Another source of information and preparation available to US firms was the US federal government. As noted in Chapter 3, the chief role in this area (as opposed to the negotiation process, for example) was given to the Department of Commerce. Although Commerce set up a quite ambitious information and advice service, particularly catering to the needs of the smaller exporting firms, it faced a number of difficulties. Among these was the fact that at the inception of the SMP, there was no direct Commerce representation in the US Mission to the EC. As a result, the Commerce operation seemed at times to be dealing at second hand with the SMP, and indeed it was said that one of its major tactics was to recommend use of the information services at the EC delegation in Washington. It also appeared to be the case that Commerce preferred to define the EC as a series of national markets, rather than analysing the impact of the SMP as a whole. While this had its uses, it did not fully meet the need. Not surprisingly, the satisfaction levels achieved were pretty variable. Interestingly, part of the gap was filled, as noted in Chapter 5, by the commissioning of state-level studies, often provided by consultancies such as KPMG.

It could thus be argued that in the provision of information or advice to firms concerned about the SMP, there was evidence of corporate success and government failure. This dovetails at least in part with the findings of government's slowness to react in the early stages of the SMP (see Chapter 3). But to conclude thus is to over simplify. In particular, it is at odds with the earlier argument in this chapter about the variety of 'US firms' engaged in the SMP, and the variety of their interests. If we are to arrive at a more discriminating analysis of the needs and the activities of US firms, we need to take into account a number of variables. Among these would be:

- whether the activities of a given firm were primarily focused on *exporting* to the EC, on *investing* in the EC or on *producing* within the EC;
- whether the firm concerned was a *new entrant* to the EC arena or a *long-established* operator within that arena;
- the extent to which a firm's operations in relation to the EC were part of a *global* organization or a *regional/national* organization;
- the extent to which a firm's EC activities were *focused on one country* within the EC arena or *generalized* across the whole of the Community.

If one draws up a set of 'firm profiles' based on this set of criteria, it is possible to arrive at a number of conclusions – including the fact that a number of the larger and longer established US multinationals were and are effectively 'European' firms. It will be seen shortly that these variations can have important implications for the interests and needs of different firms.

As a result of these elements of variety and difference, it is clear that the initial challenge of the SMP was felt in different ways by different US firms or groupings. It is also clear that different parts of the SMP would be salient to different firms or groupings; thus, exporters of consumer goods to Europe would have fundamentally different perceptions of the challenge from those interested in securing contracts for power stations from public authorities. Whatever the needs of specific firms, there was clearly a need for the building up of an information base, and this was provided by a variety of different sources: the US government, state governments, trade associations, 'trickle-down' from large companies to small. Once the initial intelligence was provided, though, there was an equally clear need for corporate restructuring and the provision of strategy and support mechanisms for continuing operations in the Single Market.

A clear implication of the analysis so far is that the Single Market for many US firms was not only or not at all a threat: it could be and was seen as a major commercial opportunity, which could be exploited with great benefit. As already noted, the planners of the SMP had envisaged these opportunities and the market stimulus as accruing particularly to EC companies. But it is equally plausible to see US firms as particularly well placed to gather the benefits of the SMP. In the first place, as noted above, many US firms were effectively 'European' because of their long established presence in the EC; it was difficult if not impossible to exclude them from many aspects of the SEM. Where they could operate freely, they often had long experience of working at the EC level and on an EC scale – experience not necessarily available to EC firms that had remained securely in their own domestic bases.[17] It is thus not surprising that trade associations representing the larger US companies were from the outset enthusiastic about the SMP. The National Association of Manufacturers, the US Council for International Business and the EC Committee of the American Chamber of Commerce in Brussels were among the most public supporters of the SMP.

For some, this assumed superiority of US firms constituted a threat to EC companies in their exploitation of the Single Market. Those of a neo-mercantilist bent in the EC spent time trying to develop means to exclude the most threatening of US (and Japanese) companies from the charmed circle, but in the case of the USA they had little success, at least with the old established firms. Where firms were new entrants, even if powerful, there was more prospect of at least shaping their involvement; this was the case with at least one or two of the major US telecommunications providers, which for historical reasons were not established on a large scale in the EC.

For many large US corporations, then, EC-92 was as much an opportunity as a threat. But even for some of the longest established US firms, there were some unsuspected challenges in the SMP. For example, in the field of semiconductor manufacture, many US corporations had established manufacturing plants in the EC as long ago as the 1960s. Given the weakness of the European manufacturers, such firms as Texas Instruments had been able to create a cosy and profitable market. The SMP threatened to upset this arrangement, not by adding strength to the EC 'champions' but by creating strong incentives for the Japanese especially to set up manufacturing operations within the EC. The same could be said of the automobile industry, where the problems of access for Japanese cars created on the one hand an incentive to set up 'transplant' operations in the EC (and particularly in the UK) and on the other hand a problem with the import of cars from the USA itself, where they had been made in Japanese 'transplant' factories.

The nature of the SMP also created institutional opportunities for US firms and trade associations. Perhaps most obviously, the programme shifted the location of much regulatory policy-making to Brussels, where there was a strong growth of lobbying activity. This growth in turn, although different in some respects from the explosion of lobbying in Washington, gave advantages to US groupings well practised in the arts of persuasion. In many cases, they could become more effective as 'outsiders' than some of the more obvious 'insider' groups cultivated by the EC and its member states. The ways in which the SMP also brought together regulatory policy with the freeing up of service provision meant that many US corporations which had been spending many years operating within such an environment had considerable advantages. Thus, in telecommunications, although there were many obstacles to the opening up of the EC market, there is no doubt that US corporations such as AT&T had a lot of experience and expertise to draw upon.[18]

This picture of variety and complexity bears out many of the initial propositions made in this chapter. It is clear that the SMP posed a challenge of perception and substance to US firms, but that this challenge was modulated through a series of filters. Crucial to this modulation were variations in size of firm, experience in the EC, experience in dealing with regulatory reform, opportunities to influence EC policy-making and specific characteristics of sectors. The importance of government does not appear self-evident, at least not if one defines it as direct sponsorship of US companies by the federal machine. Since it appears on this basis that variations in the focus and extent of business networks are central to an explanation of their responses to the SMP, the investigation now turns to a more detailed examination of this aspect.

Business networks and the Single European Market

It was noted at the beginning of this chapter that the US business stake in the EC is large and complex. It is also, as is the case with business in the broader sense, differentiated and characterized by variety. To take only two obvious dimensions of this differentiation and variety, it is clear that US business presence in the EC is spatially and functionally differentiated. In the first case, certain member states of the EC – and even certain regions within those states – are favoured by American investors, while US exporters also have long-standing links with particular areas within the Community. The most favoured member state for US business – as it is for the Japanese – is the United Kingdom, with Germany close behind. These two countries have relatively welcoming business environments, and they also are receptive to US products and services. In contrast, for a long time France was relatively unwelcoming to both US investors and US exporters. By the late 1980s, the two dominant areas (Germany, taken to include the Benelux countries, and the UK and Ireland) accounted for almost 70 per cent of US exports to the EC, and for similar levels of US FDI in the Community.[19]

US business networks related to the EC also show functional differentiation, in two ways. First, as already noted, there are clear differences between those that are exporters to the EC, those that are investors in the EC and those that are effectively 'Europeanized'. Second, there are differences between sectors of activity: in manufactures, there is a clear dominance of machinery and transportation equipment, and particularly in high-technology goods. At the same time, there is a strong US presence in many areas of services, particularly financial services. The combination of spatial differentiation with functional differentiation is at first glance striking enough to imply that there will also be important variations in interest arising from it, thus causing significant variations between activities in different business networks.

A further major area of variation and difference in US business networks as they relate to the EC and the Single Market could be labelled historical. We have already noted that some US firms have been established in the EC for a long time, and this clearly gives rise to differences in access and interest. It is also clear that the changing shape of the US business presence has been related to the historical evolution of the EC itself, with surges of investment associated with the opening up of new areas of integration or the addition of new members. It would be sensible not to overstate this phenomenon, since there are many other factors (including, for example, the value of the dollar) which can affect investment and exporting decisions, but it is important to recognize that the SMP fits into a pattern of major developments in integration which have been linked broadly to changes in the pattern of US business activity.[20]

From this general discussion it can be concluded that the differentiated pattern of US business involvement in the EC and the Single Market should lead to significant variations in business interests and the direction of business activities. In particular, the distinction between 'exporters', 'investors' and 'Europeans' has been noted by a number of commentators.[21] But this understates the complexity of the linkages between the different classes of business activity, and thus the extent to which US business networks encompass linkages across the spatial and functional divide. To take three examples:

- There are often important linkages between larger multinational firms and smaller enterprises which act as suppliers to the larger firms. Very often, in dealing with the SMP, larger firms took on the role of advisors to their smaller associates, who might look like the classic 'exporters' but who were in fact closely linked into much larger multinational networks. This can be seen, for example, in the activities of firms such as 3M and General Electric.[22]
- It is often also the case that large firms based in the USA spend a lot of their time 'exporting' to their affiliates in the EC, and for many multinationals this aspect of business networking was a major element in their response to the SMP. A very specific instance of this, which

proved problematic at times, was the fact that Japanese 'transplant' enterprises based in the USA wished to export to the EC, either to affiliates or directly to the market. As noted elsewhere, such firms as Honda in the automobile industry and Ricoh in office equipment not only pursued these aims but were also able to impress their concerns on the White House and the USTR (see Chapter 3).

- In other cases, functional networks can form important linkages. For example, the provision of financial services in the EC to US multinationals is often through US investment banks (indeed, the data show that US investment banks such as Goldman Sachs and Morgan Stanley, with their experience of large mergers and acquisitions, had some comparative advantage in working within the Single Market more generally, financing many of the cross-national mergers and acquisitions between European firms).[23]

These linkages and potential synergies were in many ways focused by the SMP, with its emphasis on the reform of the business environment in the EC. A number of institutions, of which the most salient is probably the EC Committee of the American Chamber of Commerce in Brussels, could also take advantage of these linkages in monitoring or seeking to shape EC legislation related to the SMP.[24] Overall, these features suggest important advantages in particular for US firms located in the EC, in terms of intelligence, ability to structure themselves in response to the SMP and ability to ensure market access.[25] The implication is that there are clear 'network benefits' to be captured in response to the changing business environment of the Single Market.

This does not, of course, mean that all US firms were equally well positioned in the early stages of the SMP. Indeed, variations in initial position, attitudes and interests are central to an explanation of the ways in which US businesses responded to the programme. In general, it can be argued that key elements in such variations were levels of initial awareness on the part of firms, the adaptability of their internal structures and their perceptions of challenge and opportunities. As emphasized earlier in the chapter, it is not always apparent that government in any of its manifestations has a central role to play in these essentially 'extranational' processes and positions.

Such an argument is underlined by a number of specific issues that emerged from the SMP for US businesses. At one level, these were issues of 'philosophy', particularly approaches to problems of regulation and market access. As noted in earlier chapters, the US approach – at both governmental and corporate levels – was based essentially on ideas of 'national treatment', whereas at least in the early stages of the SMP the Community seemed to be proposing various more or less threatening versions of reciprocity. Government certainly had a role here, in focusing the attention of EC officials on the fears their approach had generated. But for many firms, especially those long established in the Community, there was no problem; they were as good as European. Where there were 'late entrants', as, for example, in the telecommunications field, there were more problems, but these could be dealt with at the corporate level through joint ventures and other devices, with only the occasional nudge from government.

Another aspect of this set of problems was more specific: what to do about the EC development of a new regulatory environment and how to influence the deliberations of EC institutions. This linked at times quite directly with a number of debates about regulatory policy going on in the USA. Perhaps the most clear cut example of this was the draft Second Banking Directive, which at the same time seemed to threaten exclusion of US financial services providers from the Single Market and linked with an increasingly intense debate in the USA about the future of the banking system. At times, it appeared that banking interests in the USA – often themselves having direct involvement in the Single Market – could play one set of regulatory proposals off against another. Although this did not have a major direct effect in the USA, it demonstrates again the network linkages and interests generated in relation to the SMP.[26]

The experience of US firms in these areas was not all positive, however. It has already been noted that the initial uncertainty surrounding the SMP meant for even the most 'European' of US firms a steep learning curve. It also confronted many business actors with questions of priority and choice, coming as it did alongside the negotiation of the Uruguay Round in the GATT and of the NAFTA. For many US firms, these two latter developments were at least as important as the SMP; indeed, for many they promised to set the SMP into a context which would 'civilize' it and shape it by reference either to the multilateral trading system or to the growth of a potential regional bloc in the Americas. Thus it was far from uncommon to hear US business leaders referring to the priority accorded to the GATT as the means for framing the SMP more favourably.[27]

Another question of priorities arose for many US firms in relation to their need – or absence of it – for US government support. In terms of the big picture, concerning the philosophy of the SMP and its relationship to the multilateral system, it is clear that most businesses could see a role for the federal government. They could see a role for state governments when it came to export promotion for small and medium enterprises, or the promotion of inward investment from the EC. But it was quite difficult from the perspective of corporate leaders in 'European' US firms to see the need for Congressional involvement at anything but the broadest agenda-setting level; indeed, any attempts at congressional 'micro-management' were actively to be resisted as the kind of help that was positively unwelcome.

More important for most business networks was the tactical issue: how to take advantage of positional advantage or of network strengths in the evolving Single Market. For many companies, the central questions were those of access to specific national or regional markets, and the forming of relationships with either EC or other partners to exploit their advantages. The problems were those of adjusting production, marketing and distribution so as to make the most of new market opportunities, rather than those of reflecting on the underlying model which gave rise to Single Market legislation.[28] These considerations gave rise to significant variations in strategy (see below); they also suggest that there were significant differences of interest between different business networks operating within the EC arena.

It is logical to suppose that the differences in position and network strength identified for different types of US business network in the Single Market should have given rise to differences of interest. Early responses to the SMP revealed this by uncovering different sets of concerns and priorities for initial action.[29] More recently, research has identified important ways in which these differences can be described and assessed.[30] But it is important to note that there were a large number of cross-cutting interests at the strategic level, which contributed to a strong bias in favour of the SMP as it developed.

An example is provided by responses to the development of EC competition policy, a central thrust of the Single Market given its broadly deregulatory character.[31] This was clearly a central interest for many US firms, and it was also an issue in the USA itself, given the desire to shape EC policies through the development of joint action and consultation. It is clear that many of the larger US firms positively welcomed the development of competition policy at the EC level, since it promised to release them to some extent from the variations in national practice which had been wide in the Community before the SMP.

Corporate strategies could thus adjust to the ways in which competition policy developed, and there could be attempts to shape it through agenda-setting activities. But there came a point at which there was not only an interest in shaping the policy from within the EC, but also a desire to have the support of the US federal authorities. It was thus logical to see major US firms in the EC supporting the development of transatlantic consultation on anti-trust and other aspects. There was a clear shared interest, not only between the major firms and the US government but also between major 'European' US firms and those whose involvement in the SEM was more peripheral. Given these interests, and minimal responsiveness on the part of the EC, it was extraordinarily difficult to see how any coalition against the SMP could be generated in the USA itself.

This said, there were a number of sensitive issues on which strange alignments of different interests could be discerned among the 'US' firms involved. An example is provided by automobiles. Here, a number of the leading European producers are American by origin, while a number of potentially significant importers are American by adoption but Japanese by extraction. One of the purposes for which Mrs Carla Hills's crowbar was to be used in relation to the Single Market was to ensure that barriers were not to be erected against any of these 'transplanted' American products. At the same time, the 'European' US companies in the EC were concerned to ensure that Japanese cars should be subject to strict regulation, whether or not they came from the USA.

It is clear that alignments of interest in US business networks in their approach to the SMP are not easy to pigeon hole. A number of variables contribute to this difficulty, as they contribute to the differentiation of US business networks in general. Among the most significant are: size and organizational structure of the firm; sector of activity; length of establishment in the EC; the number of cross-linkages and potential coalitions with others, either within the EC or in the USA. The product is a complex mosaic of linkages and alignments, which also feed into consideration of strategy. One clear implication is that much of 'US policy' in this area is in fact 'extranational' in character, generated outside the United States even where it involves substantial American interests. We will return to this issue later in the book.

Business strategies and the Single European Market

In the most general terms, business strategies can be seen to aim at a number of desirable outcomes: the reduction of uncertainty; the minimization of costs and risks; and the maximization of benefits. Such strategies are not to be understood in purely financial terms, although many of them have major financial implications; often, the concern with the stability and predictability of regulatory structures, for example, is a major preoccupation in itself. It is also important to note that business strategy in a complex environment such as the SEM has to cater both for the self-evidently 'strategic' issues – those which entail long-term commitments and consequences, and which have to do with the framework for business operations – and for what Maria Green Cowles terms 'bread and butter' issues, which can still have important medium-term and sectoral consequences.[32]

The SMP in these terms was an almost unique challenge, in the sense that it combined a sweeping strategic goal with a host of important and material sectoral issues. To this was added the challenge of dealing with a complex institutional context in which expectations and assumptions were often subtly different from those in the American system.[33] For any firm, this was a demanding context for adjustment and innovation. In the earlier parts of this chapter, considerable stress has been laid on the variety of positions occupied by US firms in relation to the SMP, and the variety of cross-cutting interests to which those gave rise. Here, it is argued that these positions and interests gave rise in turn to a number of identifiable patterns of activity designed to cater for both the strategic and the more limited challenges raised by the SMP.[34]

One response at the strategic level among US firms was to become (or remain, or become more) 'European'. In other words, the strategic thrust was towards stressing their position, their interests and their credentials as participants in the SEM. Such a strategy typically had a number of features, in different combinations.

The first of these was restructuring at the European level to stress cross-national interests and activities, while at the same time remaining aware of differentiation between national contexts in EC member states. An often cited example of this feature is the strategy adopted by 3M, a wide-ranging US multinational which at an early stage of the SMP constructed a number of cross-national strategy groups and laid these over its continuing national structure for sales and marketing. By the end of the SMP, 3M had decided to go beyond this restructuring, to produce a genuinely cross-national product strategy; by doing so it intended not simply a revolution in administration, but also a cultural shift on the part of managers.[35]

The second was a stress laid on common interests with US firms in the 'European' mould. One device for doing this was active participation in trade associations or wider business groupings, such as the EC Committee of the American Chamber of Commerce (AmCham) in Brussels. Dissemination of information and debate about strategies could take place through such channels, and they could also be used to shape EC processes and legislation. Of the US-based peak organizations, the most active were the National Association of Manufacturers and the US Council for International Business. When complemented by the AmCham and by sectoral organizations, these bodies could form a substantial shaping influence on both EC and US policy-making; indeed, as the SMP unfolded, an umbrella organization was established in the shape of the United States Industry Coordinating Group, with the single aim of influencing EC policies in the interest of US firms.[36]

The third was the formation of linkages with EC firms, either through merger or more commonly, as the SMP proceeded, through joint ventures of different types. The aim of such strategies might be to forge genuine business partnerships and share the costs of development and marketing, but another aim in many cases for US companies was to gain effective access to the SEM without the start-up costs of establishing an affiliate. Thus, the strategy of AT&T for gaining access to a historically heavily protected area – telecommunications – was to seek out joint ventures with in the first instance Philips and then Stet, the Italian firm. Likewise, Whirlpool, the domestic appliance manufacturer, bought into Philips and eventually bought out its partner to become a major player in the EC white goods market.[37]

The fourth feature was the penetration of the EC policy community, either directly at the sectoral level or indirectly through such devices as 'Eurogroups'. In a sense, this is an extension of the identification and pursuit of common interests with other US or EC companies. It relies on the fact that, as Richardson and Mazey argue, EC policy communities are often unstable and open to penetration.[38] It also relies on the development of lobbying in the EC and the emergence of relationships of mutual interest between parts of the European Commission and their 'clients'. Thus it is argued by AmCham and others that they can be of use to the Commission and that a mutually beneficial relationship can emerge.[39] For many of the most 'European' of US firms, another channel was provided by their membership of groups such as UNICE, the European federation of industrial employers, which is treated as an 'insider' group by the Commission and other EC bodies. Not only this, but membership of sectoral associations such as the grouping of European motor manufacturers was available to long-established firms such as Ford and General Motors.

These differentiated strategies are not mutually exclusive; they form in various combinations an overall thrust towards 'becoming European' on the part of many US companies. The discussion here confirms a number of propositions: that the access thus gained could help US companies to shape the agenda of Single Market developments; that the roles played by US firms in the SMP were often significant, not only in material terms but also through the activities of what Reich has termed 'symbolic analysts' providing information and analysis of the problems faced in the SMP; that US business networks are far from being associated with a specific national 'base'; and that eclectic strategies give the best prospects of effective access and involvement. It could be argued – and has been argued by a number of commentators – that US firms adopting such strategies were more effective 'Europeans' than any EC firms or groupings.

For those not attracted by the strategy of 'going European' (or to whom the strategy was not available), there were still prospects for access and leverage in the SMP through what might be termed network extension. It might be thought that this is just another way of describing alliances with EC companies, but in fact such a strategy entails a number of quite distinctive aspects:

- The arm's-length use of trade associations and other bodies to provide 'inside knowledge' without the investment of large amounts of time and resources entailed in a 'going European' strategy. Thus a number of groupings in Washington as well as in Brussels (AmCham, National Association of Manufacturers, US Council for International Business) often operated together to provide insight into the SMP and its effects for those who either by choice or by force of circumstance were unable to access the EC process directly, while the EC delegation itself engaged in an intensive public and corporate education campaign during the early years of the SMP.

- The capturing of what were earlier termed 'network benefits' through alliances not only with EC firms but also with other 'outsiders' such as groups of exporters or consortia. Again from the point of view of corporate strategy, the aim was to access the SMP without the investment and risk entailed in 'going European', and this strategy was also encouraged by both federal and state governmental agencies in the USA.

- 'Piggybacking' strategies, in which links with larger companies were exploited by smaller exporters in order to gain the information and other benefits available to those more directly involved. As noted earlier, this strategy was often encouraged by regional, state or local authorities in the USA, who could see the benefits to be gained from encouraging close links between local 'champions' and smaller firms that were very often suppliers to them. In this way, the SMP linked into more general developments in US export promotion or competitiveness policies.

Although such strategies can accurately be portrayed as more 'arm's-length' than those discussed earlier, it is clear that for a wide range of smaller and more specialized firms they were appropriate responses to the SMP, reducing the information costs and the material investment implied by more ambitious efforts. Very often, as indicated, they dovetailed with the priorities of larger and more 'European' enterprises.

A third set of strategies brings the discussion back to one of the central themes of this study, since it could be labelled 'using government'. Both for the more 'European' firms and the less ambitious or heavily involved, the SMP raised important questions about the role of government and its uses to business. As indicated in Chapter 3, the US federal government experienced tensions and uncertainties about the SMP, in particular as it related to government external policies more generally. Chapters 4 and 5 have also indicated significant areas of tension and development in the roles of Congress and the states, often intersecting with the concerns of business. It is thus important to arrive at an evaluation of the role played by government as seen by business.

It is clear that there are close links between the concerns of business in relation to the SMP and the perceived role of government as the guardian of the national and international framework for business operations. It is also clear that government at both the federal and the sub-federal levels saw itself as having a significant role in forming linkages with business and providing information, especially in the early stages of the SMP. But it is also clear that there were a number of difficulties attending the government–business relationship.

First, there was a problem for many firms, both large and small, in gaining access to the US government. Particularly in the early stages of the US response to the SMP, there were complaints about the lack of a central access point for information and advice, and even when the access point was provided through the Department of Commerce, it was not always clear what its function was.

Second, at a number of crucial points, there was a problem about the 'supply' of government action. Most particularly from the point of view of the more 'European' companies, it was unclear what was driving US government policies in relation to the Second Banking Directive or telecommunications legislation (for example). One explanation for this at the government level is clearly that there was uncertainty or internal competition in respect of 'voice' and the ability to shape policy (see Chapter 3). On the other hand, there were a number of occasions on which government policy was supplied effectively and in a low-key way (for example, in the case of standards or competition policy; see Chapter 7).

Third, it is apparent that the 'extranational' nature of a number of the policy processes entailed in the SMP created some difficulties for government. The US Mission to the EC did not have the resources to cover all of the bases (although it was reinforced, almost uniquely among existing US missions, during the early 1990s). Business interests seem on a number of issues to have decided that the Washington connection was of little use to them (this applies especially to the activities of Congress) and to have proceeded on the perfectly logical basis that the EC arena was where policy was made and implemented. The priorities of the Washington government were not ignored, particularly when in the global context they intersected with the concerns of business in the EC (for example, over the GATT or NAFTA), but they were not accorded automatic priority in the calculations of those forming business strategy in the EC.

Conclusion

This chapter has been concerned not only to map the concerns of US firms as a whole with the SMP, but also to point out important areas of difference and variety across the range of US business. It is apparent from the evidence that difference and variety are central features, given additional emphasis by the scope and the uneven impact of the SMP itself. US firms in their responses to the SMP demonstrated considerable energy and creativity, influenced by their positions in the political economy of the EC itself and by their links to the US economy. As a result, it can be argued that US firms were led to a complex and sophisticated set of access strategies, some but by no means all of which entailed the search for US government support or sponsorship. In many cases, indeed, the strategies adopted required the support or sponsorship of EC institutions, of European governments or of European partners.

The tale of government–business relations in the context of the SMP is thus a fairly tangled one. At a number of junctures, the federal government showed itself concerned to police the SMP and to discipline the EU. This chimed with some but not all of the priorities of US business, and when it threatened to create dysfunctional tensions there were ways of letting government know about it. The US government – or governments, since this also engaged sub-federal agencies – wished to promote certain groups or processes in the EC context, but it is unclear whether this desire was more effectively pursued through government than through the formation of business-to-business linkages of the kind described above. Perhaps above all, the federal government in particular showed itself perfectly naturally to be concerned with the big picture rather than with the very differentiated view of business that has emerged in this chapter. The business of government, it could be argued, is the establishment of legitimated structures and frameworks for the conduct of business; at the level of the firm or the trade association, government has no standing, nor should it have, unless issues of a broad-ranging nature are raised. Such a conclusion is suggested not only by the evidence here but also by the broader arguments of those who have discerned a 'triangular diplomacy' operating between states and firms in different national or regional arenas.[40]

Even at the level of the broad framework, though, it is apparent that the US government in dealing with the SMP had difficulties in reconciling priorities, institutional preferences and political action.[41] It might have been expected that this process of flux and uncertainty would have impacted upon the effectiveness of business strategies, reducing their effectiveness. What was surprising about the SMP from an analytical perspective, however, was that these uncertainties were of such small consequence in shaping the perceptions, interests and strategies of business. Business needed government, but apparently only in small doses and at critical points in the process.

There are a number of possible explanations for this apparent weakness in the linkage between government and business in the context of US responses to the SMP. One is that for many US (large) firms, the

SMP represented not a revolution but the continuation of 'business as usual' with an added intensity. For smaller firms, the existing engagement of larger 'patrons' in the EC could often provide important benefits not available through governmental support. The growth of 'Europe-centred' strategies and of networks with strong extranational linkages clearly served to underline this tendency, and was accentuated by the demands of lobbying and government–business interaction within the EC itself. To return to arguments made in Chapter 2, it is clear that such factors set up a complex and multilayered pattern of interaction, shaped strongly by institutional contexts and market structure in the EC as well as by the more political concerns of government at home.

Notes and references

1   US Congress, Office of Technology Assessment, *Competing Economies: America, Europe, and the Pacific Rim*. Washington, DC, US Government Printing Office, July 1991, Chapter 5. See also K. Featherstone and R. Ginsberg, *The United States and the European Union in the 1990s: Partners in Transition* (2nd edn), London, Macmillan, 1996, Chapter 4; and G. C. Hufbauer (ed.), *Europe 1992: An American Perspective*. Washington, DC, Brookings Institution, 1990, Chapter 1.

2   See S. Woolcock, *Market Access Issues in EC–US Relations: Trading Partners or Trading Blows?*, London, Pinter for the Royal Institute of International Affairs, 1991; and M. Smith and S. Woolcock, *The United States and the European Community in a Transformed World*, London, Pinter for the Royal Institute of International Affairs, 1993, Chapters 1 and 3.

3   J. Stopford and S. Strange, *Rival States, Rival Firms: Competition for World Market Shares*, Cambridge, Cambridge University Press, 1991; S. Strange, 'States, firms and diplomacy', *International Affairs*, 68(1), 1992, pp. 3–15.

4   R. Reich, *The Work of Nations: Preparing Ourselves for Twenty-first Century Capitalism*, New York, Knopf, 1991.

5   K. Ohmae, *The Borderless World: Power and Strategy in the Interlinked Economy*, London, Fontana, 1992. See also the discussion in Chapter 1 of this book, pp. 7ff.

6   G. Thompson *et al.* (eds), *Markets, Hierarchies and Networks: The Coordination of Social Life*, London, Sage, 1991, especially Introduction, pp. 1–19.

7   J. Dunning, *International Production and the Multinational Enterprise*, London, Allen and Unwin, 1981. See also J. Dunning and P. Robson, 'International economic integration and multinational

corporate integration', *Journal of Common Market Studies*, **XXVI**(2), 1987, pp. 103–26; and J. Dunning, 'European integration and transatlantic foreign direct investment: the record assessed', in G. Yannopoulos (ed.), *America and Europe, 1992*, Manchester, Manchester University Press, 1992, pp. 153–76.

8   See Dunning and Robson, 'International economic integration and multinational corporate integration'.

9   See, for example, the series of surveys of the 1992 programme produced by *The Economist* from 1988 onwards, and in particular '1992: under construction. A survey of Europe's internal market'. *The Economist*, 8 July 1989.

10 M. Calingaert, *The 1992 Challenge from Europe: Development of the European Community's Single Market*, Washington, DC, National Planning Association, 1988, Chapter 7; Hufbauer, *Europe 1992: An American Perspective*, Chapter 1.

11 The details of the Airbus dispute are best summarized in two reports produced by the Congressional Research Service: J. W. Fischer *et al.*, *Airbus Industrie: An Economic and Trade Perspective*, CRS Report for Congress, Washington, DC, Congressional Research Service, February 1992; and J. W. Fischer, *The Airbus Controversy: Revisited?*, CRS Report for Congress, Washington, DC, Congressional Research Service, April 1993.

12 'The battle for Europe', *Business Week*, June 1991, quoted in C. Egan and P. McKiernan, *Inside Fortress Europe: Strategies for the Single Market*, London, Addison-Wesley/Economist Intelligence Unit, 1994, p. 63.

13 See US Congress, Office of Technology Assessment, *Competing Economies: America, Europe, and the Pacific Rim*, Chapter 5.

14 Source of Table 6.1: S. Young, M. McDermott and S. Dunlop, 'The challenge of the single market', in B. Burgenmeier and J. L. Mucchielli (eds), *Multinationals and Europe 1992: Strategies for the Future*, London, Routledge, 1991, p. 4.

15 See Burgenmeier and Mucchielli, *Multinationals and Europe 1992*, especially Part 1; also D. Julius, *Global Companies and Public Policy: the growing challenge of foreign direct investment*, London, Pinter for the Royal Institute of International Affairs, 1990.

16 See Egan and McKiernan, *Inside Fortress Europe*, especially Chapter 8.

17 US Congress, Office of Technology Assessment, *Competing Economies: America, Europe, and the Pacific Rim*, Chapter 5; Julius, *Global Companies and Public Policy*; Burgenmeier and Mucchielli, *Multinationals and Europe 1992*.

18 See Calingaert, *The 1992 Challenge from Europe*; P. Cowhey, 'Telecommunications', in G. C. Hufbauer (ed.), *Europe 1992: An American perspective*, Chapter 4, pp. 159–224.

19   S. Cooney, *Europe after 1992: Boom or Bust?*, Washington, DC, National Association of Manufacturers, June 1993, p. 8.

20   J. Dunning, 'European integration and transatlantic foreign direct investment'.

21   Dunning, 'European integration and transatlantic foreign direct investment'; Office of Technology Assessment, *Competing Economies*, Chapter 5; J. Peterson, *Europe and America in the 1990s: Prospects for Partnership*, Aldershot, Edward Elgar, 1993, pp. 88–90.

22   Interview, National Association of Manufacturers, Washington, DC, June 1993.

23   See D. Waller, 'Alive and well, and buying in Europe', *Financial Times*, 13 December 1990; A. Baxter, 'Quiet American makes a big noise in M & A', *Financial Times*, 16 January 1991.

24   See the work of Maria Green Cowles here, in particular: M. G. Cowles, 'The "business" of agenda-setting in the European Union', paper presented to the fourth Biennial Conference of the European Community Studies Association, Charleston, SC, May 1995; M. G. Cowles, 'The politics of big business in the Single Market Programme', Paper presented to the third Biennial Conference of the European Community Studies Association, Washington, DC, May 1993.

25   A pertinent example is that of semiconductor producers: see K. Flamm, 'Semiconductors', in Hufbauer, *Europe 1992: An American Perspective*, Chapter 5, pp. 225–92.

26   See the discussion in Chapter 4 of Congressional activity in this area.

27   Interviews, National Association of Manufacturers and US Council for International Business, Washington, DC, September 1988.

28   For an account of these variations, see Egan and McKiernan, *Inside Fortress Europe*, especially Chapters 8–10.

29   See, for example, the discussion in R. J. Ahearn, 'US access to the EC-92 market: opportunities, concerns and policy challenges', in US House of Representatives, Committee on Foreign Affairs, *Europe and the United States: Competition and Cooperation in the 1990s*, Washington, DC, US Government Printing Office, 1992, pp. 177–92.

30   See the work by Maria Green Cowles cited above (note 24).

31   See D. E. Rosenthal, 'Competition policy', in Hufbauer, *Europe 1992: An American Perspective*, Chapter 6, pp. 293–345.

32   Cowles, 'The "Business" of agenda-setting in the European Union'.

33   For an excellent discussion of this issue, see M. Calingaert, 'Government–business relations', in US House of Representatives, Committee on Foreign Affairs, *Europe and the United States: Competition and Cooperation in the 1990s*, pp. 31–45. See also his later revision of his 1988 book: M. Calingaert, *European Integration Revisited: Progress, Prospects, and U.S. Interests*, Boulder, CO, Westview Press, 1996, especially Part Three.

34 The general framework for this discussion draws upon Chapter 2, pp. 35–41, with its analysis of government–business relations and modes of influence.

35 See E. M. Graham, 'Strategic responses of US firms to the Europe-1992 initiative', in G. Yannopoulos (ed.), *America and Europe, 1992*, pp. 177–205; Christopher Lorenz, 'Facing up to responsibility', *Financial Times*, 15 December 1993, p. 11. Interview, 3M Europe, Brussels, April 1994.

36 See M. G. Cowles, 'The EU Committee of AmCham: the powerful voice of American firms in Brussels', *Journal of European Public Policy*, 3(3), 1996, pp. 339–58. See also the numerous AmCham publications, including the regularly revised *European Information Handbook* and *Business Guide to EC Initiatives*, both Brussels, EC Committee of the American Chamber of Commerce.

37 S. Greenhouse, 'US corporations expand in Europe for '92 prospects', *New York Times*, 13 March 1989, pp. A1/D6.

38 S. Mazey and J. Richardson (eds), *Lobbying in the European Community*, Oxford, Oxford University Press, 1993. See also M. Calingaert, 'Government–business relations'; A. McLaughlin, G. Jordan and W. Maloney, 'Corporate lobbying in the European Community', *Journal of Common Market Studies*, 31(2), 1993, pp. 191–212.

39 Interviews, AmCham, February 1994. See also M. G. Cowles, 'The EU Committee of AmCham'.

40 See the works by Stopford and Strange cited earlier in this chapter.

41 See the discussion in Chapter 3, pp. 66–70.

7

Cases

with Edward Hodson

Thus far, the argument in this book has focused particularly on the ways in which different governmental and non-governmental groupings in the USA responded to the challenge of the Single Market Programme. The concern has been to identify the ways in which the challenge was perceived and made itself felt, and the ways in which a variety of responses emerged. It is clear that those responses were characterized on the one hand by *diversity* and on the other hand by *specificity*; the range of levels and types of action that were called forth guaranteed diversity, while at the same time the responses of different players were affected by a number of organizational, sectoral and other influences which gave them distinctive characteristics.

Alongside the general finding of diversity and specificity goes another: that the different interests, needs, priorities and actions of the players intersected and interacted at a number of key points, and that this affected the processes of learning and response that were produced as Americans dealt with the SMP. Different players assumed different functions in the process, and developed different operating methods; different players also needed the support or the acquiescence of others. Thus, the US executive moved from responses governed by domestic political and economic forces towards responses conditioned by interaction with the EC and by the development of the broader political scene. Equally, US firms were more inclined to deal with the SMP as a commercial problem to be solved, but none the less one in which at key stages they might need the support of the US government. Both Congress and state governments in the USA also developed characteristic patterns of concern and conceptions of role and function in the process of response.

The evidence so far evaluated thus supports the initial argument in this book, about the changing nature of foreign economic policy and the ways in which this was likely to be exposed by challenges such as the SMP, which spanned a number of levels of policy and action and which called for innovative policy responses. More specifically, the evidence focuses the questions posed in Chapters 1 and 2, about the significance of *access and control* in the handling of novel international economic challenges. In this chapter, the aim is to focus down even more sharply, and to examine the ways in which our general findings are supported by a pair of sectoral case studies.

The chapter starts with an initial proposition, derived from our examination of the general evidence and relating to the issues of access and control. On the basis of the evidence from Chapters 3 to 6, the broad distinction between policies based on access and those based on control can now be further elaborated. We discern a central contrast in the evolution of international economic policy between two tendencies. On the one hand, there is a tendency which centres on the importance of *position, power, control and bargaining*, and which could be said to support traditional statist notions of foreign economic policy and related diplomacy. On the other hand, there is a tendency centring on *process, leverage, access and networking*, which suggests a transformation of foreign economic policy into a form of multilevel negotiation and which takes us beyond established notions of the policy arena. In our examination of the US response to the SMP, both of these tendencies can be discerned, and part of the significance of our analysis lies in the extent to which we can identify and discriminate between them as they operate in any given policy domain.

Here, we examine two sectoral case studies, those of public procurement and of standards, testing and certification. Both of these issues were central to the evolution of the SMP – in fact, they were among the necessary conditions for its attainment – both were of high significance to a range of public and private US groupings and both stimulated initial tensions and suspicion on the part of the United States. They thus provide a prima facie test of the general conclusions we have reached so far. They also provide at first examination contrasting patterns of challenge, response and outcome which will enable us to test the conclusions further. To be more specific:

- in the case of *public procurement*, there is a move from initial unilateralism, through a period of confrontation, into a period of negotiation and partial intergovernmental agreement, and towards a multilateralization of the agreement reached;
- in the case of *standards and certification*, there is a move from initial unilateralism, through a period of confrontation, into a period of networking and mutual recognition which relies upon the engagement of a range of private interests and institutions.

It is the argument here that the contrasting courses of the US–EC tensions in these two areas can be explained at least in part by the ways in which the areas did or did not conform to the traditional models of foreign economic policy, and to the two tendencies outlined above.

The chapter proceeds first by outlining some of the challenges posed by the need to influence EC policy development in the two areas, and looking at the course of events in both of the cases. It goes on to examine specifically the ways in which actions and interactions took place, in terms of the different actors engaged on the US side of the equation. It concludes with an evaluation of the two cases in terms of the general arguments made above.

The challenge of policy development in the EC

As noted at several points in Chapter 2 and elsewhere, one of the key elements in the challenge posed by the SMP for all outsiders was that of policy development and policy innovation. The SMP was explicitly based on new forms of policy development in the EC, emanating from the Single European Act (SEA): this established the institutional framework for the generation of SMP legislation, and in particular the focus on policy initiation by the Commission in conjunction with qualified majority voting in the Council of Ministers. These were not new elements in the EC's institutional make-up, but they were used in novel ways to generate momentum behind the SMP; the famous package of '300 Directives' gathered together in the 1985 Commission White Paper on completion of the Single Market also played a central role in focusing attention and generating a seemingly unstoppable momentum for the SMP. One central element of the challenge was thus that the SMP seemed to promise radical and programmatic change based on the implementation of new policy instruments.[1]

Alongside this challenge at the level of institutions went more specific challenges, two of which are particularly relevant to the case studies of public procurement and standards, testing and certification. In the first case, and particularly in the area of public procurement, the SMP promised a new opening up of policy processes hitherto subject to strong national government control. It was aimed not only at establishing rules for the handling of government contracts, but also at removing the ability of governments to maintain so-called 'excluded sectors', primarily the large public utilities. This was a challenge, therefore, for governments and firms within the EC, and one to which they responded with varying degrees of enthusiasm. For the outsider, it promised both the opening up of reserved areas of policy and the need to deal with new levels of policy determination in the EC. It also carried the implicit threat that new

EC-level policies could be used effectively to discriminate against interested outsiders (see below).[2]

In the second case, the EC itself self-consciously pursued a programme of policy innovation in conjunction with the SMP. Most obviously, in the area of standards and certification, it gave the responsibility for the formulation of particular standards to a set of quasi-private institutions (CEN, CENELEC and ETSI) which operated at arm's length from the central Community process. This novel use of what has been called 'associative regulation', relying on the concerting of policies between the public and private sectors, clearly demanded of outsiders an ability to adapt and to learn about the new policy process.[3]

It is apparent even from this brief sketch that the processes of policy development in the EC, and their implications for outsiders, are not a static target. In the case study areas of public procurement and standards, testing and certification, there were distinct and specific challenges emerging from the ways in which the internal EC process developed. Although these can be seen as distinct, it is also the case that certain common elements existed. In both of the areas, there was an expansion during the SMP period of the use of specialist working groups and advisors; technical, advisory and regulatory committees were established or expanded; and the Commission's need to develop a lot of policy on many fronts at the same time inevitably meant a proliferation of channels not only for advice but also for influence. Not only this, but national governments in member states were led to develop extensive national scrutiny and monitoring mechanisms, which themselves provided means of access to the policy process. To use a phrase coined by two analysts of the area, national government processes were strongly 'Europeified'.[4]

What this meant for the structure of policy-making in the two case study areas was essentially a growth and extension of the channels for communication, leverage and influence, at a number of interrelated levels within the EC. In both public procurement and standards, testing and certification, a range of bodies grew up to support the work of the Commission and the Council of Ministers, and to ensure the coordination of SMP issues with others. Thus, for example, the Internal Market Advisory Group or the Internal Market Normalisation Committee on the one hand went alongside the Ad Hoc Committee on the Uruguay Round on the other, in advising the Council of Ministers. Although the major part of SMP activity centred on the Commission, it must not be forgotten that both the Council of Ministers and the member states played important roles in the generation and the implementation of legislative measures.

Within the Commission itself, one of the key features of the SMP was the extent to which it forced coordination and communication on the many Directorates-General engaged in the range of issues. On public procurement, DGs I (External Relations), II (Economic Affairs), III (Internal Market and Industrial Affairs), IV (Competition) and XIII (Telecommunications, Information Industries and Innovation) could claim to be major actors in the process. While the core Directorate was to be found in DG III, with one subdivision focusing on policy development and another focusing on the application of the relevant Directives, it is clear that not only other parts of the Commission bureaucracy but also key parts of national governments had an input.

A similar picture of cross-departmental policy-making emerges from the standards, testing and certification area. Although all 'external' aspects of the problem were theoretically handled by DG I, there were others centrally and continuously involved, including DGs II, III and IV. The 'internal' aspects of technical standards were handled again by a directorate (B) in DG III, although other parts of the DG were inevitably involved in specific applications of the process. As in the case of Commission policy-making more generally, these areas were served by a range of *ad hoc* and standing committees, playing a wide range of roles in the drafting of legislation and technical consultation. For the standards, testing and certification area, the Committee on Technical Standards and Regulations had to be consulted in the drafting of legislation.

The Commission and the Council of Ministers thus stood at the centre of a process taking place at many levels and in many different specialist forums. To this could be added the European Parliament, with its structure of specialist committees and its role in the monitoring of legislation; the SEA had enhanced this role from that of 'consultation' to that of 'cooperation', with specific reference to SMP measures.

The significance of this wide-ranging process of policy innovation to the ways in which outsiders such as the USA could influence SMP measures cannot be overestimated. While in previous chapters we have sometimes stressed the essentially 'domestic' nature of US attitudes and responses to the SMP, it is clear that in order to influence policy development in areas such as public procurement and standards, testing and certification, Americans had to get to grips with the multilevel and highly interconnected processes of policy-making in the EC. Given the high stakes for which Americans were playing in both areas, this was not an optional response; but the ways in which the response was formulated and put into action could be expected to demonstrate the variety and the specificity of the US interests engaged.

Public procurement: the roads to (partial) agreement

The broad term 'public procurement' covers the whole range of purchasing by public or quasi-public bodies – everything from paper clips to nuclear power stations. Traditionally, much of this purchasing has been subject to a variety of restrictions, often with the result that public contracts have been awarded to national suppliers. Most obviously, in the great public utilities such as energy generation and supply, water supply, transportation and telecommunications there have been strong patterns of national preference, which could be seen as having a protectionist nature. The SMP, by aiming to open up public procurement within the EC to cross-EC competition, threatened a number of these rather cosy arrangements. At the same time, it could be seen as both an opportunity and a threat by non-EC interests: an opportunity because it opened up hitherto protected markets; a threat because it might lead to protection at the EC, rather than at the national, level.

This was a matter of particular concern to Americans. The public procurement market in the EC was estimated to be worth around $600 billion per annum, and much of it was of interest to American companies.[5] In the field of telecommunications, for example, the size of the EC market was estimated at ECU15 billion in 1986, with the potential to rise to ECU19 billion in 1990.[6] US companies, as we have seen in Chapter 6, were often well-placed to operate complex contracts on a continental scale; not only this, but their experience of dealing with state-level public purchasing arrangements in the USA as well as with massive US government and private utilities contracts gave them a pronounced advantage over EC companies, which had historically relied on intimate arrangements with national governments.

Around this general perception of opportunity and threat, however, lay a number of other important factors. First, the US and proposed EC systems of public procurement regulation were in many respects profoundly different. Particularly in the case of the utilities, much of the US system was based around private companies, with government having a relatively arm's-length role in regulation. At the same time, as indicated above, much public purchasing in the USA is carried out at the state level, and at that level there is a series of restrictions, known generically as 'buy-American legislation', which provides preferences for local suppliers. At the federal level, there are numerous restrictions on the range of participation in public contracts, primarily on national security grounds.[7]

In this context, the EC efforts to liberalize and unify the public procurement market were guaranteed to have not only economic but also political repercussions. Within the EC, there was the problem of extending the regime from central government to regional and local levels, and opening up reserved areas. When it came to the treatment of outsiders, the predominant concerns were in the USA. Although there were some existing US–EC agreements on access to public contracts, these were of marginal importance; many of the more significant arrangements were between the USA and individual EC member states, through (for example) treaties of friendship, commerce and navigation, often of very long standing.

Particular suspicion was aroused in US circles by the fact that the major Utilities Directive – published in September 1990 – included in article 29 a 3 per cent price preference for EC companies, accompanied by a local content requirement; in other words, US companies accounting for more than 50 per cent of any bid would be excluded if they did not bid at least 3 per cent lower than their EC rivals. The fact that this provision was based on a 6 per cent preference incorporated in much 'buy-American legislation' was not given much weight by American firms or the federal government: there was an immediate accusation of protectionism. In this atmosphere, the fact that the relevant directives also included provisions for reciprocity fed the US perception that there was a protectionist agenda in the EC's programme.[8] A final factor giving the Americans cause for concern was the fact that the GATT framework for public procurement was still in an embryonic state; in this context, the EC directives looked like an attempt to pre-empt the construction of a multilateral regime. The fact that many US public purchasing practices would also not sit happily in a GATT regime was not given salience.[9]

Between 1987 and 1991, the public procurement issue was transformed into a major focus of conflict between the USA and the EC. Significantly, from an early stage it was seen as the responsibility of the US government to take up the cause: it was seen as the means by which access for US firms could be ensured, and through which the US public procurement regime could be safeguarded. Not only this, but only the federal authorities could make the linkages between the GATT context, the bilateral US–EC context, the sub-federal context and the specific needs of US firms. By doing so, it was assumed, the USA could gain leverage over the EC and promote the interests of major areas of US industry.[10] At an early stage, US government interest was focused on a number of key areas; most prominent were heavy electrical equipment and telecommunications equipment, two areas central to the liberalization of the EC internal market and of great interest to powerful US corporations.[11]

Both sides in this emerging battle had armed themselves during the 1980s. Apart from existing bilateral agreements between the USA and individual EC member states, the Americans could draw upon a range of trade legislation. In particular, the Omnibus Trade and Competitiveness Act of 1988 had focused on unfair trading practices in a number of areas related to public procurement; the concept of 'unfair trade' had been broadened to include government contracts, and this had been given particular force in such areas as telecommunications, where the deregulation process in the USA was seen as having created a uniquely open environment. One effect of this legislation was to mandate US negotiators in the GATT Uruguay Round to take a hard line on disguised protectionism; another was to sensitize US interests to any moves on the part of the EC.

At the same time, it was clear that in the EC context there was a desire to use the utilities directive to put some pressure on the Americans. Not for nothing had the directive included a 'mirror image' of the US 'buy-American legislation' and its price preferences, and reciprocity provisions. Alongside this unilateral mechanism, with its implied bilateral overtones, there was also a desire on the part of the EC to promote the GATT as a dispute settlement process. Both the Americans and the EC were thus concerned to try and link their unilateral measures, bilateral relations and multilateral aspirations.

The problems that emerged between 1991 and 1993 reflected both the high stakes for both sides and the complexities of trying to balance the unilateral, bilateral and multilateral levels of action. In December 1990, the halting attempts to negotiate on utilities and particularly on telecommunications in the GATT Uruguay Round were brought to a halt by the setback at the Brussels ministerial meeting – a setback which arose from the failure to make progress on agriculture, but which had extensive repercussions in the area of public procurement. More hopefully, the agreement of the Transatlantic Declaration between the USA and the EC in December 1990 laid some foundations for the development of consultation mechanisms in areas central to the SMP.[12]

During 1991–2, the discussions of the utilities directives and their application to US firms continued, but also continued to make little progress. The EC developed the compliance mechanisms for implementation when the directive was adopted and came into force (this was envisaged for early 1993). The USA continued to wrestle with the fact that both negotiations with the EC and the Uruguay Round talks implied an untangling of the multilevel system for public purchasing in the USA itself.[13] At the same time, the issue emerged in the context of the negotiations for the NAFTA, which gathered momentum during late 1991. In late 1991, a draft Uruguay Round agreement was tabled, and this led in early 1992 to the development of a draft revised GATT government purchasing agreement.[14]

The public procurement issue continued to hang fire during 1992, but it was brought decisively to a head by the entering into force of the Utilities Directive in January 1993. The immediate response of the United States was to impose sanctions, focused particularly on telecommunications and heavy electrical equipment; these were suspended when bilateral talks recommenced in the early part of 1993,[15] although the EC saw no reason to halt the implementation both of the Directive and of its regime for compliance. The net result of these events was to underline the multilevel characteristics of the problem: as the EC implemented measures unilaterally, there were bilateral talks and these went alongside the Uruguay Round process, which had extended to cover the purchasing of sub-federal governments.

The bilateral talks in the spring of 1993 resulted in a partial agreement in the form of a Memorandum of Understanding. This contained a broad agreement that both sides would eliminate all remaining restrictions on access by each other's companies to central government contracts. It also contained an undertaking by the US administration that it would approach the governors of all 50 states and a range of governing bodies in the largest US cities, with a view to eliminating sub-federal 'buy-American' provisions. In addition, the understanding focused specifically on one area, that of equipment purchases by electricity generators: thus, the United States agreed to drop 'buy-American' rules for the Tennessee Valley Authority and the Energy Department's five electric power administrations, while the EC agreed to eliminate 'buy-European' rules for equipment purchases by utilities (a concession estimated at $20 billion per year).[16] Despite this apparent progress, the US administration proceeded immediately to impose sanctions on the EC because of failure to agree on access to the EC telecommunications switching equipment market. The EC retaliated, and the prospect of a trade war seemed imminent, despite the resolution of the problem over power generating equipment which had concerned the USA since the 1960s.

This was a confused and confusing situation for negotiators in both the United States and the EC, made more complex by the simultaneous need for progress in the Uruguay Round and (for the USA) in the NAFTA negotiations. Further complexity was introduced during the summer of 1993 by the US administration's attempts to deal with the sub-federal 'buy-American' provisions, and also by a dramatic defection from the EC position on the part of Germany. When at the end of May the Americans finally imposed an estimated $20 million sanctions on EC companies to register their dissatisfaction at the failure to agree in telecommunications equipment, the US Trade Representative reported on 10 June that the sanctions would not be imposed on Germany. It appeared that the Germans had decided to give precedence in their relations with the USA on this matter not to EC policy but to their treaty of friendship, commerce and navigation dating from 1954. As a result, they would not be imposing sanctions on the USA as demanded by the EC, nor would they be applying article 29 of the Utilities Directive to US telecommunications equipment suppliers.[17]

As a result, during the summer of 1993 there appeared to be a looming crisis in the EC as it confronted the penetration of its common stance by the USA, with the connivance of Germany. Opinions differed over whether this was an active conspiracy or simply an accidental convergence of interpretations and interests. The Commission responded to the use of the friendship, navigation and commerce treaty by asking all EC members with such agreements to rewrite them, giving precedence to the EC's common commercial policy. At the same time, the dispute filtered into the GATT context through continuing difficulties in the negotiation of an agreement on government purchasing in the Uruguay Round; and this in turn was seen as difficult for the USA in the context of the NAFTA negotiations.[18]

By the end of 1993, however, the dispute seemed to have been at least partially defused. Crucial to this process was the continuation of EC–US bilateral consultation at the same time that the issue was multilateralized in the Uruguay Round. Although the bilateral US–EC dispute over telecommunications was not ended, it was hived off from the central negotiations through the device of a joint study, designed to lead to a bilateral agreement during 1994; and the USA and the EC signed such an agreement in the margins of the Marrakesh conference at which the Uruguay Round agreement was finally signed. In December 1993, a revised government purchasing agreement was signed in the context of the GATT by the EC member states and 11 others, including the USA.[19]

The public procurement dispute outlined here had thus not been eliminated (and the telecommunications problem remained unresolved despite multilateral negotiations during 1995 and 1996), but it had in some ways been defused, and in some areas effectively ended. Given the high stakes, the politicization of the issue and the way in which it crossed many levels of government, it is clear that it was always likely to cause problems. The fact that those problems had to be addressed at the diplomatic level, even while they involved the interests of companies in very specific sectors or even individual contracts, added a distinctive dimension to the tensions. Meanwhile, it is fair to say that many corporations were proceeding quietly to exploit either their existing positions in the EC or newly made connections with EC partners to gain effective access in a host of government purchasing areas. To be sure, there were exceptions, and not only in telecommunications: the difficulties encountered by GE in bidding for German power station contracts during 1994 and 1995 attracted the attention of the White House and Congress.[20] But the complexities of the diplomatic context, and the need to operate simultaneously at the domestic, the bilateral and the multilateral level, bear ample witness to the development of multilevel diplomacy in this area.

Standards, testing and certification: towards dialogue and mutual recognition

As already noted, the issue of standards, testing and certification was central to the entire SMP. The thrust of the programme, towards mutual recognition rather than harmonization, and the adoption of a series of crucial directives based on the so-called 'new approach', constituted landmarks in the evolution of the SMP, and in the EC's policy process. From the point of view of US firms, as for EC firms, the process was not only of great importance in general; it often carried with it implications of major material costs and benefits, linked to the gaining of product approval and the ability to market in the whole range of EC member states. Taking the general picture, the European Commission estimated, for example, that the gains from standardization in telecommunications, through the exploitation of economies of scale, would amount to between ECU850 million and ECU1.1 billion. Removal of all technical barriers to trade in pharmaceutical products would save between 0.8 per cent and 1.6 per cent of total industry costs.[21]

The extensive involvement of US firms both in exporting to the EC and in investing or operating within the EC meant that they had an instant interest in this issue. Indeed, of the many initial treatments of the SMP referred to elsewhere in this book, the vast majority identified standards, testing and certification as a key if not the key issue facing US business. In many sectors, the combination of standards issues with problems such as those of public procurement meant that there was early and intense interest in the field; the most direct relationship can perhaps be seen in telecommunications, but other major areas included pharmaceutical products, medical equipment and office equipment – all areas in which the USA had a long-standing and significant involvement with the EC.[22]

The problems facing US interests, as noted earlier, were essentially twofold. On the one hand, the use of standards, testing and certification as flagship SMP activities created the obvious danger that they could be used as means of exclusion, and that US companies could be the target of discrimination. The fact that many US companies were well established in the EC and operated effectively as 'European' companies did not eliminate the problem, since they were confronted with the decision as to whether they should adopt EC standards as a global framework for their operations. One of the implicit aims of the SMP in this area was the 'capturing' by the EC of important influence over global standards.

On the other hand, there was the challenge created by the 'new approach' itself and by the institutional context for the SMP standards process. As noted earlier, this was distinctive, in the sense that it divided the labour between the Commission and the Council of Ministers, which were responsible for the legislative framework, and a series of semi-private bodies, which were responsible for the development of individual standards. The roles of CEN, CENELEC and ETSI were central to the standards, testing and certification issue, and raised questions about the extent to which individual firms or industry groupings could have access to the standards setting process. Decision-making in these bodies reflected the influence of national standards bodies, which could propose standards in accordance with the EC framework; but it also reflected the influence of EC firms that took a major role at the level of national technical committees and those at the EC level. Clearly, the definition of what constituted an 'EC firm' would be crucial to the access and influence of US corporations.

These roles were also a challenge to the US domestic standards system, which was highly fragmented and largely privatized, and in which the national governmental involvement was tangential, to say the least. Many standards were effectively set by market-leading corporations, and the American National Standards Institute (ANSI), the national representative body, was a weak federation of private organizations. The position of the Department of Commerce was debatable in the face of private-sector dominance, and the Department did not have an international representative role; that was reserved to ANSI. There had been an understandable tendency to focus on standards for the US market, and to ignore developments elsewhere; the SMP made this an untenable position in many crucial sectors, not least because it appeared to give the EC a dominant role in the relevant global bodies – the International Standards Organization (ISO) and the International Electrotechnical Commission (IEC) – and thus the potential to seize the initiative in newly significant areas.[23]

It can be seen from this sketch of the process that in the area of standards, testing and certification there was both a private-sector challenge and a governmental challenge to American interests. On the one hand, there was the danger of exclusion from both the process and the benefits of agreement on standards; on the other, there was the danger of 'regulatory capture' of not just EC markets but also those elsewhere in Europe, since the EC's aim was to include both members of the European Free Trade Area (EFTA) and the European Economic Area (EEA), and later Central and Eastern European countries in their orbit. Beyond this lay a form of global competition between rules, in which the EC appeared to have a structural advantage.[24]

The initial US response to these forces was none the less broadly positive. Although there were obvious possibilities of exclusion or discrimination, the move towards a European 'space' for standards, testing and certification was seen as a net gain, not least by the larger multinational corporations. Other US interests were both less aware and less affected; examples of small and medium-sized firms who found out only at a late stage about the impact of specific standards changes were frequent and sometimes startling.[25] More problems emerged when it transpired that the EC process itself was prone to delay and uncertainty. Although EC standards were supposed to be compatible with international (ISO/IEC) standards, and could even be 'taken over' by them, it was not clear what would happen in areas where there were no established ISO/IEC frameworks. Not only this, but the process generated by CEN, CENELEC and ETSI allowed for the development of voluntary standards in areas not yet mandated by the EC; what would happen when these came up against later EC mandates?

The crucial element in this set of problems was that these uncertainties applied to all or the overwhelming majority of firms operating in the EC. There might be fears that EC companies would have an inside track, but in most cases they were subject to exactly the same challenges. A more complex issue arose in the area of testing and certification. The EC aim was to establish mutual recognition agreements at the EC level, so that national testing and certification processes could be accredited. But what did this imply for the largely decentralized system in the USA? Could the accreditation of testing and certification bodies be used as a means of exerting leverage on the Americans, and forcing them into line with EC standards? Not surprisingly, this possibility claimed a good deal of attention in the US debate.[26]

US concerns could be summarized as those of access and transparency, within the general sensitivity to the significance of competition between regulatory systems. They were sharpened by the fact that the lack of a firm global regulatory structure, through either the ISO/IEC or the GATT, gave the opportunity for EC moves to have long-term and wide-ranging effects. The perception that the EC had at least twelve votes in the ISO made a deep impact on certain US commentators, as did the view that the USA had no effective presence in the EC process.

As the process unfolded during 1985 to 1988, the prime US concern at both corporate and governmental levels seemed to be with information and monitoring. The debates over the 1988 Omnibus Trade and Competitiveness Act touched on standards in the context of the Uruguay Round and in the context of moves against unfair traders (it must not be forgotten that the Japanese were seen as the arch-practitioners of regulatory discrimination). A key role was played in respect of information by the Department of Commerce, which gave the standards issue pride of place in its EC-92 programme and developed a strong knowledge base; but there was also a major push both by firms and trade associations in the US context and by US corporations and associations operating in the EC. The role of the EC Committee of the American Chamber of Commerce in Brussels, for example, was central not only to the awareness of US firms but also at times to the advising of EC and private bodies on the implications of standards proposals.[27]

The most dramatic example of US governmental commitment in this area was the call in January 1989 for a 'seat at the table' on EC standards issues, made by the Secretary of Commerce, Robert Mosbacher. This received the predictable stony response from Brussels, but it did set in train a diplomatic process by which in July 1992 Mosbacher and Martin

Bangemann, the EC Internal Market Commissioner, could announce an understanding and a process of consultation. This was accompanied by the establishment of a US–EC dialogue, conducted primarily at the private-sector level, which became a significant force in the development of the relationship. Almost immediately, CEN/CENELEC announced a change in its policy on access for non-member bodies: it was ready to give due consideration to all comments or proposals on standards projects from outside the EC, when these were made through the relevant member body of the ISO/IEC. In the case of the USA, this meant ANSI and the National Institute for Standards and Technology, recently established under the aegis of the Department of Commerce.[28] In December 1989, the EC produced a Green Paper, 'A Global Approach to Testing and Certification', which reaffirmed the basis of EC policy in international standards and also allowed for flexibility in the continuation of existing national-level mutual recognition agreements, where these had not been renegotiated at the EC level.[29]

These moves at the EC–US and EC levels clearly created momentum behind a broader multilateral convergence. Despite the collapse of the Uruguay Round talks in Brussels in December 1990, it was clear that a revised Agreement on Technical Barriers to Trade was achievable, and that the development of US–EC consultation was a key element in this. It had been agreed that the governing principle of the application of technical standards at the governmental level should be effective national treatment, and that the application of GATT dispute procedures should be investigated; there remained the issue of sub-central and local government, which the EC wished to cover but the USA did not.[30]

During 1991, the dialogue intensified. The focus was the application of the Green Paper, and the channels were those of the Transatlantic Declaration and bilateral diplomacy between Mosbacher and Bangemann. A further meeting of the two on 21 June produced broad agreement, but stressed the need for conformity with global standards; the EC was also urged to encourage the EC standards bodies to make more use of non-EC expertise in working groups and technical committees.[31] There was also a significant move by CEN/CENELEC towards a matching of their schedules and processes with those of ISO/IEC.[32] On 18 June 1992, the Council of Ministers adopted a Resolution on 'The Role of Standardisation in the European Economy'. This constituted nothing less than an EC recognition of the move away from the promotion of EC standards, and the acceptance of standards, testing and certification as a global process. To a large extent, too, it was an acceptance of the interests of US government and business.[33]

This resolution also set the scene for intensive renegotiation at the EC level of transatlantic mutual recognition agreements, which began in October 1992. The US aim was to have testing and certification of products for the EC market carried out in the USA wherever possible and appropriate. For its part, the EC wished to achieve effective reciprocity of access, and to limit the agreements in the first instance to selected sectors. Through 1993, the negotiations continued not only in this context but also in the context of the Uruguay Round. In December 1993, the Uruguay Round Agreement achieved a significant strengthening of the global standards, testing and certification regime, extending it to all members of the WTO and subjecting it to GATT dispute settlement procedures.[34]

The process through which the issue of standards, testing and certification was handled through governmental dialogue thus seems to indicate a different pattern from that observable in the case of public procurement. In place of confrontation, there was quiet diplomacy; in place of sanctions, dialogue; and in place of recrimination, consultation. It is also true to say that there was a very different role for the private sector in the process, both because of the nature of the EC process and because of the broader concerns of US and EC firms. At the same time, it is clear that the relationship between EC–US dialogue and the broader global regime, as represented by ISO/IEC and the GATT, played a vital part in the development of working principles. These general features of the process indicate both that it furnishes an interesting example of multilevel diplomacy and that it contrasts in many areas with the case of public procurement. We now proceed to an evaluation of the roles played in these cases by the key actors at different levels in the US policy arena.

Foreign economic policy and multilevel diplomacy: an evaluation

In this section, we examine the roles played in the two case study areas by the range of actors in the US policy process, as outlined in Chapters 3 to 6. The aim is to identify the variety of roles and responses and to evaluate characteristics both specific to each of the cases and of more general significance.

The executive in action

It is apparent from both of the cases that the executive branch of the US federal government had both an active interest and a significant part to play. The question, though, is the extent to which the interest and role were uniform, and the extent to which they conformed to the assumption of executive primacy contained in traditional models of foreign economic policy. On the domestic front, did the executive remain at the centre of policy formulation? In the EC–US arena, did the executive retain exclusive or primary access to the EC policy process? In both cases, what forms of adjustments to institutions and strategy were apparent?

In the early stages of both cases, it appears that the executive did retain primacy. Two factors are important: first, the fact that the executive, however imperfectly, did have information unavailable to those operating in Congress or at the sub-federal level of government; second, the fact that the interest of firms was largely confined to the large multinational investors or exporters who had a long-standing interest in EC affairs. These two forces coincided to keep the issues insulated, but not for very long. The key catalyst here was the elaboration and publication of EC policies, which made more specific the threat both to access at the EC level and to existing US domestic practices. As noted in the case of public procurement, the executive alone came to be seen as the body capable of linking the various needs and interests called into play.

As these needs and interests filtered down into the US domestic system, it is apparent that pressure on the executive to respond to specific sectoral challenges increased. By the end of 1988, the range of government departments with a public position on the SMP had widened greatly, and these departments were encouraged by the White House to enter into the debate (see Chapter 3). At the centre of all positions were the issues of public procurement and standards, testing and certification – partly at least because these areas carried the greatest stakes and the broadest range of potential effects on the US system. It was not surprising in this context that the executive felt driven to threaten sanctions against the EC, particularly in the area of public procurement (see above). Significantly, however, these threats and sanctions were not characteristic of the executive's position on standards, testing and certification, where a much more diffuse network of agencies and private bodies was to be found.

At the same time that there were diverse pressures on the executive to shape its overall position on the SMP and the two cases, there was the problem of access to the EC policy process. We have noted that this was a 'moving target', and in both of the case study areas this proved a significant factor. US business in Europe also had a central part to play, as we have seen, but in at least the early stages of policy development this was seen as subordinate to executive leadership. The position changed as executive leadership threatened to raise the stakes and the tensions, and thus to call into question the role of US companies in the EC (see below). As a result, there were occasions on which the 'European' US firms felt the need to lobby Washington (sometimes with the support of the US Mission in Brussels) in order to prevent damage to their positions and interests.[35]

As the cases developed, there was thus a developing issue of 'voice' in the federal executive's role. At one level, this was an issue of the extent to which the White House and executive agencies could express private needs; at another level, it was apparent that the multiplicity of international channels for communication and action militated against executive dominance. There is significant variation here between the public procurement case and the case of standards, testing and certification. In the first case, the politicization of the subject, its linkages to the US governmental system and its connections to the GATT regime guaranteed the executive a central and continuing role. In the second, the available channels were largely if not predominantly private and technical; thus, although the executive had a clear role in establishing and validating the broad framework, the treatment of a wide range of specialized issues was in other hands.

It is important to note, however, that the variations in role and 'voice' between the two sectors explored here occurred within a broad-based development of US–EC consultative mechanisms. In particular, these were centred on the Transatlantic Declaration of 1990; they also covered areas of intense mutual interest such as competition and anti-trust policies, which became a very active focus from 1990 on.[36] The collaboration here led to regular contacts between the European Commission and a range of US executive agencies. While this might be seen as consolidating the role of the executive as a whole, it also gave these 'domestic' agencies a new level of access to the EC process.

The wide range of involvement by executive agencies in the US–EC relationship can be linked to specific institutional developments in the handling of public procurement and standards, testing and certification. In a general sense, the need to cope with EC policy development led to institutional innovation in Washington; as noted in Chapter 3, this led to the establishment of inter-agency mechanisms, and to a fluctuating balance of initiative between the Department of State, the USTR and the Department of Commerce.[37]

This process of domestic institutional response was focused by the demands of the two case study areas, in different ways. On the issue of public procurement, it is noteworthy that the executive response was concentrated primarily in the USTR; this can be seen as a function of its linkages with the 'high politics' of trade agreements, the need to deal with both the EC level and the national level in the US–EC arena, and particularly the extent to which the issue became one of threat, counter-threat and sanctions. In the case of standards, testing and certification, there is considerable evidence of institutional innovation, but with very different implications. As noted above, the role of the Department of Commerce was central in the executive. From an early stage, Commerce assumed responsibility for information, advice and liaison among the wide variety of public and private interests engaged in the process. It had the position from which to do so, given its historic concern with such issues at the national level and its involvement in the relevant international bodies.

This meant that from the outset the Department of Commerce was the focus of institutional innovation in the executive. The National Institute for Standards and Technology (NIST) developed initiatives through which private-sector firms could be informed and it also worked closely with other federal and private-sector agencies to evaluate the product of the EC's standards development process.[38] In the context of the inter-agency task force on EC-92, Commerce chaired the working group on standards development, testing and certification, and its links with the private sector were enhanced by the President's Advisory Committee for Trade Policy and Negotiations, which also dealt with GATT-related issues. During 1990, the department established the Federal Advisory Committee on the EC Common Approach to Standards, Testing and Certification in 1992, which institutionalized access for private-sector interests to the executive machine.[39]

Commerce was also able to establish a presence in the US Mission to the EC in Brussels, which had been denied to it previously, partly on the basis of increasing demand for its services from both state governments and the private sector.[40] Once established, its representatives were able to work with and monitor the EC's process and to brief groupings both at home and in the EC. Thus, in addition to its growing role domestically, the department had extended its international network. When this is put alongside its involvement with the international standards community, either through NIST or in conjunction with ANSI, it is clear that the response to EC-92 was only a part of a broader Commerce deepening of its engagement in the world arena.

The evidence thus suggests that for the executive, the case of public procurement was largely processed through the established trade policy machinery. This did not mean that new agendas were irrelevant, since this executive response was conditioned, as we have seen, both by private sector pressures and by the need to deal with sub-federal government. But the overall pattern indicates a persistence of executive dominance and of the USTR's role as trade negotiator. In the case of standards, testing and certification, there is a far more dynamic and innovative picture, in which the dynamism of the EC's process is paralleled by policy development and institutional change in Washington and Brussels, and in which private sector forces play a major role. We shall return to a number of these conclusions in the following sections.

Congress: absent at the feast?

In Chapter 4, we discussed the ways in which the SMP impacted upon Congress, and identified four particular characteristics which gave it a specific flavour: its lack of traditional trade policy legislation, the ways in which directives came to the attention of Congress, the complexity of the technical details attending the programme and the fact that Congress depended upon pressure from firms to engage itself with the SMP process. We argued that this led to a reactive rather than a proactive response on the part of Congress, and that the legislature acted as a mediator rather than an initiator of policy.[41] The evidence from the two case study areas supports this set of arguments, and leads to important questions about legislative oversight in such areas of policy.

One function performed by Congress – although not exclusively – was the gathering of information and the commissioning of studies on the impact of the SMP. Thus, the public procurement issue was covered in a series of studies by the International Trade Commission, which also covered a range of other aspects of the SMP.[42] A series of hearings by Congressional subcommittees interested in the SMP also identified public procurement and the related issues of national content and rules of origin as a focus for their attention, while the Congressional Research Service was also active in producing assessments of the problem.[43] In the same way, although with a much more consistent focus, the standards, testing and certification issue came before Congress on a number of occasions. The Office of Technology Assessment in March 1992 produced a substantial study of global standards issues, including those raised by the SMP, and the Congressional Research Service also fed the debate.[44]

It is clear that the Congress was more inclined to give its attention to the standards, testing and certification problem, and that this reflected a number of factors. One was the perceived stakes for the US economy, both in the EC context and in the broader global political economy. A second was the nature of the EC policy process itself, which was seen as obscure and inaccessible to legitimate US interests. A third was the fact that in the US context there was no strong centralized procedure for pursuing interests in the standards area. As we have already seen, this contrasted with the perception in the public procurement field that the executive was the proper policy initiating body. By the same token, however, the trade policy aspects of both the public procurement and the standards issues fell squarely within the competence of the Congress. The 1988 Omnibus Trade and Competitiveness Act gave considerable attention to unfair trade practices, among which featured regulatory policies such as public procurement and standards setting. One of the key sectors in which these concerns came together, as indicated earlier, was that of telecommunications. Congress, having legislated the deregulation and deconcentration of the US telecommunications industry during the early 1980s, was anxious to see equivalent deregulation in the EC, which was seen as a prime target for the newly liberated 'Baby Bell' companies; the 1988 Act contained explicit provision for reciprocity in this area with any or all of the USA's trading partners.[45]

With these solid grounds for concern on the part of Congress, it is all
the more noteworthy that the legislature played very little public part in
the development of US positions in either of the case study areas. In the
case of public procurement, it can be argued that the legislative
framework and the trade policy instruments were in place, and that the
self-evident concern of the executive to ensure that the EC played the
game was sufficient reassurance; since the executive was assertive,
Congress had little opportunity to insert itself. In the case of standards,
testing and certification, the domestic concerns of Congress were amply
taken on board by the Department of Commerce, and the ways in which
they were pursued as part of broader competitiveness policy meant that
they were also not a matter of dispute. Congress did concern itself openly
with standards, at the stage when executive policy was still being formed:
the calls by Sam Gejdenson for a seat at the EC table were answered by
the same call from the Department of Commerce, and, as we have seen,
the issue was handled through quiet diplomacy and networking rather
than through confrontation. If specific regional or local interests were
affected in either area, Congress was often less able effectively to handle
them than were state authorities, the regional offices of the Department of
Commerce or trade associations such as the National Association of
Manufacturers.[46]

The states: subnational and transnational concerns

It is evident from many parts of the discussion in this book that state
governments – and at times municipal authorities in the USA – had clear
and direct interests in issues of both public procurement and standards,
testing and certification. In general, they had a concern for the fate of
exporters based in their territories and for the fortunes of investors who
had strong regional links. More specifically, they had an important role as
part of the governance and government structures in the USA. In public
procurement, as already noted, many of the most significant areas of 'buy-
American' policy were to be found at state or municipal level; thus, if
there were to be negotiations about this regime, the states and
municipalities would become involved whether they liked it or not.[47]
The EC was not slow to point out these features in its annual survey of
barriers to trade in the USA.[48] As for standards, much of the testing and
certification machinery in the private sector had inescapable links with
state or municipal regulatory structures, and this meant that policy
development in this area also had important regional or local
resonances.[49]

Although they were thus engaged in the policy process in a broad sense,
sub-federal authorities in the United States were in many ways marginal to

the transatlantic policy process. Their concerns were twofold: first, to promote 'their' industries in the EC and to protect them at home; second, to shape trade policy developments at the federal level when these promised or threatened to impact upon their economic development objectives. In pursuit of these aims, much of the early activity of the states in relation to EC-92 was in the area of information and education (see Chapter 5); as part of this, attention was paid both to issues of public procurement and to questions of standards, testing and certification. The state offices in Brussels or other EC locations played their role in providing information or in guiding local or regional concerns through the EC process, but, as noted above, they were often matched by trade associations with their sharper sectoral focus.

To this extent, the impact of EC-92 on state governments was not qualitative but quantitative, increasing the numbers pursuing export promotion or investment promotion. But there were a few key junctures at which state governments came into the explicitly political arena. The most obvious relates to public procurement. During 1992, there was increasing pressure on and among state authorities to reassess their 'buy-American' rules, and this came into a close relationship with the development of US–EC relations in this area. Indeed, the states and municipalities were a vital part of any solution to the problem, given that any effective bargaining at central government level had to be conditioned by the need to achieve assent and implementation at the sub-federal level. During 1992, the USTR requested a re-evaluation of the 'buy-American' acts, and in the autumn the National Governors Association passed a (non-binding) resolution asking that these practices be made subject to the GATT Government Procurement Code.[50]

This meant that when the Memorandum of Understanding was agreed in April 1993, there was already on the sub-federal agenda a good deal of concern with the future of public procurement. The issue was intensified by the progress in 1993 towards a revision of the GATT Agreement, which, as we have seen, came into close relationship with the US–EC diplomacy in the area. State governors and municipal leaders were thus put in the position of having to assent to agreements reached in the transatlantic or the multilateral arenas; many of them showed willing, but the response was not instantaneous or complete.

While in the area of public procurement state and municipal authorities had a material if subordinate role, in the area of standards, testing and certification their involvement was even more marginal. The development of a dialogue at the transatlantic level was primarily focused on the interaction of federal and business interests, with a strong element of transnational networking among standards agencies within the global regime. This left little space for the sub-federal authorities, except insofar as their local regulations imposed different standards on goods or services from those agreed at the US–EC or the broader level. Where this was so, it is clear that the state or municipal agencies acted more as transmission belts than as policy initiators or shapers.

US business: networking and negotiation

Chapter 6 identified not only the depth but also the range of involvement and interests characteristic of US business and the SMP. US firms are perhaps the key illustration of the ways in which the SMP evoked differentiated and sectorally specific responses on the part of the USA; as might be expected, these firms generated a wide range of responses, both in terms of the strategies they adopted and in terms of the networks within which they operated. It is also clear, as demonstrated in the earlier parts of this chapter, that US firms had key interests in the two case study areas, public procurement and standards, testing and certification. The stakes were high, and these were defined not only in terms of the firm: whole industries, many of them expanding and dynamic and many of them with global implications, were at issue. The two issues often also came together to provide a linked challenge; for example, in telecommunications or in pharmaceuticals and medical equipment.

This said, it is clear that for many of the 'European' US firms the SMP came as far less of a surprise than it did to those based at home, or to the various levels of the US government. For years if not decades they had been attempting to penetrate national policies in the EC member states, some of them with formidable closed shops in the areas of public purchasing and others with powerful and often competing national standards organizations. It was natural for many of these large and well established firms to see the SMP as operating in their favour, by attacking the cosy relationships between national utilities and favoured suppliers or by breaking down the competing national standards empires. The EC's attempt to create a level playing field in the Single Market could thus be seen (and was seen by many wary EC firms) as favouring the US multinationals, which knew how these things operated on a continental scale and could be better placed to reap the benefits.

As we have also seen, however, there were other parts of US business which were less well prepared and whose market intelligence was imperfect, to say the least. There were also important variations between both the positions and the interests of 'Europeans', 'investors' and 'exporters' which had implications for the general thrust of their policies (see Chapter 6). One of the tests of the US business response was to be the extent to which these different interests could be reconciled and linked with the services provided by the US government, in particular the executive branch, when they were required. Business, unlike many parts of government, was confronted with the daily challenge of organising to deal with the evolving and fluid EC regimes in the two case study areas. As a result, it was to be expected that its response would be pragmatic and flexible, guided by corporate strategy objectives rather than by any sense of US national needs.[51]

It is at this point that one can discern important differences of emphasis between the responses of US firms to the public procurement and standards issues. On the one hand, even those US companies long located in Europe had had problems dealing with the 'insiderness' required for effective access to public procurement markets. The opening up of these markets, therefore, created potential problems even for the biggest and the best organized; and the Utilities Directive provisions on local content and price differentials meant that many 'European' US companies could still find themselves on the wrong end of the result (see above). Exporters from the USA, or those trying to invest in local production for these historically protected markets, had equal problems. Thus it was logical even for those well established in the EC to call for the intervention of the federal government, which had the potential to wield the big stick against the EC. Where there were large corporations newly entering dynamic markets, such as AT&T in the EC telecommunications market, there was a need to enlist the flag alongside the trade associations and the lobbyists to ensure that the playing field remained relatively level.

In the case of standards, testing and certification, it was not so clear that US firms needed the US government. Equally, they needed to be alert to the culture of the EC standards-setting process and able to respond to it. An example is furnished by AMSCO International Inc, a corporation based in Pittsburgh, which had traditionally exported its medical equipment not so much to the EC as to the Middle and Far East. After initial uncertainties, AMSCO decided to immerse itself in the European process and to become involved in the relevant technical committees. By the time it did so, it was made aware very quickly that the process moved very slowly and on the basis of traditional EC practices. This was not an intentional manifestation of a 'Fortress Europe' policy; rather, it reflected the conservative nature of EC business elites faced with the newly dynamic market.[52]

What is of interest here is not simply the problem faced by AMSCO, but also the response it adopted. Faced with conservative inertia in the EC, they decided to go global – in other words, to try to use the ISO to generate international standards that would then shape the EC debate. Thus, in 1990, at the instigation of ANSI and with the support of the US Association for the Advancement of Medical Instrumentation, the ISO convened discussions of global sterilization standards. The aim was to achieve an 'end-run' around the EC process and thus to change the terms in which the race for the global standard was conducted. The lesson, though, was not just in terms of the EC process; in the course of this episode, US corporations became far more inclined to use the ISO as a standards generator, rather than simply insisting on the superiority of standards generated in the US context. They also realized that multiple strategies using the Department of Commerce, ANSI and other channels to access the EC process could pay dividends, not only in the setting of standards but also in the accreditation of testing and certification procedures.[53] In Brussels, the newly established ANSI office occupied rooms next door to the EC Committee of the American Chamber of Commerce – a significant juxtaposition.

The process of network extension visible in this and other standards cases is not as evident in the public procurement domain. Here, the protagonists tended to be not technical institutes and firms, but national authorities, sub-federal authorities and firms in the role (implicit or explicit) of 'national champions'. Such was certainly seen to be the case for US firms in the telecommunications sector, as illustrated by the efforts made by AT&T to gain access. Its first attempt, joining forces with Philips to try to gain control of the French company CGCT, was thwarted by a variety of administrative factors, mainly at the national level. Only when it joined forces with Olivetti to gain access to the Italian system, and thereby to establish itself as a European operator, was it able to claim any success; but increasingly as the Single Market opened up and the telecommunications sector globalized, US companies were able to gain important presence in all national markets. This did not altogether relieve the pressure in Congress for legislation enjoining reciprocity on non-US producers, on the basis that the US market was the most open in the world and that everyone else must in some way or another be playing the game unfairly.

In the power generating equipment sector there was an intense sharing of interests by the US government, specifically the USTR, and the large manufacturers such as GE. It was thus no accident that the Memorandum of Understanding of April 1993 focused on this area; it was here that the confluence of interests, bargaining power and control over the market was at its greatest. Even in the USA, the peculiar status of the Tennessee Valley Authority and the Department of Energy's undertakings meant that intergovernmental agreement could deliver the goods. In standards, the diffusion of access and leverage meant that outcomes were much less predictable.

In both the areas under study, there was a prominent role for trade associations and business networks, both at the industry level and across sectors. Within the USA, the NAM conducted an exhaustive campaign to alert US companies to the issues in public procurement and standards. With respect to procurement, the emergence of the Utilities Directive led the NAM to undertake a sustained lobbying campaign, both on its own account and in conjunction with the AmCham and the US Council for

International Business. This campaign was conducted not only in Brussels, and specifically in relation to the Commission, but also in Washington, with the aim of influencing the position of the USTR. When much later in the public procurement dispute there was a need to ensure movement at the sub-federal level in accordance with the Memorandum of Understanding, the NAM was active here too, lobbying state and municipal authorities and reminding the USTR of the need to be realistic in its demands.[54]

The NAM was also to be found informing, lobbying and advising in the standards domain. In Congress, its representatives gave evidence and argued consistently for an industry-based approach to the problems encountered; they also exploited close links with the Department of Commerce to bring about the kind of networked collaboration which was appropriate to the area. When the EC produced its Green Paper in December 1990, the NAM was again to be found clarifying the position. In Brussels, meanwhile, the AmCham was pursuing an energetic campaign to ensure access for US interests to the EC process, with considerable success. While many of the more specific measures were dealt with at the industry level, it is clear that these operations by peak associations were effective both in gaining access to the standards setting process and in reminding potentially troublesome groups in the USA of their interest in a constructive outcome.

The net result of these efforts was greatly to enhance the sensitivity of US policy responses, both in the sense of government policy and in the sense of business strategies. Secretary of Commerce Mosbacher admitted that the success of his campaign to enhance US access to the EC standards process was owing 'in large part to the Secretary's consultation of and reliance on the US private sector standards and business communities in addressing the implications of incompatible standards and pursuing remedies'.[55] While this gave the US government a significant role at the level of regime formation and the diplomatic framework, it is clear, particularly in the case of standards, that the framing of specific measures was almost entirely the preserve of firms and of specialist associations, which had increasingly effective access to the EC process. This supports the arguments made earlier in this chapter and in the book that business networks could adopt a variety of access strategies, and that government was often marginal to the ways in which those strategies were designed or operated in specific sectors. Some caveats must be entered, though: it is clear that the more distant firms were from the EC market, the more they could see a use for both ANSI and the various programmes operated by the Department of Commerce. This fits with the earlier argument that there are important distinctions to be made between firms on the grounds of size, structure, location, sector and history of involvement with the EC (see Chapter 6).

In general, therefore, it appears that the roles, interests and strategies characteristic of US business in relation to public procurement and standards, testing and certification bear out many of the general conclusions reached in Chapter 6. It is equally clear, though, that there are important areas of variation between the two cases and within them. At the level of the cases, the public procurement issue saw business adopting an explicitly government-oriented position, looking to the executive for diplomatic support in regime formation and informing government at all levels of the ways in which it actions impacted on the interests of business. Standards, on the other hand, demonstrated a much greater diffusion of attention and leverage, with a range of strategies available and the potential for business to link levels; for example, between the USA, the EC and the global arenas. Within the cases, there is much support for the contention that business networks and business strategies demonstrate diversity and specificity, with the key elements being the nature of the businesses' existing involvement with the EC machine, their sectoral focus and their business structure, including size and location.

Conclusion

At the beginning of this chapter, a pair of general propositions was advanced. It was contended that there were two visible tendencies in the ways in which different US actors approached the SMP, and interacted with respect to it.

- First, there was a tendency centring on the importance of *position, power, control and bargaining*, which corresponds largely to traditional notions of foreign economic policy.
- Second, there was a tendency centring on *process, leverage, access and networking*, which goes beyond the notion of foreign economic policy to identify forms of multilevel negotiation in a complex policy arena.

While it was not contended that these tendencies were mutually exclusive, it was argued that they would be found in different balances in different domains of the US–EC relationship, and that the SMP in general would dictate a shift from the first to the second in US policy, because of both its focus on new international economic agendas and its association with policy innovation in the EC itself. How far is this borne out by the evidence?

It seems clear that neither of the cases precisely fits the template provided by the qualities outlined above, but it seems equally clear that each occupies a different point on the spectrum defined by the two sets of tendencies. In brief, the case of public procurement tends towards the end of the spectrum which might be labelled 'foreign economic policy': there is evidence of strong state involvement, with a focus on position, on the mobilization of power and on the use of bargaining, with some coercive features, to gain control over the situation and over outcomes. But this is only part of the story. Public procurement also engages the participation of both sub-central government and private corporations, which occupy crucial positions in the bargaining context, and who have at least some power over outcomes. In order to produce results, there was also a need to go beyond arm's-length diplomacy and to engage with domestic structures in the public procurement issue area. In addition, there was a strong linkage between domestic structures, governmental action and the multilateral trade regime in the shape of the GATT. Thus, although the case tends towards the foreign economic policy end of the spectrum in some ways, in others it has strong elements of multilevel diplomacy and a focus on access, process, leverage and networking across levels.

In the case of standards, testing and certification, the initial conclusion must be that it sits well towards the end of the spectrum characterized by process, leverage, access and networking. The role of government in many ways was itself a networking role, with agencies building linkages between both governmental and non-governmental actors and using a wide range of institutional and informational resources. Alongside government, though, and in many ways more prominent than government, went the non-governmental networks of business and technical interests, which at anything other than the broadest regime-shaping level had a determining influence. The ways in which business networks could make themselves felt and shape the agenda were many and various, reflecting themselves the diversity of needs, interests and resources highlighted in Chapter 6. The roles of Congress and sub-federal government are less prominent here, with the emphasis firmly on the specialized agencies of government and their interaction in an institutionalized environment with technical and business participants.

Given these different patterns of participation and influence, it is not surprising that the two issues followed the path that they did within the broad context of US–EC relations. What is clear, though, is that the assumption of governmental predominance and control in both areas is subject to question, with the emphasis being rather on institutional innovation, interaction and communication as means of achieving preferred outcomes. This is broadly what would be expected in a situation of multilevel diplomacy, and it is to be expected that it would be replicated, albeit with distinct sectoral variations, in other areas of US policy towards the SMP. The argument would also suggest that in such areas there would be examples of the kinds of learning process which were central to the ways in which both case study areas developed and were managed during the late 1980s and early 1990s. Besides equipping themselves to play roles and fulfil functions within the US–EC arena, participants learned to adapt, adjust and mobilize new resources as they proceeded. This does not mean that the process was unproblematic and free of tensions or conflicts; it does mean that for all participants in policy arenas characterized by multilevel interactions, the capacity to learn and to innovate is perhaps the most important of all.

Notes and references

1   See, for example, D. R. Cameron, 'The 1992 initiative: causes and consequences', in A. Sbragia (ed.), *Euro-politics: Institutions and Policymaking in the 'New' European Community*, Washington, DC, Brookings Institution, 1992, Chapter 2; R. O. Keohane and S. Hoffmann, 'Institutional change in Europe in the 1980s', in R. O. Keohane and S. Hoffmann (eds), *The New European Community: Decisionmaking and Institutional Change*, Boulder, CO, Westview Press, 1991, Chapter 1.

2   This point is made in a number of the general studies. See, for example, M. Calingaert, *The 1992 Challenge from Europe: Development of the European Community's Internal Market*, Washington, DC, National Planning Association, 1988; G. C. Hufbauer (ed.), *Europe 1992: An American Perspective*, Washington, DC, Brookings Institution, 1990; US House of Representatives, Committee on Foreign Affairs, *Europe and the United States: Competition and Cooperation in the 1990s*, Washington, DC, US Government Printing Office, 1992.

3   See S. Woolcock, *Market Access Issues in EC–US Trade Relations: Trading Partners or Trading Blows?*, London, Pinter for the Royal Institute of International Affairs, 1991, pp. 97–9; M. Egan, ' "Associative regulation" in the European Community: the case of technical standards', paper presented at the Second Biennial Conference of the European Community Studies Association, Washington, DC, May 1991.

4   S. Anderssen and K. Eliasson (eds), *Making Policy in Europe: the Europeification of National Policy-making*, London, Sage, 1993.

5   US Congress, International Trade Commission, *The Effects of Greater Economic Integration Within the European Community on the United States*, USITC Publication 2204, Washington, DC, US Government Printing Office, July 1989, pp. 5–7. See also Woolcock, *Market Access Issues*, p. 83. Woolcock is the best concise treatment of both the public procurement and the standards, testing and certification issues up to 1991.

6   Commission of the European Communities, *Research on the Costs of 'Non-Europe'*, Brussels, Commission of the European Communities, 1988, vol. 1, pp. 333–5.
7   See Woolcock, *Market Access Issues*, pp. 79–85.
8   See A. Cox and J. Sanderson, 'From the mobilisation of bias to trade wars: the making and implementation of the European Community utilities procurement rules', *Journal of European Public Policy*, 1(2), 1994, pp. 263–82. For details of the various directives and of US reactions, see G. Harrison, *The EC's Government Procurement Directive: has 'Fortress Europe' Arrived?*, CRS Report for Congress, Washington, DC, Congressional Research Service, April 1993.
9   'Public procurement: brought low', *The Economist*, 27 February 1993, pp. 82–4.
10 See Hufbauer, *Europe 1992: An American Perspective*, pp. 41–4; Calingaert, *The 1992 Challenge from Europe*, Chapter 9; D. Mayes (ed.), *The External Implications of European Integration*, Hemel Hempstead, Harvester-Wheatsheaf, 1993, pp. 105–6.
11 See Woolcock, *Market Access Issues*, pp. 83–6; P. Cowhey, 'Telecommunications', in Hufbauer, *Europe 1992: An American Perspective*, Chapter 5, pp. 225–92.
12 See R. Schwok, *US–EC Relations in the Post-Cold War Era: Conflict or Partnership?*, Boulder, CO: Westview Press, 1991; M. Smith and S. Woolcock, *The United States and the European Community in a Transformed World*, London, Pinter for the Royal Institute of International Affairs, 1993.
13 Woolcock, *Market Access Issues* pp. 86–90; R. J. Ahearn, 'US access to the EC-92 market: opportunities, concerns, and policy challenges', in US House of Representatives, *Europe and the United States*, pp. 177–92; S. Cooney, *Europe After 1992: Boom or Bust?*, Washington, DC, National Association of Manufacturers, June 1993.
14 See S. Woolcock, 'The European acquis and multilateral trade rules: are they compatible?', *Journal of Common Market Studies*, 31(4), 1993, pp. 539–58.
15 Harrison, *The EC's Public Purchasing Directive*.
16 'US, Europe reach partial settlement', *Washington Post*, 22 April 1993; 'EC and US reach partial pact', *New York Times*, 22 April 1993.
17 'US, Germany reach deal on contracts, shun sanctions', *Journal of Commerce*, 11 June 1993; see also *Inside US Trade*, 11 June 1993.
18 J. Wolf, *Wall Street Journal*, 24 October 1993. See also D. Dodwell, 'GATT fears ease over procurement hurdle', *Financial Times*, 26 October 1993.
19 D. Dodwell, 'Government contracts to be opened up', *Financial Times*, 19 December 1993, p. 2.

20   M. Lindemann, 'German government contracts deal opposed', *Financial Times*, 3 July 1996, p. 2.

21   Commission of the European Communities, *Research on the Costs of 'Non-Europe'*, vol. 1, Chapter 10.

22   M. Calingaert, *The 1992 Challenge from Europe*, Chapter 8; Hufbauer, *Europe 1992: An American Perspective*, Chapter 1.

23   Woolcock, *Market Access Issues*.

24   Woolcock, *Market Access Issues*, pp. 92–4; Calingaert, *The 1992 Challenge from Europe*, Chapters 4 and 5; Hufbauer, *Europe 1992: An American Perspective*, Chapter 1.

25   See, for example, W. S. Mossberg, 'As EC markets unite, US exporters face new trade barriers', *Wall Street Journal*, 19 January 1989.

26   Woolcock, *Market Access Issues*, pp. 101–4; Hufbauer, *Europe 1992: An American Perspective*, pp. 367–9; Calingaert, *The 1992 Challenge from Europe*, pp. 91–2; Mayes, *The External Implications of European Integration*.

27   Interviews, AmCham, Brussels, February 1994.

28   S. Cooney, *Europe after 1992: Boom or Bust?*; V. Kendall, 'Current problems in technical harmonisation', *European Trends*, 3/1993, p. 75.

29   Cooney, *Europe after 1992: Boom or Bust?*; Kendall, 'Current problems in technical harmonisation'; T. Duesterberg, 'Federal government responses to the EC 1992 challenge in standards, testing and certification', *Business America*, 24 February 1992, p. 6.

30   Duesterberg, 'Federal government responses'; Kendall, 'Current problems of technical harmonisation'; Cooney, *Europe After 1992: Boom or Bust?*

31   Woolcock, *Market Access Issues*, p. 108. Efforts were made to produce codes of good practice for application at the sub-central level.

32   Duesterberg, 'Federal government responses'; Cooney, *Europe After 1992*.

33   Kendall, 'Current problems in technical harmonisation', p. 65.

34   *Ibid.*; F. Williams, 'Uruguay deal boosts world standardisation', *Financial Times*, 4 February 1994, p. 5.

35   Interviews, Brussels, April 1994; Woolcock, *Market Access Issues*, Chapter 2.

36   M. Smith and S. Woolcock, 'Learning to cooperate: the Clinton administration and the European Union', *International Affairs*, 70(3), 1994, pp. 459–76.

37   See Chapter 3, pp. 57–66.

38   Duesterberg, 'Federal government responses', p. 6; Interview, Center for Strategic and International Studies, Washington DC, April 1994.

39   K. B. Bonine, 'US 1992: how the US government is preparing for the Single Market', *Europe*, April 1990, pp. 14–17.

40   Interviews, US Mission to the European Communities, Brussels, March 1994.

41   See Chapter 4, pp. 81–91.

42   US Congress, International Trade Commission, *The Effects of Greater Economic Integration within the European Community on the United States; Fifth Follow-up Report*, Washington DC, USITC Publication 2628, 1993, Chapter 4 (standards, testing and certification) and Chapter 5 (public procurement).

43   Harrison, *The EC's Government Procurement Directive: Has 'Fortress Europe' Arrived?*

44   US Congress, Office of Technology Assessment, *Global Standards: Building Blocks of the Future*, Washington, DC, US Government Printing Office, March 1992; Lennard G. Kruger, 'EC standards and conformity assessment', in US House of Representatives, Committee on Foreign Affairs, *Europe and the United States: Competition and Cooperation in the 1990s*, pp. 293–309.

45   P. Cowhey, 'Telecommunications', in Hufbauer, *Europe 1992: An American Perspective*, Chapter 5; Calingaert, *The 1992 Challenge from Europe*, Chapters 8–9.

46   See below, pp. 173–5.

47   Woolcock, *Market Access Issues*, pp. 112–13.

48   See, for example, Commission of the European Communities, *Report on United States Trade and Investment Barriers, 1993: Problems of Doing Business with the US*, Brussels, Commission of the European Communities, April 1993, pp. 27–34.

49   Commission of the European Communities, *Report on United States Trade and Investment Barriers 1993*, pp. 55–63.

50   *Inside US Trade*, 5 July 1991.

51   On corporate responses see S. Dryden, 'Europeanising US Business', *Europe*, September 1990, pp. 13–14; R. Guttman, 'Doing business in 1990s Europe', *Europe*, September 1990, pp. 16–19. For a more general treatment, see J. Greenwood (ed.), *European Casebook on Business Alliances*, London, Prentice Hall, 1995; C. Egan and P. McKiernan, *Inside Fortress Europe: Strategies for the Single Market*, London, Addison-Wesley/Economist Intelligence Unit, 1994.

52   J. Burgess, 'Competing in a diverse market: US firms seek unity on product standards in Europe', *Washington Post*, 2 December 1991, pp. A1/A6.

53   Burgess, 'Competing in a diverse market'.

54   Bonine, 'US 1992: how the US government is preparing for the Single Market'.

55   Duesterberg, 'Federal government responses', p. 6.

8

Conclusions

At the beginning of this book, two interrelated aims were set out: first, to investigate the nature of foreign economic policy in the world of the 1990s; second, to explore the shaping of foreign economic policy in the context of a recent and highly significant set of events, the US response to the Single European Market. The book has pursued the two aims in a number of stages. First, it developed a view of the changing nature of foreign economic policy, of the context in which the USA faced the challenge from the Single Market Programme and of the most challenging characteristics of the SMP. Second, it took a number of slices from the concept of 'the United States', by taking apart the key levels of action and policy formation: the federal executive, the Congress, state governments and firms. Finally, the book applied the arguments derived from both the general context and the more specific dissection of US policy formation to the analysis of two case studies, those of public procurement and standards, testing and certification.

In a sense, therefore, the process of the book has been first to take policy apart and then to reassemble it in relation to the case studies. Although there are many other procedures and focuses that might have been adopted, this one has the merit of delineating clearly the questions and paths of analysis which are suggested by each of the steps. The task of this conclusion is to revisit the starting point of the process, and to deal in a systematic way with the questions raised and the answers suggested by each of the intervening chapters. This will make possible a judgement on the two central issues noted above: the nature of the US response to the SMP and the changing nature of foreign economic policy more generally. It will also lead to some suggestions about the current agenda of US–EU relations insofar as it constitutes a continuation of the process dealt with in the book.

Revisiting foreign economic policy

In Chapters 1 and 2, it was argued that the analysis of foreign economic policy in the 1990s carried with it a set of important analytical concerns, arising from the changing nature of statehood and the world political economy. To summarize, those concerns were: the importance of 'boundary problems', between foreign policy and foreign economic policy and within the domain of foreign economic policy itself; the emergence of multilayered policy milieus in which networks of governmental and non-governmental actors were implicated; the generation of novel policy processes in which the objectives, methods and interactions of participants posed new demands; and the overlapping pressures of change and differentiation which surrounded the attempt to produce coherent strategies. These four areas of analytical concern, of course, also refer to areas of substantive concern for policy-makers, whoever or whatever they represent.

The analytical and policy concerns arising from the four tendencies outlined above were focused in a concentrated yet wide-ranging form by the emergence of the SMP: a complex and demanding process of policy innovation and institutional change in an arena where the stakes for the USA were (and remain) at the core of its national welfare. But at the same time that the SMP posed a national challenge, it also posed a challenge differentiated sharply in terms of its impact and implications for different parts of the US political economy. The argument in Chapters 3 to 7 has attempted to identify the ways in which the challenge made itself felt for different groups of Americans, and also to chart the ways in which those groups and institutions representing them responded. As a result, it is possible to draw some conclusions about the four analytical concerns set out above: 'boundary problems', multilayered policy milieus, policy processes and the pressures of change and differentiation.

'Boundary problems'

The first area of analytical and policy concern outlined in Chapter 1 was the ways in which boundaries have been challenged by developments in the world political economy during the 1990s. At one level, these boundaries are those between foreign policy and foreign economic policy: has the balance between economics and security remained the same in the 1990s as it was historically assumed to be, particularly during the Cold War? The evidence gathered here suggests that there is considerable force to interpretations focused on the increasing salience of economic and welfare issues. The American concern with national economic security, and the European desire to establish competitive advantage through the unification of the market, appear at many junctures to have interacted to create tension and misunderstanding. These tensions and misunderstandings were given added force by the broader systemic development of the world political economy, in which the USA was seen by many as an ailing if still dominant power. The federal executive undoubtedly placed the SMP in the context of intercontinental competition, and was concerned to impress on the EC that it was watching for adverse effects. Some arguments would go further, to place the US response to the SMP in the context of a nascent 'world of blocs', in which the major economic groupings would engage in a struggle for world market share and competitive advantage.

This is a neo-mercantilist view of the US response to the SMP, and although there is some evidence from the research that this was a significant thread – both rhetorical and substantive – in US policy formation, there is also strong evidence that this thread was woven into a much broader picture of interdependence and interpenetration. That is to say, the salience of foreign economic policy and of the SMP in particular did not represent a situation in which foreign economic policy had *become identical to* foreign policy. There are two specific lines of argument which are important here. First, as pointed out at many stages of the argument, the policy process in the USA in response to the SMP was quite strongly fragmented and diffused. At different stages of the response, different institutions, agencies and groupings played different roles. The priorities were not set in accordance with some supposed national strategy; rather, they drew upon the insights and inputs of many different participants. The federal executive could and did play an important role in connecting up the parts of the response, and in presenting the concerns of significant US groupings. But the executive itself was often faced with problems of coordination and of policy design, given the differential impact of the SMP on important 'customers' for its policies. Such 'customers' were represented at several points in the process, through Congressional pressures, through subnational governments in the form of the states and through corporate channels. As a result, the executive faced problems of both a conceptual and a procedural nature in framing its actions.

A second line of argument qualifying the neo-mercantilist view of US responses to the SMP can be termed the 'reassertion of foreign policy'. As argued in Chapter 3, although at times in the late 1980s it appeared that foreign policy could be reduced to foreign economic policy, this was an illusion. The events of 1989 and thereafter in Europe produced a dramatic refocusing of executive attention on the high politics of the post-Cold War era, and thus put the SMP in a very different context. Thus, as the Bush administration in particular framed its response to the SMP, it was shaped inexorably by the new political priorities of the 1990s. In many ways, the same could be said of the Clinton administration, despite the 1992 campaign rhetoric of economic priorities and the espousal of avowedly domesticist aims. The reassertion of political and security internationalism was far from a foregone conclusion, but what it did do was to change the atmosphere in which the SMP was discussed and decisions were taken about US responses.

If there was a shifting boundary between foreign policy and foreign economic policy in US responses to the SMP, what can be said about the boundaries within the foreign economic policy domain? In Chapter 1, two such boundary problems were identified: the domestic–international divide and the public–private divide. On the one hand, it could be argued that foreign economic policy in the changing world political economy was eroding the boundaries not only between 'us' and 'them', between the national and the international level, but also the boundaries which had separated foreign economic policy-making from policy-making at the subnational or the local level. At the same time, it appeared that the growing influence of non-state groupings in the private domain would have important implications both for inputs into policy-making and for the ways in which policy was conducted.

The evidence from the research gives strong but not unqualified support for such arguments. It is clear that in examining US responses to the SMP, it is insufficient to present the notion of 'the US government' as monolithic, dominated by the executive at every stage. At important points in the framing of US responses, both Congress and state governments had important messages to convey, and these were not always conveyed through the federal executive. In the provision of information and the raising of awareness, although the executive played a key role, it was not the only actor on the stage. In the shaping of the policy agenda, likewise, the influence of Congressional and state authorities could be discerned. It has already been noted that on important aspects of the SMP, the executive itself had little in the way of a coherent or coordinated policy, at least in the early stages. There is considerable evidence that the inherently cross-national–cross-departmental nature of the SMP made the pursuit of any unified US governmental response quixotic. Yet it is also clear, not least from the case studies conducted in Chapter 7, that there were areas in which the executive was seen as the only possible actor: in particular, these were areas in which the exercise of a high diplomatic function was required, and areas where the broader international trade or other regimes were at issue.

The evidence for the erosion of boundaries between levels of government is considerable but not unqualified, and the same might be said of the ways in which the public–private boundaries operated to shape US responses to the SMP. At the level of the institutional and diplomatic framework, there is no doubt that central government retained a vital role: this much is clear, for example, from the diplomacy of public procurement, where there was a need for an intergovernmental accord (even if there were then severe limitations to the ability of both the USA and the EC to deliver subnational or sub-EC level actors). But at the level of operations within the framework, and the shaping of the agenda for governmental action, there was a central and consistent role for corporate and other private actors. To a degree, this was a function of the ways in which corporate actors were often involved across the apparent boundaries between the US arena and the EC arena, and this is an important finding in terms of what was earlier termed the growth of 'extranational policy-making' (see below). It was also a reflection of the fact that the presence, the experience and the expertise of the US firms in the Single Market was an important asset for US policy responses. To the extent that US government officials recognized this, gave it space to operate and allowed it to shape the US posture, it can be said that they showed the capacity to learn and adapt to the multilayered policy milieu. Where they did not, they were sometimes sharply reminded of their distance from the real world of firms' strategies and actions.

The multilayered milieu

It was argued in Chapter 1 that many aspects of foreign economic policy were profoundly influenced by the development of a multilayered policy milieu. Much of the argument about 'boundary problems' is intimately linked to such a view of the policy environment, and thus need not be repeated here. Three aspects of multilayered policy environments do demand attention, though, since they are crucial to an understanding of the effectiveness of policy responses. First, there is the issue of mutual dependency, in which a variety of governmental and non-governmental actors are bound together by perceptions of need and the practicalities of action. Second, there is the issue of scope, in which networks of mutual dependency can extend beyond the traditional boundaries of national policy-making. Finally, there is the question of strategy, in which the focus is on the relationship between broad frameworks for policy and the tactical demands imposed by involvement in specific sectors of activity.

On the first of these questions, the evidence is that US responses to the SMP showed important areas of mutual need between participants, and important variations according to the policy issues confronted. As noted above, the executive was indispensable to the framing of policy and the taking of action at the level of US–EC institutional exchanges, and this need was recognized by other participants. In many other areas, the situation was much more fluid, and depended upon the capacity to act of the particular constellations of forces involved. Here, the most important aspect of action by the US executive was either getting out of the way or acting as a catalyst to link together the aims and resources of a wide range of participants. Where action was desired within the EC institutions themselves and on particular sectoral concerns, there was often much more to be said for the influence of trade associations or of well established corporations, and this was recognized by many smaller US companies in their search for access.

The second significant aspect of multilayered policy environments in this part of the analysis is strongly connected with the boundary problems and with the situations of mutual dependence outlined above. Put simply, it is clear that much significant policy-making affecting US responses to the SMP went on not only outside the confines of the federal executive but also outside the USA itself. In a word, policy-making was often effectively extranational, with the major inputs coming from firms or other groupings operating in the Single Market, with their resultant expertise and information. Such an extension of policy-making did not detach it completely from the national base, since at many points it fed back into US policy processes and into the strategies of non-governmental groupings at home. But the institutional contexts that mattered, and the inputs that mattered, were distanced from the territory of the USA in what was termed in Chapter 1 a reticulated diplomatic milieu. This raises important issues of control and coordination in policy-making by both governmental and non-governmental actors. At times, the processes of control and coordination evaded the US federal government altogether, in ways recognized and usually accepted by Washington.

The third aspect of multilayered policy environments to be reviewed here is that of strategy itself. Implicit in the arguments made above is the conclusion that conceptions of national industrial or competitiveness strategies should be handled with particular care in a multilayered policy milieu. Networks of need and activity do not operate in a vacuum, and they are clearly influenced, as has been noted, by the agreements reached at the level of governmental diplomacy. But the attempt to go beyond recognition, sensitivity and awareness to the active coordination of strategies is one fraught with danger. The reality of the situation, as revealed especially in the case studies, is a process of continuous mutual adjustment among governmental and non-governmental actors, with an awareness of each others' needs and agendas. At times, this adjustment is bound to be less than smooth and efficient, as can be seen from the evidence relating to public procurement and standards, testing and certification. It is not detached from institutional frameworks and explicit rules of the game. But it is an iterative process, in which change at the level of the broad framework feeds into adjustments made among actors at the sectoral and even at the enterprise level. Such evidence might be used by some to argue against the possibility of strategy; the conclusion here is that sensitivity to the multilayered and reticulated character of policy settings is an integral element of effective strategy. Where this was demonstrated, in both case study areas and on both the European and the American 'sides', important progress could be made.

Novel policy processes

It was argued in Chapter 1 that the combination of 'boundary changes' and the related development of multilayered policy environments created the conditions for the emergence of new policy processes. To be specific, the contrast was drawn between policies focused on *access* and those focused on *control*: the first of these reflected the impact of the new conditions for foreign economic policy, while the second represented the residue of the traditional focus on sovereignty and territoriality in the formulation and pursuit of foreign economic policies.

From the evidence explored in Chapters 3 to 7, it seems clear that the challenge of the SMP raised important problems of both access and control. The SMP itself was at one and the same time a broad strategic programme and a mass of technical (but not politically insignificant) measures, covering a wide variety of sectors. Processes of decision-making and implementation in the EC were both complex and multilayered, so that it was difficult to identify the key points either for access or for the exertion of control. As a result, the many actors with an interest in the development of the EC's policies were led to explore new channels for access, and new agents through which to exercise leverage or control. Access to information, to the policy-making process and to the mechanisms of implementation was a key target for all of the actors concerned, and it was not to be found only in Brussels. In some cases, as noted in Chapters 6 and 7, access to the US government itself was not easy to establish; and control of the US government on occasions when it might have undertaken inappropriate escalation of disputes was a concern for a number of participants. What this implies is that even where control was attempted, it was not in the ways or even with the aims implied in traditional views of foreign economic policy.

On the basis both of the chapters dealing with US policy-making and of the case studies, it is possible to develop the distinction between policies of access and those of control into a broader contrast between two modes of policy-making and implementation (see Chapter 7). The first is based upon *process, leverage, access and networking*; the second, upon *position, power, control and bargaining*. Elements of both are present in the US response to the SMP, but the key question concerns the extent to which and the ways in which they vary between different policy settings. It is not sufficient to say that the more the processes take place at the level of intergovernmental 'high politics', the more they will conform to the pattern of traditional foreign economic policy. As has been demonstrated in several of the chapters, governments themselves are often much 'softer' and more characterized by permeability than might be imagined: they are challenged in particular by the development of widespread institutional innovation, as well as policy innovation of the kind represented by the

SMP. Agreements negotiated at the highest political level may require inputs from a wide variety of expert participants, and may require implementation not only by central government but also by sub-central and private mechanisms. Such was undoubtedly the case in US–EC dealings over public procurement. On other occasions, government itself may need to act rather as a pressure group and to base its policies not on confrontation but on the generation of dialogue and access at the expert level, as arguably occurred with issues of standards, testing and certification. It is also clear that government in Washington was itself penetrated and reshaped by many of the influences emanating from the Single Market (although not the Single Market alone).

This does not mean that the politics of position, power, control and bargaining are or were irrelevant to US foreign economic policies, and particularly to the ways in which the SMP was dealt with. Indeed, it is possible to point to important junctures at which the exercise of relatively traditional methods was not only necessary but also indispensable to a resolution. Even such methods, though, were deployed in changed circumstances. The tangled tale of sanctions against the EC in the crisis months of the public procurement dispute demonstrates the difficulties encountered. It also demonstrates the validity of questions about mutual need in multilayered policy environments: to what extent did US companies really need the federal government to impose sanctions, and to what extent did the growth of transnational alliances between US and EC companies render the notion of transatlantic confrontation redundant?

Such questions relate strongly to conceptions of international negotiation processes. If one possible product of a foreign economic policy based on process, leverage, access and networking is a kind of continuously negotiated order, does this bear out the arguments made in Chapter 1 about international negotiation as a form of management process, rather than as an expression of interstate rivalry? It is clear from the evidence that the US response to the SMP was strongly based on aspirations for negotiated order, but also that this was not seen as simply a neutral or technical state of affairs. In other words, the outcomes mattered, and they mattered a lot. They also mattered in different ways at different levels, ranging from the benefits of custodianship of the international institutional order to the profit and loss accounts of individual US firms. The stakeholders in this process of negotiated order may be different from those engaged in traditional interstate diplomacy, but the stakes are no less important for many groupings.

This means that there is much of interest in the ways in which individual bargains are reached and in the ways in which governmental and non-governmental participants can bring resources to bear on the shaping of these bargains. As noted in Chapter 1, the world political economy is increasingly an information-rich and a participant-rich environment; governments have not held the whip-hand in important areas for many years. This means that there is a premium for governments on active adjustment to changing contexts and on the manipulation of resources such as information or communication channels. The SMP posed this challenge in a concentrated form, and the evidence from this study shows the often patchy and halting ways in which the US government adjusted to the changing demands made upon it. The specific bargains reached in public procurement and in standards, testing and certification reflected not only the mutual needs and relative resources of the participants, but also the ways in which these could be mobilized or catalysed, partly but not wholly through government actions. The extent to which these bargains could be institutionalized, and integrated into a developing US–EC negotiated order, was also crucial not only to short-term gains and losses but also to long-term strategies.

The USA, the SMP and foreign economic policy

When we evaluate the ways in which the evidence supports the earlier arguments about foreign economic policy in the 1990s, it is clear that any answer will be in terms of trends and tendencies rather than absolutes. It can be strongly argued, on the evidence assembled here, that US responses to the SMP went (and had to go) well beyond traditional conceptions of foreign economic policy. They exhibited distinctive policy styles and policy problems, and they demonstrated a number of changing roles and functions, not only for government but also for other participants. Perhaps most importantly, they showed that a key feature of the contemporary world political economy is its dynamism and the consequent demand for constant mutual adjustment on the part of those involved in it. This leads to important implications for the further analysis of foreign economic policy.

One set of implications relates to policy style. US Presidents and administrations have typically placed a good deal of weight on the creation of distinctive and effective policy styles, partly for domestic electoral reasons. The evidence here shows that this is not a guaranteed route to success in foreign economic policy. The ability to conjure up appropriate mixes of policy styles and policy instruments, and to adjust them if and when circumstances require it, is a key to achievement in a multilayered policy environment, and many of the most important attributes may not be those that appear most dramatic on prime-time news.

A second set of implications relates to the role of government itself. International economic transactions are in many ways increasingly governed, but they are not always governed by national governments. This may seem a trite conclusion, but it goes to the heart of the functions of government in such cases as US–EC relations. The evidence examined here does not deny a strategic and even a coercive role for national governments in the world political economy, but it does point to the fact that government is not only a strategic actor. It can take the role of catalyst, bringing together those with an interest and with the expertise to make things happen. It can be seen not only as the monolithic expression of national interests but also as an expression of the 'active state' sensitive to demands and opportunities and to the mutual needs of those engaged in particular issues or sectors. In this guise, it can operate through or in conjunction with agents from a wide variety of sources, and speaking a wide variety of 'languages'.

Third, there is a set of implications for international negotiations. The evidence suggests that in the interactions between the USA and the EC over the SMP, there emerged a strong sense of the interaction between policy arenas, with US policy-makers concerned to respond to and to shape what was going on in the EC arena, and the EC sharing this concern with respect to the US arena. This was not present in all its facets at the start of the process; indeed, the process of learning was not always very smooth or productive in the short term. But it was a process of learning and of mutual adjustment. Not only this, but it encapsulated a role for governmental authorities which went beyond that of the traditional 'gatekeeper' or barrier between different arenas. Instead, it strengthened a tendency noted in Chapter 1 and earlier in these conclusions towards the extranationalization of foreign economic policy; that is to say, towards intervention in the 'domestic' milieu of others' policies in order to shape events at the international level. It might be argued that this has always happened in foreign economic policy. But it is clear that US–EC relations demonstrate the tendency in a consistent and institutionalized form, which goes beyond the rather static conceptions of government contained (for example) in the notion of 'two-level games'. Government, it appears, is soft and mobile as well as hard and permanent.

Finally, there are implications for the relationship between complex bilateral relations and the broader world arena. The focus in this study has been firmly on the US–EC relationship as concentrated by the SMP, but it is clear that broader political and economic factors must be built into the analysis. National political change in the shape of electoral politics and the electoral cycle is an issue, not only because governments may change but also because they need to learn, as evidenced by the experience of the Bush administration. The intersection of political change in one arena with the changes taking place in another (in this case, in the EC) is also a potent qualifying factor for many negotiation processes. Perhaps of even more importance, though, in the case of the USA and the SMP, is the impact of system change at the broader European and international levels. When the USA began to respond to the SMP, it was Cold War; when it finished, it was not. Not only this, but the institutional context of interactions within the world political economy had also undergone considerable change, with the conclusion of the Uruguay Round and the establishment of the WTO. As noted at many points in this study, the intersection of not only economic but also political and institutional change is central to the general course of US–EC relations, but also more specifically to the ways in which Americans approached the challenge of the Single Market.

The USA and the Single Market: towards the future

In a sense, this study is a historical one. It deals with an episode which could be said to have begun in 1985 and ended in 1993, and this has been its empirical focus. But it also contains broader messages about the nature of foreign economic policy, as explored above, and about the nature of relations between the USA and the EU. At the end of 1995, the USA and the EU agreed a New Transatlantic Agenda and a Transatlantic Action Plan, which covered a very wide variety of subjects. In many ways, these agreements could be seen as the logical outcome of many of the processes described in this study; they dealt with the need for networking and mutual recognition in the transatlantic arena, and they explicitly gave the governmental authorities in question a catalytic and facilitating role. Not only this, but they were paralleled by the establishment of a Transatlantic Business Dialogue, with the central aim of reinforcing and deepening the processes of consultation among major firms on both sides of the Atlantic.

This represents a further institutionalization of the process which has been described in this book; the creation of a multilayered and increasingly interpenetrated policy space in the Atlantic area, in which differences can be handled and mutual adjustment accomplished. While not extending to the fuller integration implied in a Transatlantic Free Trade Area, it establishes mechanisms through which interconnectedness can be managed without the abandonment of strategic government action. It is not without potential complications, given the uncertain impact of economic and monetary union in the EU and of regional initiatives in the American or the Asia-Pacific regions; and radical political developments in the wider Europe or the Middle East could shake it fundamentally. It does, however, provide a setting in which foreign economic policies of the kind described in this book might be fostered and furthered.

Bibliography

While not claiming to be an exhaustive list of US–EC relations during the period covered by the book, the bibliography lists the major sources used in preparing the study. In addition to these, we conducted approximately fifty interviews, the details of which are not listed here, mainly for reasons of confidentiality.

Documents

This section contains publications and papers from both governmental and private sector organizations.

Ahearn, R.J., *US Access to the EC Market: Opportunities, Concerns and Policy Challenges*, Washington, DC, Library of Congress, Congressional Research Service, 16 June 1992.

Bulletin of the European Communities (various, 1985–95).

Calingaert, M., *The 1992 Challenge from Europe: Development of the European Community's Internal Market*, Washington, DC, National Planning Association, 1988.

Commission of the European Communities (COEC), *Research on the Costs of Non-Europe: Volume 1, Basic Findings, Executive Summaries: Volume 5, The Costs of Non-Europe in public sector procurement,* Consultants in association with Eurequip SA, Roland Berger and Partner, Eurequip Italia, *Volume 6, Technical Barriers in the EC*, Groupe Mac. *Volume 16, The International Markets of North America. Fragmentation and Integration in the US and Canada*, J. Pelkmans in cooperation with Marc Vanheukelen, Brussels, 1988.

COEC, *Proposal for a Council Directive Relating to the Co-ordination of Procedures on the Award of Service Contracts*, Brussels, COM (90) 372, 1990.

COEC, *General Overview of EC/US Trade Relations*, Brussels, DG 1, Internal, 7 May 1991.

COEC, *Standardisation in the European Economy – Communication from the Commission*, Brussels, COM (91) 521 final, 16 December 1991.

COEC, *General Overview of US–EC Relations*, Brussels, DG 1, Internal, 3 July 1992.

COEC, *European Symposium – Auto Emissions 2000*, Brussels, 21 September 1992.

COEC, *Report from the Commission Concerning Negotiations Regarding Access to Third Countries' Markets in the Fields Covered by the Utilities Directive*, Brussels, COM (93) 80 final, 3 March 1993.

COEC, *Report on United States Trade and Investment Barriers – Problems of Doing Business with the US*, Brussels, April 1993.

Colgan, C.S., *Forging a New Partnership in Trade Policy between the Federal and State Governments*, Washington, DC, National Governors' Association, 1992.

Commerce, US Department of, *EC Testing and Certification Procedures Under the Internal Market Programme*, Washington, DC, International Trade Administration (ITA), 1 April 1992.

Cooney, S. (NAM), *EC'92 and US Industry*, Washington, DC, National Association of Manufacturers, February 1989.

Cooney, S. (NAM), *Europe 1992: Long Term Implications for the US Economy*, Statement to a Hearing of the Joint Economic Committee, US Congress, Washington, DC, US Government Printing Office, 1989.

Cooney, S. (NAM), *An NAM Report on Developments in the European Community's Internal Market Programme and the Effects on US Manufacturers*, Washington, DC, National Association of Manufacturers (NAM), International Economic Affairs Division, 1990.

Cooney, S. (NAM), *The Third NAM Report on Developments in the European Community's Internal Market Programme and the Effects on US Manufacturers*, Washington, DC, NAM International Economic Affairs Department, 1991.

Cooney, S. (NAM), *The Fourth NAM Report on Developments in the European Community's Internal Market Programme and its Effects on US Manufacturers*, Washington, DC, NAM International Economic Affairs Department, 1992.

Cooney, S., *Europe after 1992: Boom or Bust?*, Washington, DC, National Association of Manufacturers, 1993.

EC Committee of the American Chamber of Commerce (ECAmCham), *EC Information Handbook*, Brussels, ECAmCham, 1993.

European Parliament, *European Standardisation and Certification*, OJC 240, 16 September 1991.

GATT, *Multilateral Trade Negotiations*, The Uruguay Round, Marrakesh, GATT Secretariat (Trade Negotiations Committee), 15 April 1994.

Harrison, G., *The European Community's Plan: An Overview of the Proposed 'Single Market'*, Washington, DC, Congressional Research Service, 21 September 1988.

Harrison, G., *EC'92 and the United States*, Washington, DC, Congressional Service, 29 August 1989.

Harrison, G., *The EC's Government Procurement Directive: Has 'Fortress Europe' Arrived?*, Washington, DC, Congressional Research Service, 9 April 1993.

Jacob, R. (ed.), *EC–US Yearbook, 1992*, Washington, DC, European-American Chamber of Commerce, 1993.

KPMG Peat Marwick, *Europe 1992: Implications for California Business*, California State World Trade Commission/California European Trade and Investment Office, 1989.

Levine, J., *Going Global: A Strategy for Regional Cooperation*, Denver, CO, Western Governors Association, 1989.

National Governors Association (NGA), *America in Transition: The International Frontier. Report of the Task Force on Foreign Markets*, Washington, DC, 1989.

National Governors Association (NGA), *Governors' Weekly Bulletin*, 23(25), 1989.

National Governors Association (NGA), *Going Global: A Governors Guide to International Trade*, Washington, DC, 1992.

Office of the United States Trade Representative, *National Trade Estimate Report on Foreign Trade Barriers*, Washington, DC, 1992.

Roberts, B., *Competition Across the Atlantic: The States Face Europe 1992*, Denver, CO, National Conference of State Legislatures, 1991.

Roberts, B., *Investment Across the Atlantic: New Competition and Challenges for States*, Denver, CO, National Conference of State Legislatures, 1992.

Trade Promotion Coordination Committee, *National Export Strategy: Third Annual Report to the US Congress*, Washington, DC, October 1995.

US Chamber of Commerce, *Europe 1992: A Practical Guide for American Business*, Washington, DC, International Division, US Chamber of Commerce, 1990.

US Congress, Congressional Research Service, *Airbus Industrie: An Economic and Trade Perspective*, Washington, DC, CRS Report for Congress, February 1992.

US Congress, Congressional Research Service, *The Airbus Controversy: Revisited?*, Washington, DC, CRS Report for Congress, April 1993.

US Congress, International Trade Commission, *The Effects of Greater Economic Integration Within the European Community on the United States*, Washington, DC, USITC Pub. 2204, US Government Printing Office, July 1989.

US Congress, International Trade Commission, *The Effects of Greater Economic Integration Within the European Community on the United States: Fifth (of Six) Follow-up Report*, Washington, DC, USITC Pub. 2628, US Government Printing Office, 1992.

US Congress, Joint Economic Committee, *Europe 1992: Long-term Implications for the US Economy*, Hearing before the Joint Economic Committee, Washington, DC, US Government Printing Office, 26 April 1989.

US Congress, Office of Technology Assessment, *Competing Economies: America, Europe and the Pacific Rim*, Washington, DC, US Government Printing Office, July 1991.

US Congress, Office of Technology Assessment, *Global Standards: Building Blocks for the Future*, Washington, DC, TCT-512, US Government Printing Office, 1992.

US Council for International Business (USCIB), *Meeting the Global Business Challenges of the 1990's – Annual Report*, New York, USCIB, 1992.

US General Accounting Office, National Security and Affairs Division, *European Single Market: US Government Efforts to Assist Small and Medium-sized Exporters*, Report to the Chairman, Subcommittee on International Trade, Committee on Finance, US Senate, Washington, DC, February 1990.

US Government, Interagency Task Force on the EC Internal Market,

Completion of the European Community Internal Market: An Initial Assessment of Certain Economic Policy Issues Raised by Aspects of the EC's Program, Public Discussion Document, US Government, 1988.

US Government, US Mission to the European Community, *Declaration on US–EC Relations*, 23 November 1990.

US House of Representatives, *European Community's 1992 Integration Plan – Executive Summary*, Subcommittee on International Economic Policy and Trade, of the Committee on Foreign Affairs, Washington, DC, US Government Printing Office, 31 May 1989.

US House of Representatives, *Europe and the United States: Competition and Cooperation in the 1990s*, Study papers submitted to the Subcommittee on International Policy and Trade and the Subcommittee on Europe and the Middle East, of the Committee on Foreign Affairs, Washington, DC, US Government Printing Office, June 1992.

US Trade Representative, Office of European and Mediterranean Affairs, *Response of the Government of the United States of America to the European Community Green Paper on the Development of the Common Market for Telecommunications Services and Equipment*, Washington, DC, USTR, mimeo, 1987.

Newspapers

Business America
Christian Science Monitor
The Economist
Financial Times
The Journal of Commerce
The New York Times
San Francisco Chronicle
USA Today
Wall Street Journal
Washington Post

Books

Aho, C.M., *European Trade Policy at a Critical Juncture*, New York, Council on Foreign Relations, 1990.

Anderssen, S. and Eliasson, K. (eds), *Making Policy in Europe: The Europeification of National Policy-making*, London, Sage, 1993.

Audretsch, D., *The Market and the State: Government Policy towards Business in Europe, Japan and the USA*, London, Harvester Wheatsheaf, 1989.

Barfield, C. and Schambara, W. (eds), *The Politics of Industrial Policy*, Washington, DC, American Enterprise Institute, 1988.

Bergsten, C.F., *America in the World Economy: A Strategy for the 1990's*, Washington, DC, Institute for International Economics, 1988.

Brown, S., New Forces, Old Forces, and the Future of World Politics (post-Cold War edn), New York, HarperCollins, 1995.

Burgenmeier, B. and Mucchielli, J.L. (eds), *Multinationals and Europe 1992: Strategies for the Future*, London, Routledge, 1991.

Buzan, B. *et al.*, *The European Security Order Recast: Scenarios for the Post Cold War Era*, London, Pinter, 1990.

Cafruny, A.F. and Rosenthal, G.G. (eds), *The State of the European Community Volume 2: The Maastricht Debates and Beyond*, Boulder, CO, Westview, 1993.

Calingaert, M., *European Integration Revisited: Progress, Prospects and US Interests*, Boulder, CO, Westview, 1996.

Cecchini, P., *The European Challenge of 1992: The Benefits of a Single Market*, Aldershot, Wildwood House, 1988.

Choate, P., *Agents of Influence: How Japan's Lobbyists in the United States Manipulate America's Political and Economic System*, New York, Knopf, 1990.

Cohen, B., *The Public's Impact on Foreign Policy*, Boston, Little Brown, 1973.

Cohen, S.D., *The Making of United States International Economic Policy: Principles, Problems and Proposals for Reform* (2nd edn), New York, Praeger, 1981.

Cohen, S.D. Paul, J.R. and Blecker, R.A., *Fundamentals of US Foreign Trade Policy: Economics, Politics, Laws and Issues*, Boulder, CO, Westview, 1996.

Destler, I.M., *Making Foreign Economic Policy*, Washington, DC, Brookings Institution, 1980.

Destler, I.M., *American Trade Politics: System under Stress* (2nd edn), Washington, DC, Institute for International Economics and the Twentieth Century Fund, 1992.

Destler, I.M., *American Trade Politics: System under Stress* (3rd edn), Washington, DC, Institute for International Economics and the Twentieth Century Fund, 1995.

Dicken, P., *Global Shift: The Internationalisation of Economic Activity*, (2nd edn), London, Chapman, 1992.

Duchacek, I.D., *The Territorial Dimension of Politics: Within, Among and Across Nations*, Boulder, CO, Westview, 1986.

Dunning, J., *International Production and the Multinational Enterprise*, London, Allen and Unwin, 1981.

Edwards, G. and Regelsberger, E. (eds), *Europe's Global Links*, London, Pinter, 1990.

Egan, C. and McKiernan, P., *Inside Fortress Europe: Strategies for the Single Market*, London, Addison-Wesley and the Economist Intelligence Unit, 1994.

Evans, P.B., Jacobson, H.K. and Putnam, R.D. (eds), *Double-edged Diplomacy: International Bargaining and Domestic Politics*, Berkeley, University of California Press, 1993.

Fallik, A. (ed.), *The European Public Affairs Directory*, Brussels, Landmark, 1990.

Fallik, A. (ed.), *The European Public Affairs Directory* (2nd edn), Brussels, Landmark, 1993.

Featherstone, K. and Ginsberg, R., *The United States and the European Community in the 1990s: Partners in Transition*, London, Macmillan, 1993.

Featherstone, K. and Ginsberg, R., *The United States and the European Union in the 1990s: Partners in Transition* (2nd edn), London, Macmillan, 1996.

Fosler, R.S., *The New Economic Role of American States: Strategies in a Competitive World Economy*, Oxford University Press, New York, 1988.

Garten, J.E., *A Cold Peace: America, Japan Germany and the Struggle for Supremacy*, New York, Times Books, 1992.

Glickman, N.J. and Woodward, D., *The New Competitors: How Foreign Investors Are Changing the US Economy*, New York, Basic Books, 1988.

Greenwood, J., Grote, J. and Ronit, K., *Organised Interests in the European Community*, London, Sage, 1994.

Greenwood, J. (ed.), *European Casebook on Business Alliances*, London, Prentice Hall, 1995.

Haftendorn, H. and Tuschoff, C. (eds), *America and Europe in an Era of Change*, Boulder, CO, Westview, 1993.

Herman, C.F., Kegley, C.W. and Rosenau, J.N. (eds), *New Directions in the Study of Foreign Policy*, Boston, Allen and Unwin, 1987.

Hill, C. and Beshoff, P. (eds), *Two Worlds of International Relations: Academics, Practitioners and the Trade in Ideas*, London, LSE/Routledge, 1994.

Hinckley, B., *Less than Meets the Eye: Foreign Policy-making and the Myth of the Assertive Congress*, Chicago, University of Chicago Press/ Twentieth Century Fund, 1994.

Hobbs, H.H., *City Hall Goes Abroad: The Foreign Policy of Local Politics*, Thousand Oaks, CA, Sage, 1994.

Hocking, B., *Localizing Foreign Policy: Non-central Governments and Multilayered Diplomacy*, London/New York, Macmillan/St Martin's Press, 1993.

Hocking, B. (ed.), *Foreign Relations and Federal States*, London, Leicester University Press, 1993.

Hocking, B. and Smith, M., *World Politics: An Introduction to International Relations* (2nd edn), London, Prentice Hall/Harvester Wheatsheaf, 1995.

Hufbauer, G., *Europe 1992: An American Perspective*, Washington, DC, Brookings Institution, 1990.

Jackson, J.H., Louis, J.V. and Matsushita, M., *Implementing the Tokyo Round: National Constitutions and International Economic Rules*, Ann Arbor, University of Michigan Press, 1984.

Julius, D., *Global Companies and Public Policy: The Growing Challenge of Foreign Direct Investment*, London, Pinter, RIIA, 1990.

Kahler, M., *Regional Futures and Transatlantic Economic Relations*, New York, Council of Foreign Relations Press, 1995.

Kahler, M., *International Institutions and the Political Economy of Integration*, Washington, DC, Brookings Institution, 1995.

Karvonen, L. and Sundelius, B., *Foreign Policy Management*, Aldershot, Gower, 1987.

Kenen, P.B. (ed.), *Managing the World Economy: Fifty Years After Bretton Woods*, Washington, DC, Institute for International Economics, 1994.

Kennedy, P., *The Rise and Fall of the Great Powers*, London, Unwin Hyman, 1988.

Kennedy, P., *Preparing for the Twenty-first Century*, New York, Random House, 1993.

Keohane, R.O. and Hoffman, S. (eds), *The New European Community: Decision-making and Institutional Change*, Boulder CO, Westview, 1991.

Keohane, R.O., Nye, J.S. and Hoffman, S. (eds), *After the Cold War: International Institutions and State Strategies in Europe, 1989–91*, Cambridge, MA, Harvard University Press, 1993.

Kirchner, E., *Decision-making in the European Community*, Manchester, Manchester University Press, 1992.

Lodge, J. (ed.), *The European Community and the Challenge of the Future*, London, Pinter, 1989.

Low, P., *Trading Free: The GATT and US Trade Policy*, New York, Twentieth Century Fund, 1993.

MacMillan, J. and Linklater, A. (eds), *Boundaries in Question: New Directions in International Relations*, London, Pinter, 1995.

Mann, T.E. (ed.), *A Question of Balance: The President, Congress and Foreign Policy*, Washington, DC, Brookings Institution, 1990.

Mayes, D. (ed.), *The External Implications of European Integration*, Hemel Hempstead, Harvester Wheatsheaf, 1993.

McGrew, A., *Empire: The United States in the Twentieth Century*, London, Hodder and Stoughton, 1994.

Nau, H., *The Myth of America's Decline*, New York, Oxford University Press, 1990.

Nelson, M.M. and Ikenberry, G.J., *Atlantic Frontiers: A New Agenda for US–EC Relations*, New York, Carnegie Endowment for International Peace, 1993.

Nicoll, W. and Salmon, T., *Understanding the New European Community*, New York/London, Harvester Wheatsheaf, 1994.

Nothdurft, W.E., *Going Global: How Europe Helps Small States Export*, Washington, DC, Brookings Institution, 1992.

Nye, J. Jr, *Bound to Lead: The Changing Nature of American Power*, New York, Basic Books, 1990.

Odell, J.S. and Willett, T.D. (eds), *International Trade Policies: Gains from Exchange Between Economics and Political Science*, Ann Arbor, University of Michigan Press, 1993.

Ohmae, K., *The Borderless World: Power and Strategy in the Interlinked Economy*, London, Fontana, 1992.

Palmer, J., *1992 and Beyond*, Luxembourg, European Communities, 1989.

Peterson, J., *Europe and America in the 1990s: Prospects for Partnership*, Aldershot, Edward Elgar, 1993.

Peterson, J., *Europe and America in the 1990s: Prospects for Partnership* (2nd edn), London, Routledge, 1996.

Princen, T. and Finger, N. (eds), *Environmental NGOs in World Politics: Linking the Local and the Global*, London, Routledge, 1994.

Redmond, J. (ed.), *The External Relations of the European Community: The International Response to 1992*, London, Macmillan, 1992.

Reich, R., *The Work of Nations: Preparing Ourselves for 21st Century Capitalism*, New York, Knopf, 1991.

Richardson, J. and Mazey, S., *Lobbying in the European Community*, Oxford, Oxford University Press, 1993.

Ripley, R.B. and Lindsay, J.M. (eds), *Congress Resurgent: Foreign and Defense Policy on Capitol Hill*, Ann Arbor, University of Michigan Press, 1993.

Rosenau, J.N., *Turbulence in World Politics: A Theory of Change and Continuity*, Hemel Hempstead, Harvester Wheatsheaf, 1990.

Sandholtz, W., Borrus, M., Zysman, J., Conca, K., Stowsky, J., Vogel, S. and Weber, S., *The Highest Stakes: the Economic Foundations of the Next Security System*, New York, Oxford University Press, 1992.

Sbragia, A.M. (ed.), *Euro-politics: Institutions and Policy-making in the 'New' European Community*, Washington, DC, Brookings Institution, 1992.

Scholte, J.A., *International Relations of Social Change*, Buckingham, Open University Press, 1993.

Schwok, R., *US–EC Relations in the Post-Cold War Era: Conflict or Partnership?*, Boulder, CO, Westview, 1991.

Servan-Schreiber, J.J., *Le Défi Americain*, Paris, Denoel, 1967.

Skidmore, D. and Hudson, V.M. (eds), *The Limits of State Autonomy: Societal Groups and Foreign Policy Formulation*, Boulder, CO, Westview, 1993.

Smith, D.L. and Ray, J.L. (eds), *The 1992 Project and the Future of Integration in Europe*, Armonk, NJ, Sharpe, 1993.

Smith, M., *Western Europe and the United States: The Uncertain Alliance*, London, Allen and Unwin, 1984.

Smith, M. and Woolcock, S., *The United States and the European Community in a Transformed World*, London, Pinter, RIIA, 1993.

Snow, D.M. and Brown, E., *Puzzle Palaces and Foggy Bottom: US Foreign and Defense Policy-making in the 1990s*, New York, St Martin's Press, 1994.

Steinberg, M., *The Technical Challenges and Opportunities of a United Europe*, London, Pinter, 1990.

Stephanopoulos, G., *Europe, America and the Single Market*, London, Macmillan, 1992.

Stopford, J. and Strange, S., *Rival States, Rival Firms: Competition for World Market Shares*, Cambridge, Cambridge University Press, 1991.

Stubbs, R. and Underhill, G., *Political Economy and the Changing Global Order*, Basingstoke, Macmillan, 1994.

Swann, D. (ed.), *The Single European Market and Beyond: A Study of the Wider Implications of the Single European Act*, London, Routledge, 1992.

Tolchin, M. and Tolchin, S., *Buying into America: How Foreign Money Is Changing the Face of Our Nation*, New York, Berkeley, 1989.

Treverton, G. (ed.), *The Shape of the New Europe*, New York, Council on Foreign Relations, 1992.

Thompson, G., Frances, J., Levacic, R. and Mitchell, J. (eds), *Markets, Hierarchies and Networks: the Co-ordination of Social Life*, London, Sage, 1991.

Twiggs, J.E., *The Tokyo Round of Multilateral Trade Negotiations: A Case Study in Building Domestic Support for Diplomacy*, Lanham, MD, University Press of America, 1987.

Urwin, D. (ed.), *The European Community Encyclopedia and Directory, 1992*, London, Europa Publications, 1991.

Wallace, C.D. and Kline, J.M., *EC92 and Changing Global Investment Patterns: Implications for the US–EC Relationship*, Washington, DC, Center for Strategic and International Studies, 1992.

Walters, R.S. (ed.), *Talking Trade: US Policy in International Perspective*, Boulder, CO, Westview, 1993.

Woolcock, S., *Market Access Issues in EC-US Relations: Trading Partners or Trading Blows?*, London, Pinter, RIIA, 1991.

Yannopoulos, G. (ed.), *Europe and America*, 1992, Manchester, Manchester University Press, 1992.

Zysman, J. and Tyson, L. (eds), *American Industry in International Competition: Government Policies and Corporate Strategies*, Ithaca, NY, Cornell University Press, 1983.

Articles and conference papers

Advisory Commission on Intergovernmental Relations, 'State and local governments in international affairs: ACIR findings and recommendations', *Intergovernmental Perspectives*, 20(1), 1993/4, pp. 33–7.

Alger, C.F., 'Local, national and global politics in the world: a challenge to international studies', *International Studies Notes of the International Studies Association*, 5(1), 1978, pp. 1–13.

Alger, C.F., 'Perceiving, analysing and coping with the local–global nexus', *International Social Science Journal*, 117, 1988, pp. 321–40.

Blanchard, G., 'Public procurement: working with the new rules', *European Trends*, 3rd Quarter, 1993, pp. 54–63.

Bonine, K., 'US 1992, how the US government is preparing for the Single Market', *Europe*, 1990, pp. 14–18.

Bony, E. de, 'Lobbying the EU: the search for ground rules', *European Trends*, 3rd Quarter, 1994, pp. 73–80.

Brack, D., 'Balancing trade and the environment', *International Affairs*, 71(3), 1995, pp. 497–514.

Bradshaw, J., 'Constitutional reform after Maastricht', *European Trends*, 1st Quarter, 1994, pp. 58–70.

Burke, D.E., 'Export promotion partnerships: working together to help exporters', *Business America*, 113(23), 1992, pp. 2–4.

Bustin, G.L., 'A view of Fortress Europe', a speech to the UK Association for European Law, King's College, London, 20 July 1990.

Carter, R.G., 'Congressional trade politics in the post-Cold War era', paper presented at the International Studies Association Convention, San Diego, 16–20 April 1996.

Click, C., 'Virginia: state profile', *Europe*, 310, October 1991, pp. 29–31.

Cohen, B.J., 'Toward a mosaic economy', *Fletcher Forum of World Affairs*, 15(2), 1991, pp. 39–54.

Cooney, S., 'The Impact of Europe 1992 on the United States', *Proceedings of the Academy of Political Science*, 38(1), 1991, pp. 100–12.

Cowles, M.G., 'The politics of big business in the Single Market Program', paper presented to the 3rd Biennial Conference of the European Community Studies Association, Washington, DC, May 1993.

Cowles, M.G., 'The EU Committee of AmCham: the powerful voice of American firms in Brussels', *Journal of European Public Policy*, 3(3), 1996, pp. 339–58.

Cowles, M.G., 'The "Business" of agenda-setting in the European Union', paper presented to the 4th Biennial Conference of the European Community Studies Association, Charleston, SC, May 1995.

Cox, A. and Sanderson, J., 'From the mobilisation of bias to trade wars: the making and implementing of the European Community utilities procurement rules', *Journal of European Public Policy*, 1(2), 1994, pp. 263–83.

Dryden, S., 'Europeanising US business', *Europe*, 1990, pp. 13–16.

Duesterberg, T., 'Federal government response to the EC 1992 challenge in standards, testing and certification', *Business America*, February 1992, pp. 1–32.

Dunning, J.H., 'A new multinational–governmental partnership?', *Atlantic Outlook*, 51, 1993, pp. 7–8.

Dunning, J. and Robson, P., 'Multinational corporate integration and regional economic integration', *Journal of Common Market Studies*, 26(2), 1987, pp. 103–25.

Egan, M., ' "Associative Regulation" in the European Community: the case of technical standards', paper presented at the second Biennial Conference of the European Community Studies Association, Washington, DC, May 1991.

Elazar, D.J., 'States as polities in the federal system', *National Civic Review*, 70(2), 1981, pp. 77–82.

Europe, 'Awareness of 1992 on the way up among the states', *Europe*, April 1990, pp. 18–20.

Falconer, P., 'US Congressional oversight as a victim of overexpectation: a review article', *Politics*, 12(1), 1992, pp. 9–14.

Forrestal, R.P., 'Europe's economic integration in 1992: implications for the United States', *Vital Speeches of the Day*, 55(20), 1989, pp. 633–5.

Fuchs, G., 'Policy-making in a system of multilevel governance – the Commission of the European Community and the restructuring of the telecommunications sector', *Journal of European Public Policy*, 1(2), 1994, pp. 177–95.

Fulbright, J.W., 'The legislator as educator', *Foreign Affairs*, 57, 1979, pp. 719–32.

Gafour, A. and Osbourne, M., 'The impact of 1993 on public procurement', *European Trends*, 1st Quarter, 1993, pp. 58–64.

Gardner, J.N., 'Lobbying European style', *Europe*, 311, November 1991, pp. 29–30.

Garsson, R.M., '1992 countdown: fear and longing in the US', *American Banker*, 25, 1989, pp. 9–10.

Garten, J., 'The United States and Europe: towards the twenty-first Century', a speech to the American Council on Germany, 1995.

Goetz, K.H., 'National governance and European integration: intergovernmental relations in Germany', *Journal of Common Market Studies*, 33(1), 1995, pp. 91–117.

Golden, J.R., 'Economics and national strategy: convergence, global networks and co-operative competition', *The Washington Quarterly*, 16(1), 1993, pp. 91–113.

Goldsborough, J.O., 'California's foreign policy', *Foreign Affairs*, 72, 1993, pp. 88–96.

Goldstein, J., 'Ideas, institutions and American trade policy', *International Organisation*, 42(1), 1988, pp. 179–219.

Grubel, R.M., 'Foreign trade policies in the American states: innovation in times of budgetary stress', 34th Annual Convention of the International Studies Association, Acapulco, Mexico, 23–27 March 1993.

Guttman, R., 'Doing business in 1990s Europe', *Europe*, September 1990, pp. 16–20.

Guyett, S.J., 'Indiana: state profile', *Europe*, 307, June 1991, pp. 17–19.

Haas, P., 'Introduction: epistemic communities and international policy co-ordination', *International Organisation*, 46(1), 1992, pp. 1–37.

Halliday, F., 'International relations: is there a new agenda?', *Millennium*, 20(1), 1991, pp. 57–73.

Hanrieder, W.F., 'Dissolving international politics: reflections on the nation-state', *American Political Science Review*, 72(4), 1978, pp. 1276–88.

Harris, S., 'International trade, ecologically sustainable development and the GATT', *Australian Journal of International Affairs*, 45(2), 1991, pp. 196–212.

Hauser, T.J., 'The European Community Single Market and US trade relations', *Business America*, 114(5), 1993, pp. 2–5.

Held, D., 'Democracy, the nation-state and the global system', *Economy and Society*, 20(2), 1991, pp. 138–72.

Hirst, P. and Thompson, G., 'The problem of "globalization": international economic relations, national economic management and the formation of trading blocs', *Economy and Society*, 21(4), 1992, pp. 357–96.

Hopkins, R.F., 'The international role of "domestic" bureaucracy', *International Organisation*, 30(3), 1976, pp. 405–32.

Hormats, R., 'Redefining Europe and the Atlantic link', *Foreign Affairs*, 68, 1989, pp. 71–92.

Ikenberry, G., Lake, D. and Mastanduno, M., 'Introduction: approaches to explaining American foreign economic policy', *International Organisation*, 42(1), 1988, pp. 1–14.

Ingram, H.M. and Fiederlein, S.L., 'Traversing boundaries: a public policy approach to the analysis of foreign policy', *Western Political Quarterly*, 41(4), 1988, pp. 725–47.

Kapstein, E.B., 'We are US: the myth and the multinational', *The National Interest*, Winter 1991/2, pp. 55–62.

Kendall, V., 'Current problems in technical harmonisation', *European Trends*, 3rd Quarter, 1993, pp. 63–73.

Krasner, S., 'State power and the structure of international trade', *World Politics*, 28(3), 1976, pp. 317–47.

Kresl, P.K., 'The response of European cities to EC 1992', *Journal of European Integration*, 15(2/3), 1992, pp. 151–72.

Lemov, P., 'Europe and the states: free trade but no free lunch', *Governing*, January 1991, pp. 49–52.

Levine, J., 'American state offices in Europe: activities and connections', *Intergovernmental Perspectives*, 20(1), 1993–4, pp. 44–6.

Lind, M., 'The catalytic state', *The National Interest*, 27, 1992, pp. 3–11.

Luttwak, E.N., 'From geopolitics to geoeconomics', *The National Interest*, 20, 1990, pp. 17–23.

McLaughlin, A. and Greenwood, J., 'Regulating lobbying in Brussels: the tip of an administrative ice-berg?', *European Access*, October 1993, pp. 9–13.

McLaughlin, A., Jordan, G. and Maloney, W., 'Corporate lobbying in the

European Community', *Journal of Common Market Studies*, 31(2), 1993, pp. 191–212.

Manning, B., 'The Congress, the executive and intermestic affairs', *Foreign Affairs*, 55(2), 1977, pp. 306–25.

Mathews, T., 'Redefining security', *Foreign Affairs*, 68(2), 1989, pp. 162–78.

Mazey, S. and Richardson, J., 'Environmental groups and the EC: challenges and opportunities', *Environmental Politics*, 1(4), 1992, pp. 109–29.

Mitchell, D., 'Interest groups and the "democratic deficit"', *European Access*, April 1993, pp. 14–18.

Moravcsik, A., 'Negotiating the Single European Act: national interests and conventional statecraft in the EC', *International Organisation*, 45(1), 1991, pp. 19–57.

Ohmae, K., 'The rise of the region-state', *Foreign Affairs*, 72, 1993, pp. 78–88.

Ougaard, M., 'The US state in the new global context', *Co-operation and Conflict*, 27(2), 1992, pp. 131–62.

Putnam, R.D., 'Diplomacy and domestic politics: the logic of two-level games', *International Organisation*, 42(3), 1988, pp. 427–61.

Roberts, B., 'EC 1992: opportunities and challenges for state and local governments', *Government Finance Review*, December 1990, pp. 11–14.

Roberts, B.B., Burnett, S.H. and Weidenbaum, M., 'Think tanks in a new world', *The Washington Quarterly*, 16(1), 1993, pp. 169–82.

Ryerson, D.R., 'Looking homeward: regional views of foreign policy from Des Moines?', *Foreign Policy*, 88, 1992, pp. 48–52.

Sandholtz, W. and Zysman, J., '1992: recasting the European bargain', *World Politics*, 42(1), 1989, pp. 95–129.

Santos, L.E., 'Trade politics of the American Congress', *Journal of World Trade Law*, 29(6), 1995, pp. 73–8.

Schaefer, M. and Singer, J., 'Multilateral trade agreements and US states: an analysis of potential GATT Uruguay Round agreements', *Journal of World Trade Law*, 26(6), 1992, pp. 31–59.

Schneider, V., Dang-Nguyen, G. and Werle, R., 'Corporate actor networks in European policy-making: harmonising telecommunications policy', *Journal of Common Market Studies*, 32(4), 1994, pp. 473–98.

Schwab, S., 'Building a national export development alliance', *Inter-governmental Perspectives*, 16(2), 1990, pp. 19–22.

Seay, D. and Smith, W., 'Free trade's forgotten amigos: why governors want NAFTA', *Policy Review*, 65, 1993, pp. 57–64.

Shuman, M.H., 'Dateline Main Street: courts v local foreign policies', *Foreign Policy*, 86, 1992, pp. 158–78.

Smith, M., 'Clinton and the EC: how much of a new agenda?', *The World Today*, April 1993, pp. 70–3.

Smith, M. and Woolcock, S., 'Learning to co-operate: the Clinton Administration and the European Union', *International Affairs*, 70(3), 1994, pp. 459–76.

Southwick, J., 'Building the states: a survey of state law conformance with the standards of the GATT Procurement Code', *Journal of International Business Law*, 13, 1992, pp. 57–100.

Spero, J.E., 'The mid-life crisis of American trade policy', *The World Today*, 45(1), 1989, pp. 10–14.

Stanley Foundation, 'The changing face of American foreign policy: the new role of state and local actors', Report of a New American Global Dialogue Conference, Warranton, VA, 27–29 October 1994.

Stokes, B., 'Organising to trade', *Foreign Policy*, 89, Winter 1992–3, pp. 36–53.

Strange, S., 'States, firms and diplomacy', *International Affairs*, 68(1), 1992, pp. 3–14.

Stueneberg, B., 'Decision-making under different institutional arrangements: legislation by the European Community', *Journal of Institutional and Theoretical Economics*, 150(4), 1994.

Ullman, R., 'Redefining security', *International Security*, 8(1), 1983, pp. 129–53.

Vernon, R., 'European Community 1992: can the US negotiate for trade equality?', *Proceedings of the Academy of Political Science*, 37(4), 1990, pp. 9–16.

Wapner, P., 'Politics beyond the state: environmental activism and world civic politics', *World Politics*, 47(3), 1995, pp. 311–41.

Weiler, C., 'Free trade agreements: a new federal partner?', *Publius*, 24(3), 1994, pp. 113–34.

Winham, G.R., 'Negotiation as a management process', *World Politics*, 30(1), 1977, pp. 87–114.

Woolcock, S., 'The European acquis and multilateral trade rules: are they compatible?', *Journal of Common Market Studies*, 31(4), 1993, pp. 539–58.

Yeo, P., 'Congressional response to European integration', Royal Institute of International affairs discussion paper (mimeo), London, May 1990.

Index of authors

General index